I0890117

THE

National Pastime

A REVIEW OF BASEBALL HISTORY

CONTENTS

Editor: James Charlton   Copy Editor: John Paine

Designated Readers: Dick Thompson, Norman Macht   Designer: Glenn LeDoux

THE NATIONAL PASTIME Number 22. Published by The Society for American Baseball Research, Inc. 812 Huron Rd., Suite 719, Cleveland, OH 44115. Postage paid at Kent, OH.

A Note from the Editor

My cap is off to my predecessor Mark Alvarez, the Connie Mack of SABR publications directors, who toiled in the job for ten years. Mark is a long-time friend and, as it happens, lives in the same county in Connecticut; he has been generous and helpful during this transition. Having been in this job for a few months, I have an even greater appreciation for Mark's excellent work.

Before him there were other fine and capable editors, each of whom built on the work of earlier people. These include John Holway, Bob Tiemann, and John Thorn, who edited the premiere issue of *The National Pastime*, in 1982. The *Baseball Research Journal*, begun in 1975, was for years edited by Bob Davids. Special editions of *TNP* were edited or co-edited by Pete Bjarkman, Paul Adomides, and Mark Rucker.

Issue 22 of *The National Pastime* includes a variety of articles, a few of which have been in the works for several years. I particularly recommend Brian Turner's beautifully researched discovery on early integration. Bill Mead, author of *Even the Browns*, is one of my favorite writers, and his profile of Doc Hyland, the long-time Cards' physician, is most enjoyable; the estimable Gene Karst, probably SABR's senior member at 96, adds a wonderful anecdote. While I don't think I'll ever reach my goal of having a complete issue of *TNP* devoted to the Chicago Cubs, Art Ahrens' fine piece on the 1927 team is a good start. Dixie Tourangeau brings to life baseball's opening day one hundred years ago, and Lance Richbourg's affectionate and knowledgeable portrait of his father is the cover article.

I want to thank the SABR members who served as peer reviewers for the articles here, as well as in the forthcoming *BRJ*: Ed Hartig, Phil Birnbaum, John Pastier, Steve Boren, Voros McCracken, Marshall Wright, Kevin Saldana, David Vincent, Dick Thompson, Rob Neyer, Jeff Orleans, Leslie Heaphy, Rob Wood, Gene Karst, Lyle Spatz, Neal Traven, Fred Ivor-Campbell, Bill Deane, Eric Enders, and Pete Bjarkman.

JIM CHARLTON
NOVEMBER, 2002

My Father, Lance Richbourg

by Lance Richbourg, Jr.

In 1951 my father, Lance Richbourg, was named one of three outfielders on the all-time Boston Braves team. He was the regular right fielder and leadoff hitter for the Braves in the late 1920s, batting .308 over the course of eight seasons in the majors. Perhaps just as impressive is his lifetime .328 batting average in a minor league career that spanned nearly two decades. But for many fans my father's most distinguishing characteristic was his gentlemanly demeanor. Several years ago I received a letter from an elderly man who was six years old when he started going to baseball games in Milwaukee. His mother attended games on Ladies Day and said that Lance Richbourg was her favorite player because "he didn't wipe his nose on his sleeve like the others."

When my father was born in 1897, northwest Florida was a vast forest of yellow pine. A person could not wrap his arms completely around the trunk of any of those great trees that had stood in place so long there was no underbrush. The forest was as clean as a park and one could see for a quarter-mile. By the time my father was playing in the majors, that forest had been devastated: first by turpentine workers who drained the gum by cutting deep, cup-like wells in the tree's trunk; then by lumber mills that leveled the woodland. My father took the destruction of that forest as a personal loss. For the rest of his life he had an abiding reverence for the pine tree and a crusading zeal for conservation and reforestation, an environmental consciousness that was years ahead of its time. The depth of his feeling impressed on me what an awesome place that old forest must have been.

Dubbed by one critic as "America's foremost baseball artist," Lance Richbourg, Jr., is an art professor at St. Michael's College in Colchester, Vermont, and a member of the Gardner-Waterman Chapter of SABR. His work is represented by O.K. Harris gallery in New York City. The author wishes to thank Tom Simon and Elaine Segal for their editorial assistance.

The details of family history leading up to my father's birth are pieced haphazardly in my mind, based on memories of tales I heard when growing up. Recently a relative in Georgia informed me that research on the family had established the identity of its progenitor in America: one Claude Phillippe de Richebourg, the pastor of a Huguenot church who arrived in Virginia in 1690 and had migrated to Santee, South Carolina, by the time of his death in 1718. The Richbourgs' connection to the Huguenots, a Protestant sect that was persecuted in 17th-century France, as well as their connection to South Carolina and cattle, had been a part of family lore for as long as I can remember. The economic function of Georgia and the Carolinas in the 18th century was to provide food for slave plantations on the sugar-producing islands of the Caribbean, and South Carolina's main product was beef.

By the late 19th century a handful of South Carolina families had drifted down to northwest Florida, the Richbourgs among them. Those cattle clans managed their herds simply by turning them loose in the forest.

The cattle grazed in low places along the river branches and swamps, becoming nearly as wild as deer. Their range extended from Crestview, Florida, to the northwest shore of Choctawatchee Bay, an area about the size of Rhode Island. Every so often a bunch of cows would be gathered up and herded to a railhead in Florala, Alabama, where they were sold off for a nickel a head. "But it was all profit," my father would hasten to add.

Those periodic round-ups were called "cow hunts." They were carried out by men and boys mounted on skinny horses riding in U.S. Army cavalry saddles, the most minimal and cheapest of gear, and using dogs with powerful jaws that would clamp down on a cow's muzzle and hold it in place. There were celebrated dogs and horses whose names are lost in the fog of time, but one I do remember was Dillard, a horse renowned for his quickness and skill as a cow pony, as well as his longevity—some 18 years in service. For weeks at a time the cow hunters lived in the forest in pursuit of cattle. To me, as a boy hearing those tales, it all sounded like a huge, glorious camping trip, compounded by the romance and excitement of careering through the wild on horseback. But my Uncle Clint, who had been born into the final days of cow-hunt life, used to shake his head and mutter about the absurdity of riding a horse for fun.

Once my father took sick while out on a hunt. For a couple days he could barely sit on his horse. When my grandfather finally noticed his boy's indisposition, all he said was, "Son, you don't look so good. You'd better go home." Going home meant a 20-hour ride through the forest—alone. When my father finally reached his destination, he spent the next two months in bed with some unnamed fever. No one knew what it was, though he nearly died of it. I thought to ask him how old he was at the time: "Twelve," he replied.

My father told of riding through the forest from cow-hunt encampments to play in ball games. When he was about 16 he went to boarding school in Defuniak Springs, Florida, and played baseball there. He spoke of a teacher, a woman who was in charge of the school's athletics, who told him he had the ability to play baseball for a living. Volume II of SABR's *Minor League Baseball Stars* lists Lance Richbourg as having played in the Dixie League with Dothan, Alabama, as early as 1916. He is listed as having played 48 games for Newport News of the Virginia League in 1918, which must have occurred while he was in the Navy because I have discharge papers dated December 7 of that year. After his discharge, my father enrolled at the University of Florida. A story he liked to tell was of standing on the porch and watching the festivities of his fraternity's dance through a window

Lance Richbourg stands third from left in this circa 1926 photo of the Walton H.S. team from Defuniak Springs, Florida. He boarded at the school because his family's ranch was 25 miles away.

because all he had to wear was his navy issue.

In the spring of 1919 my father lettered in baseball and was discovered and signed by the New York Giants. It came about like this: The Giants were working their way north after spring training, playing exhibition games along the way. One was in Gainesville against the University of Florida team, and beforehand the college president addressed the team. "Who knows but someday one of you might wear the colors of the New York Giants," he said. One story has it that my father, playing third base, charged in on batter Heinie Zimmerman, expecting a bunt. Instead, Zimmerman lashed a line drive that my father miraculously gloved. As dramatic as that anecdote is, it seems he would have needed to perform deeds of more consequence—perhaps lining a couple of his signature triples—to have caught the eye of John McGraw. Whatever my father did, the next day he was sitting in the bleachers watching the Giants work out when the legendary manager approached him and said, "Son, did you ever consider a career in professional baseball?" McGraw signed him then and there for $250 per month, which my father took to be all the money in the world.

That summer he went up to New York. The intrateam competition was so ferocious, he told me, that McGraw would have to clear the way so my father could get in a few swings during batting practice. "Those old veterans weren't going to make some kid who might take their job feel welcome to it," my father said. He never did get into a game that season and the next he tested McGraw's patience by not reporting until his college term was done in May (he eventually earned a B.S. in agriculture in 1922). As a consequence, the Giants farmed him out to Grand Rapids, where he hit .415 in 87 games. The next year, 1921, McGraw sent him to the Philadelphia Phillies in a trade for Casey Stengel. Reporters considered it crazy to trade the "fleet-footed Richbourg" for the "clumsy Stengel," but Casey went on to become a World Series hero for the Giants while my father played only ten games for the Phillies.

In 1923 my father, playing for the Nashville Vols, was enjoying a fantastic season. He and Kiki Cuyler composed two-thirds of what sportswriters were calling the best outfield ever in the Southern Association. It was broken up in midseason, however, when my father, batting .378 at the time, split the large bone in his lower left leg while sliding into third, beating out a triple. The Nashville *Tenneseean* wrote, "If somebody had to break his leg why couldn't it be Warren G. Harding or the King of Spain?" Just days earlier my father had been purchased by the Washington Senators, and the injury seriously interrupted the trajectory of his career; while Cuyler moved on to Pittsburgh in 1924, capitalizing on his prime to build a Hall of Fame career, my father reported to the Senators, not fully healed. Washington had Goose Goslin in left field and Sam Rice in center, but right field was up for grabs; nonetheless, my father was unable to beat out the likes of Nemo Leibold, George Fisher, and Carr Smith. The Senators ended up sending him to Milwaukee in a deal for Wid Matthews, and that third outfield slot eventu-

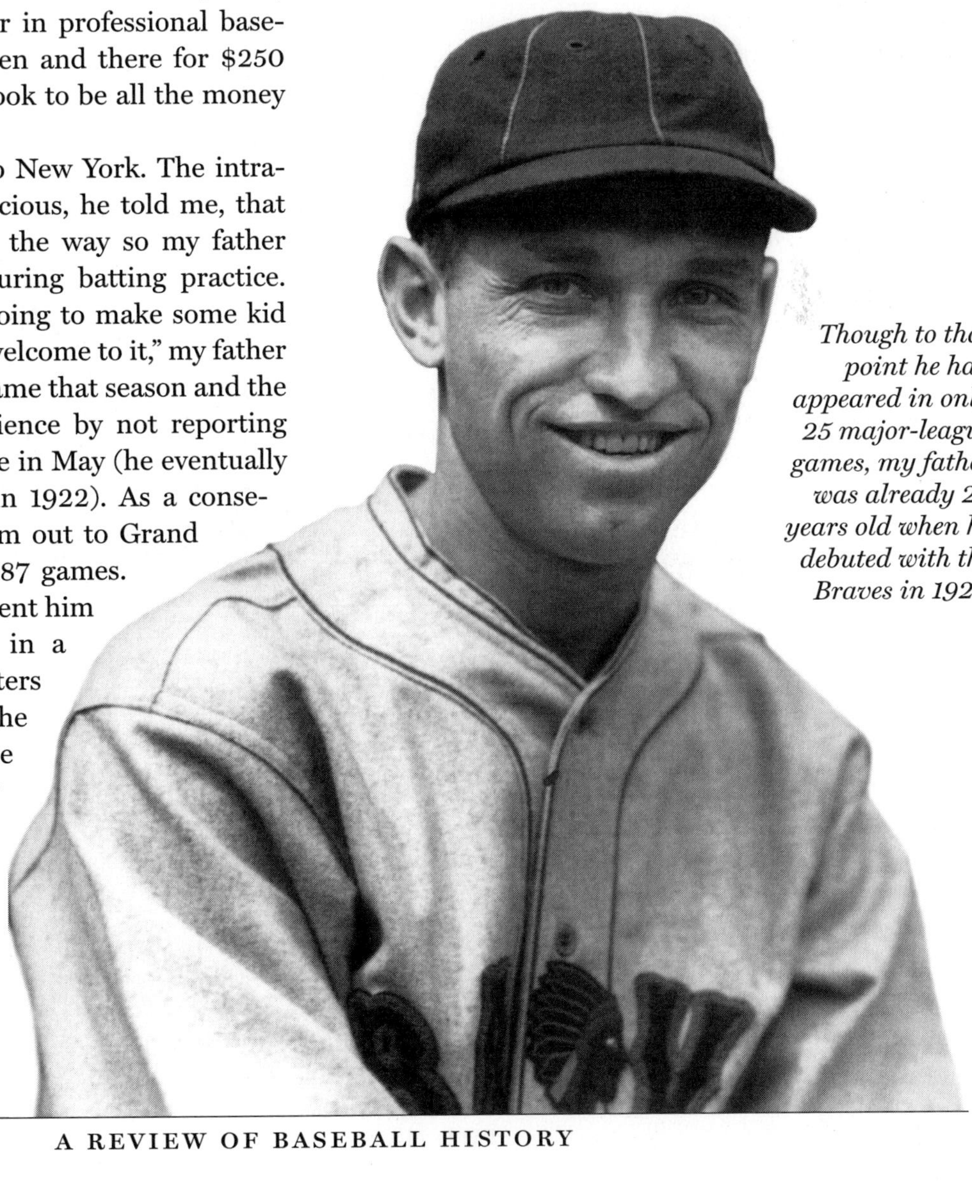

Though to that point he had appeared in only 25 major-league games, my father was already 29 years old when he debuted with the Braves in 1927.

ally fell to Earl McNeely, whose famous "pebble hit" won the seventh game of the 1924 World Series.

In 1975 my father recollected his final at-bat with the Senators to Ed Barfield of the Pensacola *News Journal*: "We were playing Boston in Washington and were tied up 2-2 in the bottom of the ninth. Bucky Harris, our manager, had told us before the last inning that if our leadoff hitter, Muddy Ruel, got on base, then Fred Marberry, our pitcher, would have two swings to bunt him down. If he were to fail after two strikes, then I was to pinch hit. Well, Ruel got on base, Marberry got two strikes on him trying to bunt, and I came in to pinch hit. The count got to 3-2, and then I lined one over the third baseman's head just fair for a triple. We won 3-2. As I was walking up the long ramp from the dugout, Harris came up, slapped me on the back, and said: 'Way to hit the ball, kid. Pack your bags, you're going to Milwaukee.'"

That story serves well to invest the narrative of my father's career with drama and bittersweet irony, but it never really occurred. The game that comes closest took place in Detroit on June 4, only a few days before his release, when he pinch hit and drove home the go-ahead run in the top of the eighth inning. The Tigers, however, scored in their half of the eighth and eventually won the game in extra innings. In the mind of my father—as scrupulous a person as anyone I've ever known—that story had become the truth. That he had come to believe it, in my opinion, shows the measure of his pain in failing to hang on with a team that became world champions.

My father had three solid seasons with Milwaukee. In 1926 he had a standout year, leading the American Association in runs, hits, triples, and stolen bases. From 1927 to 1931 he played right field for the Boston Braves, posting his best season in 1928, when he batted .337 and ranked fourth in the National League with 206 hits. That year his manager was Rogers Hornsby. Determined to win the NL batting title and convinced that the Braves didn't have a chance of finishing out of the second division, Hornsby instructed my father to tag up and attempt to advance on any of his long flies because at the time hitters were not charged with a time at bat for fly balls that advanced a runner. "Richbourg's speed on the bases must have meant eight or ten points to my average," recalled Hornsby, who won the batting title with a .387 average.

My father was with the Braves in 1930, when the team wore sleeve patches adorned with a pilgrim hat to celebrate Boston's tricentennial. That year was his fourth straight 300+ season, and his last as a regular.

Though hardly beloved by his players, Hornsby seemed to get along fine with my father. Accepting an occasional dinner invitation from a fan, he would warn his host that he could talk about only one subject, then invite my father along to ensure that there was at least one other person at the table who could talk baseball.

Because my father was a left-handed batter and fast, he often bunted for hits. He practiced throughout the season, spending mornings in Boston trying to place bunts into a cap that his partner, an old pitcher, would move around the infield. Once, playing in Cincinnati, opposed by Hall of Fame pitcher Eppa Rixey, my father laid down a bunt that rolled backwards. Catcher Bubbles Hargrave charged blindly over the ball. When my father got to first base, he looked back and saw the ball sitting in the center of home plate—reportedly the shortest base hit in the history of baseball. On May 14, 1927, Lance Richbourg made it into baseball's official record book—as well as *Ripley's Believe It or Not*—by playing right field throughout 18 innings of a doubleheader without a single fielding chance, thereby setting the standard for a single day's idleness. On July 31, 1929, my father entered the record book again when he hit three triples in one game, tying the major league mark.

I have a newspaper clipping in which Paul Shannon of the Boston *Post* describes my father snagging a scorching line drive in his bare hand. "By way of a desperate spring, he managed to intercept the sphere though he took it over his head," Shannon wrote. "The ball landed squarely on the tips of the fingers of his "Meat Hand." The article goes on to describe my father finishing that game and playing through the second game of the doubleheader, "though he was seen to shake his hand after swinging and many of the spectators figured he must have been hit by a foul tip." X-rays after the game showed that his finger had been broken at the top joint. I remember that there was not a single straight finger on either of my father's hands; apparently they all had been broken at one time.

Another Shannon clipping describes Richbourg as a "brittle type of athlete." When I asked my father about that remark, he said, "I just took chances those other guys wouldn't take." One of those chances came in 1931, when my father ran into the outfield wall while chasing a fly ball. The resulting injuries limited him to 97 games that season, and his .287 batting average was his lowest with the Braves. That December he was traded to the Chicago Cubs.

My father was a Florida cowboy, spending nearly every off-season tending to a herd of cattle on the family ranch in Crestview.

One time in Chicago my father and some teammates were taken to a restaurant, something of a private club from his description. Upon seeing a couple of dark, dapper gents across the room, their host quickly made his way over to their table and introduced them to his ballplayer guests. One of those gentlemen was "Legs" Capone, Al's brother. "I had to let them know who you were," their host explained, "otherwise they might bomb my store or something." After 44 games with the Cubs, my father was sent down to the International League, where he batted .371 in 75 games. "There is no greater gulf than the gulf between the major and the minor leagues," my father used to say. He was called back to Chicago in September, but not in time to be eligible for the 1932 World Series, when Babe Ruth supposedly made his famous "called shot."

After the Series, Cincinnati acquired my father, who refused to report when the Reds tried to send him back to the International League with Rochester. Henceforth he was sold to his old team from bittersweet 1923, the Nashville Vols, and in midseason 1935 he was named player-manager. "Richbourg is too much a gentleman to be a successful manager," wrote one reporter when he was fired at season's end, but he was soon rehired and continued as player-manager in Nashville through the 1937 season.

In 1938 he received a similar appointment in Richmond, Virginia, where I was born at the end of the season. My birth marked the end of my father's playing career in organized baseball. After managing one more season in Richmond, he bought a ranch near Ft. Pierce, Florida, merging it with a much larger ranch owned by Alto Adams, a boyhood friend and successful lawyer who was soon appointed to the Florida Supreme Court and later ran unsuccessfully for governor. For a few years my father managed the 20,000 acre ranch, also managing the Ft. Pierce baseball team in his spare time.

By the mid-1940s my father was in charge of the Farm Security Program at Escambia Farms, Florida. That program helped returning World War II veterans acquire small farms, with a new house, barn, and mule composing the package to get them going raising cotton, corn, or peanuts. Perched on a little rise behind the Escambia Farms General Store, my father's office was a small prefab house identical to those on the veterans' farms, and that place, as well as the drives out dusty farm roads to visit FSP farmers, form some of my earliest memories. The knowledge my father had gained from his lifelong experience working with cattle was a valuable resource in a community where there was no large animal veterinarian. Once a full-grown stallion was brought to our house for my father to castrate. "Can you castrate a horse?" my mother asked. "I can castrate anything," my father replied.

In 1948 my father was elected County Superintendent of Education, winning the election 5,281 to 1,226. That landslide could be read as an index of his popularity, but it also might have been attributable to disenchantment with the incumbent. My father said that when he first took office, the school system's credit was so bad that "we couldn't even think of asking for a loan, we needed a court order to buy anything." It took one year for an auditor working full-time to assess the total indebtedness, which was estimated at nearly $500,000, but my father got the schools back in the black within two and a half years by operating on sheer frugality. During his 16 years as superintendent, 17 new schools were constructed and his operating budget grew from $900,000 to $7,428,000. On my father's retirement in 1964, U.S. Representative Bob Sikes telegrammed, "I can think of no finer tribute to a man in Public Life than to say he gave every fiber of his being to the job."

Lance Richbourg then turned his attention full-time to the ranch in Crestview, which had been homesteaded by his family a couple generations before him. I worked with him there during the last years of his life, finding the ranch to be a break-even proposition but rewarding if raising cattle was one's passion, as it was for my father. He had a keen knowledge of each of the 200 cows in the herd. When the calves came, for instance, he always knew which calf belonged to which cow, though it took me several weeks to learn, and even then I could never match them all. We worked many long, hard days together. His stamina and energy seemed youthful, which might have been an effect of his lifelong discipline to hard work. My father claimed to take a teaspoon of turpentine every day in winter to ward off colds, and he never had any serious illness.

When I left the ranch in 1975 to take a teaching job in Vermont, my father decided to cut back the herd. Early in the morning of September 10, he loaded a truck with cattle to send to market. After he got them all aboard, he sat down next to the cattle chute and died. He was 77-years-old.

Shortly thereafter, Red Barber, the famous radio voice of the Brooklyn Dodgers, remembered my father in his column in the Tallahassee newspaper:

> *I only saw him once and at a distance. It was at a ball game in a small town and in a very small ballpark. It was just an exhibition game in the spring of 1927. The Boston Braves were playing the then-minor league Milwaukee Brewers in Sanford, Florida. This man I saw that one afternoon took my eye every time a fly ball was hit to his area. He was slender, and he moved with a fluid, certain grace. It was a joy to watch him judge where a ball would come down, glide to the spot and with a soft yet sure hand catch the ball....*
>
> *Years later Branch Rickey explained what I had seen and would see many, many times in the big cities of the land—in his phrase, "the pleasing skills of the professional." And it came back to me in a flash when and where I first became in any way aware of it: 1927, Sanford, watching Lance Richbourg play the outfield.*

June Peppas and the All-American League

Helping the Kalamazoo Lassies Win the 1954 AAGPBL Championship

by Jim Sargent

By the time she pitched and won the final game of the Shaughnessy Championship Series for the Kalamazoo Lassies on Sunday, September 5, 1954, June Peppas had twice been selected as an All-Star in the All-American Girls Professional Baseball League (AAGPBL). She became the league's first team first baseman in 1953 and 1954, even though she often pitched.

During what turned out to be the All-American League's final season in 1954, Peppas hurled 13 games and posted a 6–4 record with a 3.32 ERA. She also batted .333, her team's best average and the league's fifth highest mark for qualified players. When Kalamazoo played the Fort Wayne Daisies for the league title, June came through big-time.

"Pitcher June Peppas, a former Daisy player," the Fort Wayne *Journal-Gazette* (all game stories for this article came from the *Journal-Gazette*) reported about the final playoff game, "was the villain of the piece. In addition to holding the Daisies to five safeties, she slammed out three hits in five trips to the plate and batted in four runs."

Leading her club to the 1954 league title, the southpaw batted .450 and won twice in the five-game series—including the 8–5 finale in the AAGPBL's last-ever game.

Jim Sargent is a Professor of History and Dean of the Social Science Division at Virginia Western Community College in Roanoke. He has written many profile articles about former big leaguers and All-Americans.

When the All-American (as the league was often called) disbanded after the season, June Peppas, who worked in printing during the off-seasons in Kalamazoo, began working full-time at the trade. After earning Bachelor's and Master's Degrees from Western Michigan University in Kalamazoo during the late 1960s, June taught vocational-education graphic arts. Later, she operated her own printing business, retiring in 1988.

Today she's best known for her part in reviving the All-American League. In 1980 June and a few friends began assembling a list of names and addresses of former players. Her work turned into a newsletter and resulted in the AAGPBL's first-ever reunion at Chicago's Wrigley Field in 1982. A Players Association was formed in 1987, and most former All-Americans continue to enjoy reunions—which became annual events in 1998.

Peppas should be remembered for many contributions to the All-American League. The daughter of George and Edna Peppas, she was born on June 16, 1929, in Kansas City, Missouri. The family soon moved to Fort Wayne, Indiana, where she grew up playing sandlot sports, notably fast-pitch softball. June graduated from Elmhurst High in 1947.

June's baseball career, which spanned the years 1948 through 1954, reflects the experiences of many women who played in the All-American's era of overhand pitching. In 1943 the AAGPBL began by playing fast-pitch softball—featuring an underhand delivery. The pitching motion was switched to a modified sidearm in 1946, to sidearm in 1947, and to overhand in 1948.

During those years the league's ball decreased in size. Beginning with a 12-inch diameter softball in 1943, the AAGPBL used an 11.5 inch ball in 1944 and 1945, an 11-inch ball in 1946 and 1947, and a 10 3/8-inch ball in 1948—the first overhand season. Midway through the 1949 season, the league introduced a 10 inch ball. In the final season of 1954, the AAGPBL's ball switched to the size of a regulation major league baseball.

Likewise, the league gradually lengthened the basepaths and the pitching distance from the mound to the batter's box. For example, batters faced a 40-foot pitching distance and ran 65-foot basepaths in 1943. But in 1948 players adjusted to a 50-foot pitching distance, the overhand delivery, and 72-foot basepaths. In 1954 the pitcher stood 60 feet away from home plate and the runners hustled around 85-foot basepaths, both just short of the men's distances.

For women like Peppas who began after the 1947 season, therefore, competing in the All-American meant playing a tough brand of baseball that continued to grow closer to the men's professional game.

A child of the Depression, she shared her memories in a 1998 interview:

"I was truly a stubborn left-hander. I liked baseball, softball, any sport, when I was growing up.

June Peppas of the Kalamazoo Lassies, c. 1952

"My folks were in the restaurant business, so we were good friends of Harold Greiner, owner of the Bob-Inn Restaurant in Fort Wayne. Harold fielded men's and women's softball teams. I played for him from 1942 through 1947 and we won state titles in 1944 and 1945. He scouted for the All-American and recommended me for tryouts. Harold also managed the Daisies in 1949.

"I went to spring training at Opa-Locka, Florida, in 1948 and was assigned to the Fort Wayne Daisies. As a pitcher, I was very erratic, but I could hit. It was tough being a home-town product, and in 1949 Harold traded me to Racine."

June had a solid rookie season, playing in 20 games and hitting .264. She pitched 16 times, finishing with a 4–12 record and an ERA of 4.62. In 1949 she had mixed success, due partly to injuries. She batted .116 in 50 games (39 with Racine), but her pitching record improved to 3–4 with a 2.25 ERA.

"At Racine I got my control," she recalled, "thanks to the teaching of manager Leo 'Pop' Murphy. I had a good bat, and also played first base. In '48 I tore my right knee up. I had it repaired over the winter, and in '49 I tore up my left knee, but I continued to play. I waited until '50 to have it repaired. In 1949, after being traded, I learned how to slide, thanks to Sophie Kurys of the Belles. Also, I did double duty like many others. I pitched every fifth turn, and I played first base the rest of the time."

Once she overcame knee injuries, June's career blossomed. She spent the rest of 1949 and all of 1950 with Racine. However, because of financial difficulties after the '50 season, the Racine franchise was moved to Battle Creek, Michigan.

In 1950, her only full season with the Belles, "Pep," or "Lefty," as she was also called, bounced back. She hit .268 with 11 doubles, five triples, four home runs, and a career-best 52 RBI. She also posted a 4–4 pitching mark with a 4.57 ERA. Her main problem continued to be control: she walked more hitters than she struck out. For example, in 1950 she passed 41 batters while fanning 21. In 1951 she walked 31 and struck out 20.

In mid-1951 June was traded to the Kalamazoo Lassies. During her three full seasons in Kazoo, the last two as an All-Star at first base, she continued to

NORTHERN INDIANA HISTORICAL SOCIETY, INC.

1954 Kalamazoo Lassies, with June Peppas second from left in front row (kneeling).

hit well. Her averages improved from .262 to .271 to .333. In 1954 the southpaw fashioned a 6–4 record, her only winning season as a hurler.

"I was fortunate in making the All-Star team in 1953 and 1954," June observed. "I always said the only way I made it was when Rockford's Dot Kamenshek retired [after the 1952 season]."

She added, modestly, "My team, the Kalamazoo Lassies, won the Shaughnessy Trophy in the last year of the league, 1954. I was lucky enough to be the winning pitcher in two ball games."

Pretty, personable, and multi-talented, the 5'-5½" 145-pound brunette kept improving her game. She was a hit on and off the field. Recalled teammate Elaine Roth, "June had a good voice, played the piano, and when dressed up, she looked like a movie star."

On the diamond in 1948, the AAGPBL peaked with ten teams and the league's attendance reached an all-time high of 910,000. The All-American returned to eight teams in 1949, 1950, and 1951, fell to six teams in 1952 and 1953, and ended with five clubs in 1954.

During the overhand years, the Rockford Peaches won the Shaughnessy Playoffs in 1948, 1949, and 1950. After Rockford's run (the Peaches also won in 1945), the South Bend Blue Sox won back-to-back titles in 1951 and 1952. The Grand Rapids Chicks won league crowns in 1947 and 1953 (and the Milwaukee Chicks took the title in 1944). Finally, the Lassies won Kalamazoo's only championship in 1954.

But attendance declined and team revenues fell. After the 1953 season, the league's debt jumped to $80,000. While Peppas thinks the lack of good business management hurt several teams more than anything else, the impact of television hurt minor league baseball and doubtless affected the AAGPBL as well.

In any event, on the diamond in 1954, the girls played exciting ball. Hitting a regulation-sized baseball, "Jolting Jo" Weaver of Fort Wayne led the All-American with a remarkable .429 average in 93 games. She also paced the league in home runs with a best-ever 29. Jean Geissinger of the Daisies hit .377 with 26 home runs and a league-high 91 RBI. Betty Foss, another Fort Wayne slugger, hit .352 with 14 homers and 54 RBI. And Betty Francis of South Bend averaged .350 with eight home runs and 58 RBI.

Nineteen players averaged at least .300. South Bend's Wilma Briggs batted an even .300 while clubbing 25 homers and driving home 73 runs. Peppas averaged .333 with 16 homers and 49 RBI, making her one of the league's best hitters.

In the first round of the Shaughnessy Playoffs, regular-season champ Fort Wayne (54–40 record) won on a forfeit from third-place Grand Rapids (46–45). A dispute erupted when, due to an injury to Fort Wayne's regular catcher, the league voted to allow the Daisies to add Rockford All-Star Ruth Richard to the roster.

Tempers flared. Grand Rapids, claiming that using a new player was unfair, played the first game under protest—and won, 8–7. Attempting to resolve the matter the following night in Fort Wayne, Chick manager Woody English, a former major leaguer, and Daisy pilot Bill Allington ended up fighting at home plate. Later, the Chick players voted not to play, so the Daisies advanced to the championship round.

Meanwhile, fourth-place Kalamazoo (48–49) surprised second-place South Bend (48–44) in three games. Lassie Gloria Cordes hurled and lost the opener, but pitchers Nancy Warren and Elaine Roth won games two and three, respectively.

On Wednesday, September 1, the best of five championship round opened at Kalamazoo's Catholic Athletic Association Field.

Based on interviews, letters from players, and game stories that appeared in the local newspaper, Kalamazoo's usual lineup (the stats are for 1954) featured the following players:

2B—Nancy Mudge, an All-Star in 1954 who hit a career-best .232

1B/P—Peppas (Jean Lovell often played first when June pitched)

OF/C/RHP Chris Ballingall, a "Home Run Twin" who slugged 17 dingers

SS—Dot Schroeder, a slick fielder who was the league's only 12-year player

3B—Fern Shollenberger, the four-time All-Star third sacker who hit .268

OF/1B/C—Jean Lovell, a versatile player who hit .286 with 21 homers

CF— "Home Run Twin" Carol Habben, who connected for 15 homers

C/OF—Jenny "Rifle Arm" Romatowski, an All-Star catcher who hit .258

OF/1B—Mary Taylor, a second-year outfielder who averaged .251 lifetime

RHP—Nancy Warren, with a lifetime mark of 114–93, was a key starter for Kazoo

RHP—Elaine Roth, a spot starter and reliever, compiled a career 45-69 record

RHP—Gloria Cordes, an All-Star in 1952 and 1954, was 12–7 with 2.92 ERA

○ **Game one:** *Lassies 17-Daisies 9, Peppas 2-for-4*

Kalamazoo hitters blasted the pitching of the league's top winner, Maxine Kline. Although she had an 18–7 record with 3.23 ERA during the season, Kline gave up 11 runs in six innings, and Kazoo scored six more in the eighth off Virginia Carver.

Performing before a crowd of 1,299 (a total of 8,230 paid to see the five games), Pep started for the Lassies, pitched seven solid innings, and rapped two hits—including a homer in the first inning. She tired in the eighth, yielding solo homers to Katie Horstman and Jo Weaver. Nancy Warren relieved, got Jean Geissinger to hit into a double play, and saved the victory.

Hitting dominated the loosely-fielded opener, as the two clubs combined for seven home runs and 11 errors (seven by the Daisies). Horstman connected for two four-baggers, while Weaver, Peppas, and three more Lassies—Carol Habben, Fern Shollenberger, and Chris Ballingall, who hit a grand slam—slugged one each.

○ **Game two:** *Daisies 11-Lassies 4, Peppas 1-for-3*

In the second game favored Fort Wayne bounced back at "home run heaven," as Kalamazoo's bandbox CAA Field was dubbed, hitting five round-trippers to win, 11–4. Gloria Cordes started for the Lassies. Due to a mix-up over the game's starting time, the umpires did not allow her to warm up. Starting cold, Cordes allowed five runs before getting a batter out. After a leadoff walk to Mary Weddle, Katie Horstman homered for a 2–0 Daisy lead. Ruth Richard and Jo Weaver singled, and Betty Foss slugged a three-run homer for a 5–0 edge.

Right-hander Elaine Roth relieved Cordes and completed the game. But Fort Wayne slammed three more homers. Kalamazoo countered with leadoff shots by Nancy Mudge in the third inning, Peppas (who played first base) in the seventh, and Dottie Schroeder in the ninth, but the game's outcome was never in doubt.

○ **Game three:** *Daisies 8-Lassies 7, Peppas 1-for-4*

After moving to Fort Wayne's spacious Memorial Field for the rest of the series, the Daisies won a close one, 8–7, fueled by the heavy hitting of Jo Weaver. The AAGPBL's best batter produced a double, a triple, and a three-run homer in five at-bats, driving in four runs.

Still, Kalamazoo got off to a 3–0 lead in the fourth frame, thanks to a single and three Daisy errors. In the fifth Nancy Mudge doubled and scored from second when Peppas lifted a long flyball to deep right field. Maxine Kline, doing double duty as an outfielder, caught the ball. But when she fell backward on the banked earth, the speedy Mudge raced home.

In the decisive seventh inning Peppas added a base hit to spark a three-run Lassie rally, which was capped by Chris Ballingall's two-run single. But the Daisies came back in the bottom of the inning, scoring twice off Nancy Warren for the final 8–7 margin.

○ **Game four:** *Lassies 6-Daisies 5, Peppas 2-for-4*

Without the confusion preceding game two, Cordes, this time properly warmed up, pitched a complete game. Allowing five runs on nine hits, Gloria helped Kalamazoo tie the series. With Fort Wayne leading 5–2 in the eighth, Kalamazoo rallied for four runs by combining a walk, a sacrifice bunt, and five singles—by Mudge, Ballingall, Fern Shollenberger, Jean Lovell, and Carol Habben, with Habben driving home the winning tally. Bill Allington summoned Phyllis Baker in relief of Kline, but it proved too late.

Ballingall led the visitors with three hits, including a double. Peppas contributed a single, a double, and one RBI; Dot Schroeder rapped a base hit and a solo home run; and Shollenberger added two singles—as the first seven batters in the line-up produced 13 hits.

○ **Game five:** *Lassies 8--Daisies 5, Peppas 3-for-5*

Saving her best for last, June enjoyed a three-hit night and pitched a clutch game, yielding four singles and one double. She had plenty of hitting support from Mary Taylor, who had a perfect 5-for-5 game with two doubles, and Ballingall, who went 3-for-4.

Peppas made one big error. With her club ahead 5–1 going into the bottom of the fifth, she yielded two singles and a walk to load the bases. With two outs she dropped a pop fly, allowing two Daisies to score, but the left-hander got the third out with no further damage.

June gave up a run in the bottom of the eighth, but her teammates scored three in the last two frames. The game-winner came home in the top of the eighth on Schroeder's big double. Also, a base hit plus RBI singles by Peppas and Ballingall added two markers in the ninth.

In the end, the inspired Lassies rose to the challenge and batted .337 as a team, while the usually heavy-hitting Daisies averaged .275.

The All-American League was unable to return in 1955 and soon faded from most memories. Finally, in 1980, Peppas launched the newsletter project to get in touch with friends, teammates, and opponents. "I missed an organizational meeting," the former All-Star recalled, "and was elected president, which I held for four years. We accomplished becoming a Players Association, getting the permanent display on 'Women in Baseball' at the Baseball Hall of Fame in Cooperstown, and the movie, *A League of Their Own*.

"We are quite proud of our accomplishments," June Peppas reminisced, "and we hope the All-Americans will not be forgotten again. We were a proud lot."

EXCEPTING TONY GWYNN'S .394 IN THE ABORTED 1994 SEASON, *no one has come closer to batting .400 in the last sixty years than George Brett did in 1980. After a slow start, Brett had a 34-for-76 streak in late Spring that raised his average to .337. A foot-injury sidelined him for 26 games in June and July, whereupon he returned and continued hitting at a torrid pace. He reached .400 for the first time on August 17, a game in which he went four-for-four to stretch his consecutive-game batting-streak to 29.*

In early September an injured wrist, which caused him to miss ten games, and a slight slump dropped him temporarily below the magic mark. But once again, he bounced back. By September 19, Brett had accumulated 161 hits in 403 at-bats. That figured out to .3995, which rounded to .400, with just 14 games remaining in the season. The next night, September 20, Oakland right-hander Matt Keogh held him hitless in four at-bats, dropping his average to .396.

Brett would never reach .400 again. He "slumped off" to a .333 pace (14-for-42) in his remaining games to finish with a.390 average. It was still 38 points higher than runner-up Cecil Cooper of Milwaukee, and it earned Brett his second batting title and his first Most Valuable Player Award. —LYLE SPATZ

Found in a Trunk

by Frank Keetz

Twenty years ago, an ordinary 93-year-old childless widow named Edna Crotty died in Waterford, a small upstate New York village. Somewhat later, the usual estate sale was held to dispose of all her belongings from the house and barn—mostly the normal furniture, decorative figurines, appliances, tools, books, maybe a few antique items. A small, very dusty, grit-covered trunk was hauled out of the barn and opened, probably for the first time in a half century. Attendees (antique dealers, collectors, bargain hunters, plain curious folk) watched as the man in charge pulled out one item after another. An old pair of heavy woolen baseball pants, some undershirts, a small peaked cap, some old postcards, a belt, a couple woolen baseball shirts with names of cities across the fronts, a tiny baseball glove, 22 old letters, frayed newspapers, baseball shoes, towels. One lady eventually observed, "Somebody in this family must have liked baseball." Soon the trunk was empty. All the items were sold but to five or six different purchasers including both antique dealers and collectors. The contents went in different local geographic directions—some here, some there.

Eventually most of the contents were consolidated in one location. After a brief perusal of the letters and newspaper clippings, it was apparent that the "somebody" was a Walter Hammersley. But who was Walter Hammersley and how did all these cloth, leather, and paper items get into the trunk? And how were these items related to the lately deceased Edna Crotty?

Some of the letters ultimately answered the second question, since there were letters from a wife Edna to a husband Walter and vice versa. Edna lived in the Waterford area and Walter played in the Greensboro, North Carolina, area. The letters were dated either 1909 or 1910, so examination of the old Reach and Spalding Baseball Guides proved very helpful. A tiny "Hammersley, Greensboro" line appeared a couple times in the batting, fielding, and pitching statistics of the Carolina Association, a Class D league situated in the western regions of North and South Carolina.

Old National Association of Professional Baseball Leagues (minor leagues) contract records located in the Baseball Hall of Fame Library in Cooperstown as well as occasional mentions in *The Sporting Life* and *The Sporting News* led to "leads" and more bits of useful information about Hammersley's baseball career. The old tattered newspapers from the trunk confirmed much of what the baseball guides and official contracts indicated and added one surprising development.

Meanwhile, research in the Waterford area led to a small Waterford Historical Museum and some crucial facts. The museum had a town history written by a Colonel Sidney E. Hammersley which was dedicated to his three daughters. One daughter, then Frances Hammersley Child, was Walter's niece and still living.

Frank Keetz joined SABR in 1980, the same year that the Hammersly trunk was discovered. It took him twenty-two years to research and complete this, his seventh SABR article.

She readily solved many of the puzzling gaps in the story.

Walter was born in England, was one of eleven children, "was a vivid redhead," married Edna Shufelt, was "after baseball" a lock operator on the state barge canal in Waterford, and died young in October 1921 at age 37 of pulmonary tuberculosis. Edna had married a William Crotty sometime after Walter's death, which explained the different name at the estate sale. Mrs. Child identified the single gravestone in the local cemetery where Walter, Edna, and William's names appear next to each other. The obituary in the nearby Troy *Record* verified much of the above and said Hammersley "had considerable of a base ball career."

Yes, Hammersley had "considerable of a base ball career." After learning the pitching craft in local amateur and semiprofessional outings, he made the ultimate step into professional baseball in the spring of 1908. At age 24, he went South for a tryout with the Norfolk, Virginia, team. They released him, but he soon hooked up with Greensboro, which had the Class D team in the Carolina Association. It was a six-team league composed of Charlotte (population 34,014) and five smaller towns. Greensboro's population totaled 15,895.

Hammersley had a fabulous 1908 season as he helped pitch the Greensboro Patriots to the league title with a 22-8 win-loss record. He led the league in both wins and innings pitched. The Patriots clinched the pennant with victories in an exciting season-ending series against second-place Greenville, South Carolina, whose featured player was none other than the legendary 19-year-old "Shoeless Joe" Jackson. "Shoeless Joe" from Pickens County, SC, acclaimed by many to be the greatest natural hitter of all time, led the league with a .346 batting average. Nevertheless, one newspaper clipping from the "trunk" documents that Hammersley held Jackson hitless in five plate appearances in a brilliant mid-season game described in the local press as "the best contest ever seen on the local diamond." Greensboro won that contest, a 12-inning 1-0 complete game, five-hit masterpiece by Hammersley before 800 fans in one hour and 55 minutes. In another clipping, he won both games of a doubleheader 2-1 and 4-1. It was an "iron man" feat, as both were complete games. Hammersley, who had a spitball in his repertoire, pitched more than 200 innings that year. Of course, it was the "dead ball" era, which was to his advantage. Extra-base hits were few, batting averages and game scores were low. There was, however, no doubt that Walter was a hero in the then-small Carolina town.

The first and only 1909 "trunk letter" was written by Walter in Greensboro to Edna in upstate New York on April 9, 1909. Written to *"My dearest little Girl,"* he is about to leave on a ten-day spring training road trip to three Virginia towns—Danville, Lynchburg, and Roanoke. Despite a remarkable passing comment (*"I beat Boston* [National League Pilgrims] *here today 7-0. That is good for a kid don't you think so"*), he is more concerned with Edna's absence. *"I want you to write me and tell me in your next letter all about your leaving. The board will cost us the same as last year."* Two more times he repeats his wish and ends, *"Be sure & come down & do what I say. with love & kisses from your own boy X X X X X"*

Hammersley was back on the mound at wooden Cone Athletic Park in Greensboro when the official 1909 season started, and the Patriots (now called "the Champs") again won the Carolina Association pennant, edging Anderson, South Carolina, by three games. His win-loss record, however, declined to 14-15, although he again pitched over 200 innings. He lost a 16-inning 1-0 complete game in Greenville. Then there was a 12-inning scoreless tie game with Winston-Salem. Again he completed both games of a double-header, winning the opener 3-1 before dropping the nightcap to Anderson. With a roster of only 12-13 players (and no Sunday games), these teams usually had three-man pitching rotations. Even the local paper commented, "Hammersley meant well, but 10 innings straight is too much for any pitcher." (There was also one 1909 canceled July postcard from Kalamazoo, Michigan, in the trunk from an outfielder and 1908 teammate Cogswell to Walter. The message read, *"Hello Kid I am leading the League in hitting and Fielding how are you and the Bunch."* Cogswell's claim has been verified.)

The Greensboro Patriots had a disappointing season in 1910 under a new manager. It was also a bad year for Walter Hammersley if judged by his won-lost record. The team finished the season in last place, in part because it had a team batting average of .208 and also fielded poorly. The batting and fielding did not help Hammersley, who left Greensboro at the end of July with a 4-12 record. It was during this season that most of the revealing "trunk letters" and newspaper clippings from Walter and Edna Hammersley give a little insight to the obscure pitcher on the obscure Class D team.

Two high points of any minor leaguer would be to pitch against major league teams. Walter had done that in 1908 and repeated the same task in early April during two exhibition games against the New York National League Giants and the New York American League Highlanders. (Both were second-place finishers in 1910.) Hammersley pitched three innings against the mostly Giant regulars, allowing two runs as his team lost 9-2. The Highlanders won 11-3 with Hammersley allowing eight runs in four innings. Four errors did not help his cause. If nothing else, excitement and two capacity crowds benefited the Patriots' financial situation.

Two days later, Walter wrote, *"My dear Edna,"* from Roanoke. He was pitching the next day and commented, *"There is lots of money up on the game."* Then *"Most of our team was drunk tonight. This is a wet town and they all took advantage of it and got piped up. Pug Hicks (a shortstop) and Eldridge (a pitcher) near had a fight."* Unlike Roanoke, he wrote, *"Greensboro is all locked up on Sundays. you cant bye a cocola on sunday nor any candy. Just amagine me going all day sunday with out a drink or a little candy. They even locked a man up for putting up bills advertising a show. because it had girls drested in short closes. The town has gone to the bad."*

Three days later in Danville, still on the exhibition trip, he got mad when told no mail had been forwarded from Greensboro *"for I knew you had wrote me one letter at least. Then Bentley came in from some pool room with two one from you & one from Mother."* Later, he reports, *"This has been a very hot day and all the dirt seemed to stick to me,"* which led to an hour in the hotel bath tub. Before ending he said, *"I got so lonesome on sunday afternoons I dont know what to do or where to look. I near go crazy. Well it wont be very long before you will be here to cheer me up."*

A week later, he wrote that he was *"getting along fine"* but *"to morrow is sunday and it will be another lonesome day. I wont here any music and see you or any of my folks but will cheer up for I see you soon."* He also recorded, *"There was a nigger game here this afternoon and they played 5 innings and got in a fight and quit and went home. The A & M team & the Orangburg team from south carolina."* (The daily Greensboro newspaper verified this Negro college game and event between visiting Claflin College and local North Caroline Agricultural and Mechanic College.) To add to his woes, *"Mr. Collins dont let us in to his show any more. He has a sign up (no free list here) so we are strung up then."*

Next day, he wrote, *"My dear little Neddie"* that he had pitched five innings on a very cold (*"almost to cold to play ball"*) day. *"My arm is quite sore and weak and it gets tired when I write."* But he *"got a hit with two men on base and scored them both. Then I scored." "Some doctor took me in and fixed me up (with turkish bath)."* He ends, *"I wish I had you here to go to bed with me to night and you can amagine how I feel while I am writing this to you." "Be sure & be good and Ill be the same. I send you lots of love & lots of kisses. I am as ever your own Boy X X X X X X"*

Walter is really angry a week later when Edna has still not left upstate New York. *"I think you had better stay in one place and quit your running around so you can get my mail and do as I say. . . . And I wrote and told you I would be gone away after Apr 30 and asked you as nice as any one could ask you to be here before I went away. Well suit yourself come when you please."* He signs off, *"I am still your true Walt."*

The season opened on April 28. A second championship flag was raised after *"a parade in auto mobiles and the minister threw the first ball over the plate."* He pitched the opening game and lost 6-3. *"Well that won't be the only game I will lose. I wish it was but Ill lose more than that."* However, most of the letter still discusses Edna's absence without the anger that appeared in the previous letter. This letter ends with *"good by with lots of love I am ever your boy. X X I hurt my finger & cant write good by come soon. X X X X X"*

He is pleased the following night, having received a card from Edna. The team lost to Winston-Salem and already had many injuries. *"I have a boil on my arm my right one at that."* He expects her to arrive by May 14 *"and if you are not here I don't know what I'll do. I might come after you."* He closes with two thoughts. *"They are just ordering me a new suit so they must intend to keep me. Well good by my little wife and hope you have not talked to any men even than I have women."*

Edna finally arrived in Greensboro, and Walter's only problems are now baseball-oriented. Naturally the teams play "on the road" half the time, so Walter and Edna still write each other. His very tired team arrived in Spartanburg, South Carolina, at 12:40 p.m., woke to an intermittent rain but *"not enough for to stop us playing."* Later, he stumbled during pre-game practice in the outfield and *"hit my left shoulder and it hurt very bad."* The Patriots then lost a 2-1 extra inning game on a "bad" umpire decision at the plate. One player says *"those Northern Umpires always give the southern managers the worst end of the deal."* Greensboro manager C. Beusse was a southerner. It was not the best of days for Walter.

Edna got another pessimistic letter the following day. The Patriots lost 4-3. Walter's left shoulder is still troublesome. *"I tell you it is just as bad as my right one was. But I am going to try and pitch to-morrow game."* He then confides to Edna, *"I can't see where we have any chance of winning with the club we have here now. All they think of is to go out and get the game over with."* Two days later from Greenville—*"Your poor old boy lost his fourth game."* (He pitched a four-hitter. His win-loss record dropped to 1-4.) He had to end the letter quickly as the train was about to leave for Anderson.

There were three letters from Edna to Walter in the trunk. Walter received the first letter when he arrived in Anderson. It opened *"Dearest Walter"* and ended *"So will close with lots of love from your own kid. X X X X X X."* Edna was *"awful sorry to hear that you lost again"* and then told what she had done that day. *"We all set up last night until 12 o'clock but didn't see any thing of the comet."* Edna, Mrs. Morris, and Miss Beasley *"went to prayer meeting. Mrs. Morris treated us to a drink & I took pepsi-Cola & they each took Cocoa-Cola and the clerk spilt some on my white skirt."*

Walter received the second letter the following day. Edna told how *"eight of us went to the graduating exercises last night up to the Opera house the music was good but I got awful tired listening to the long address."* Edna seemed to have lots of friends in both New York and North Carolina. Other letters to Edna from friends in upstate New York and to Walter from his mother were newsy while featuring comments about farm animals, Methodist church attendance, constant hard work, and family illness. Naïve Edna also had one question which concerned all baseball players. *"The paper said that Smith saved himself from getting the pink slip maybe you know what that means."* The third letter contained a short three-lined Christian prayer to be copied and mailed to a friend on each of nine days. Failing to do so would lead to misfortune. Instructions ended with *"do not break chain."* The letter is unsigned but clearly in Edna's handwriting.

The Patriots made six errors a week later as Hammersley lost a ragged 4-2 home game to Greenville, whose outstanding player was catcher Ivy Wingo, a Georgian bound to spend 17 years in the National League. A local paper used the adjective "miserable" to describe the fielding. Hammersley scribbled in pencil on that sports page *"can't win with this bunch behind me."* In his final "trunk letter" from Spartanburg, he told Edna they had a rare 5-0 win that day while praising specific teammates who had made crucial *defensive* plays. (Does that sound like a pitcher?) He continued, *"I am going to pitch to morrows game and hope they make five runs for me and I know Ill win my game."* Getting personal, he told Edna, *"I saw a nice pair of Dorothy Dod slippers here"* but *"I lost your size"* and ended *"Well be a good girl and I be good."* The trunk did contain a five-inch sterling silver hat pin with an attractive three-quarter-inch baseball on one end—no doubt a gift to Edna at one time. Money issues are seldom mentioned in the letters, although Class D player salaries were very low in 1910. Few of these players could afford to bring their wives to a distant city, yet neither Edna nor Walter appear to have come from great wealth.

The final "trunk letter" was mailed to *"My dear Edna"* from Greenville. Walter told of damp beds in the hotel, how a teammate *"got some fellow to take us out on a fine ride in an auto,"* an unusual victory before 198 fans, and how the local authorities *"are not going to allow them to show the pictures of Jeffries and Johnson fight."* (Jeffries of course was the "great white hope" brought out of retirement to fight champion Negro Jack Johnson, who defended his heavyweight title with a 15th-round KO.) The team must leave town at 8 p.m. for Charlotte. Evidently, he and Edna had a spat. He wrote, *"Well Edna let us try and get along to-gether with out fighting. There is nothing in rangling with each other."* He ended, *"I am as ever your boy X X"*

Something happened shortly after this letter. Hammersley left last-place Greensboro and returned north. It appeared that *his* season was completed. But it was not. Newspapers and clippings in the trunk cover some August and September 1910 dates. The common factor in all these paper items is a pitcher for Utica, New York, in the higher-classification New York State League named "Harding." In reality, "Hammersley" and "Harding" were the same person. Eventually, in 1913, the ruse was discovered in another league, an unaffiliated league at that, when he again assumed the "Harding" moniker. (Official minor league baseball records have him "reserved" by Greensboro on October 21, 1910 [for the next season] but then "released" on March 14, 1911.) Anyway, illegal "Harding" pitched a shutout in his first game at Utica, then hurried back to Troy for his father's funeral (which may have been the reason he left Greensboro), and finished the season with four more losses, although three were well-pitched games against Binghamton, Syracuse, and Wilkes-Barre.

The Waterford righthander spent the 1911 summer pitching semipro games in the Troy-Albany area. Based on his 1911 showing, Hammersley spent all of 1912 in the New York State League. He started with Albany, lost all four decisions (including a 1-0 defeat), was released but quickly signed with Troy. He won at least six games including two shutouts for the Trojans but lost at least ten games. He was a hard-luck twirler, losing many 1-0, 2-1, 3-0 games. He even had an 11-inning 1-1 no-decision game. The local press often referred to him as the "Waterford curver," the "Waterford spitballer," "the Waterford boy," although he was now 29. Nevertheless, he also hurled two complete exhibition games against the Chicago Cubs, whose main attraction was local hero Johnny Evers. Hammersley was pounded in an 11-3 loss at Green Island but won 5-2 in Albany.

Hammersley opened the 1913 season with Troy winning at least one 2-1 game before joining Pittsfield, Massachusetts, of the Class B Eastern Association, where he won six of 14 decisions. He seemed to have the misfortune to play for second-division teams after the initial two Greensboro years. Near season's end, he, as "Harding" again, was winning games for Bellows Falls, Vermont, in the unaffiliated Twin States League. The ruse was discovered by the Greenfield team. The local paper reported, "Harding is Hammersley, who recently traveled with the Pittsfield Eastern Association team."

Two 1913 Bellows Falls team photo postcards showing him as a member were in the trunk, as was one postcard of the Keene, New Hampshire, baseball field. The Keene postcard was mailed to Edna. Its message read, *"Hello Neddie. I am all right. I am playing outfield and pitching for the rest of the season. Will write soon. Will be home next Sunday for good. Hammy"*

Hammersley's professional career was almost over. During the winter he tried to hook up with Binghamton but received a pleasant typewritten rejection from J. C. Calhoun, the Binghamton manager. It was the last correspondence in the trunk. He did start the 1914 season with York, Pennsylvania in the Class B Tri-state League, where he won at least two games before the team folded and moved to Lancaster. He ended with Northampton, New Hampshire, back in the unaffiliated Tri-State League as "Hammersley" this time, where he won at least seven games, all verified in the final newspaper clippings in the trunk. Two of the wins were in another iron-man doubleheader effort, 7-2 and 9-0. Perhaps illustrative of human nature, Hammersley saved accounts of only his well-pitched games—victories or tough losses. Seven years later, he was dead.

The letters give a brief glimpse of a serious full-time ballplayer's life during a losing season as well as that of the player's wife. These mostly 1910 letters were often negative in scope, partly reflecting a 4-12 win-loss record on a last-place team. (Letters written in 1908 would probably differ, since they would have reflected a 22-8 record on a pennant winner.) There was daily effort in 1910 but less opportunity for the exuberance that only a hit, a catch, a pitch, a win can bring. His was a competitive, sometimes injury-prone experience with players coming and going based on performance. There was often sweltering heat, boredom, constant travel, and frequent loneliness with few "to lean on." These letters sure contrast with those in "You Know Me Al" written by Ring Lardner in 1914.

(Hammersley appears in many of the "trunk photographs" usually as a team member but also in a couple photos wearing a formal bowler hat as well as a swimming suit. He seems to be a bit smaller in height and heft than most of his teammates. And yes, like most of those teammates, he can be seen on black-and-white 1909 Contentea and red-bordered 1910 Old Mill cigarette baseball cards.)

The Deacon, Chief and Henry Schmidt Clutch Stardom

Remembering Opening Day a Century Ago

by Dixie Tourangeau

After two years of unlawful contract signings and other roster-jumping shenanigans that produced endless lawsuits, baseball's Great Tampering War settled down as the 1903 NL campaign began on Thursday, April 16, in Cincinnati and St. Louis. Though personal disgust and distrust may not have subsided between all franchise owners, a signed truce between the long-time NL and upstart AL existed. It was inked in late January after a series of volatile meetings in Cincinnati. More amicable discussions followed as NL and AL reps met to negotiate non-conflicting schedules and coordinate the adoption of similar rules.

Headlines centered around AL President Ban Johnson's eventual agreement to enforce the standing NL foul rule, counting foul balls as strikes one and two. Johnson's spin claimed the change was supposed to speed up the game and prevent the best willow handlers from prolonging an at-bat to boring lengths while waiting for a perfect pitch to whack. Fans and sportswriters heatedly debated the move's pros and cons. Minus the strike penalty, the upstart ALers outhit their rivals by .010 in 1901 and .015 in 1902. On an even playing field in 1903, league stats readjusted and the NL hit .269 to the AL's .255, indicating that many AL bats were perhaps as overrated as the Senior Circuit often charged.

Manager/LF Fred Clarke's (.351) Pittsburgh Pirates had simply demolished the NL in 1902 with a 103–36 record. Wins (91) were to be only slightly more difficult for them in 1903. In 1902 the Reds finished 70–70 with Sam Crawford as their top batter (.333 in 1902). Crawford jumped to AL Detroit in 1903 while Pittsburgh lost its '02 mound ace Jack Chesbro (28–6) to the new AL franchise in New York. Manager/utility man Joe Kelley's Reds opened against the Pirates and Charles "Deacon" Phillippe. The gallant Phillippe (25–9) also would pitch Pittsburgh's last game that year, the final October contest of the first World Series, which he lost 3-0 in Boston. The nine-game event (one tie) gave Phillippe a probably never-to-be-broken single Series mark of 3 wins and 2 losses.

Deacon started his year off masterfully in Cincy, two-hitting the hosts, 7-1 in under two hours. Unfortunately, gloomy, drizzly weather blotted out the beautiful new stands at the spruced-up Palace of the Fans. Still, 12,000 cranks showed up and watched the Pirates rap out 11 hits off Jack Harper (6–8). Rookie C Ed Phelps (.282) had three hits, while CF Clarence "Ginger" Beaumont (.341, 1903 NL hit leader, run leader, and 1902 bat champ) and Phillippe (no hits) each scored twice. Batting champ of '03, SS Honus Wagner (.355) had two singles. Slugging CF Cy Seymour (.342) and vet SS Tommy Corcoran (.246) managed the Cincy safeties. Cy's bunt hit and Deacon's wild throw allowed Seymour to score on a subsequent groundout in the seventh. Manager Kelley (.316) did not play in his team's opener.

Boston park ranger Dixie Tourangeau supplies SABRites with box seats and scorecards for classic Openers most of us missed.

After a one-day rain postponement out in St. Louis, only 4,500 people populated the Robison Field (also called League Park) stands on Vandeventer Avenue to witness a 2-1 victory by the locals. In a pitchers duel, Cardinal Clarence Currie (5–14) bested Chicago "Colt," Jack "Brakeman" Taylor (21–14), a 22–11, 1.33, 8-shutout hurler in 1902. Leadoff Card 2B Johnny Farrell (.272) got three singles, an RBI, and scored, while rookie SS Otto Williams (single) came home with the other run. For Frank Selee's Chicagoans rookie 2B Johnny Evers (.293) and 3B Joe Tinker (.291, two errors) slashed out three of the four (or five) Colt hits. Tinker singled and scored in the eighth inning when Currie committed a fielding error, botching his own shutout, according to one news account. However, the Chicago *Tribune* claimed 1B Bill Hanlon (played just eight ML games, .095) knocked Tinker home on a "lucky" bounce hit, but neglected to give Bill credit for the scratch in its box score. Cardinal manager/RF Patsy Donovan, who guided his club to a cellar finish of 43–94, went hitless, but his fly ball plated Farrell. Tinker and C Johnny Kling botched a simple rundown play at third base that gave Farrell an extra "life." Canadian Currie was 15–23 in his two-year career.

In 1986 SABR voters retroactively selected Iowa native "Tornado Jake" Weimer (20–9) as NL rookie of the year for 1903. He started the next day for Chicago, but blew a 6-0 lead to his hosts. Chicago won in the tenth, 7-6 as Jock Menefee (8–8), beginning his last season of a nine-year career, picked up the relief victory. Left fielder Jimmy Slagle (.298) had three hits and scored twice for the Colts. Farrell smacked two doubles and scored twice, but made three errors for St. Louis. Weimer, who in 1902 won 25 games and topped the Western League with 209 Ks for champion Kansas City under manager "Kid" Nichols (27–7), led the NL in 1903 in allowing the fewest hits per nine innings, was third in ERA at 2.30 and fifth in whiffs. Jake, already 29, was one of only a handful of southpaws in the league in that year.

Games scheduled in New York and Philadelphia were postponed due to rain and cold.

On Friday, the other four NL squads opened as Boston visited Philadelphia and New York's borough rivals battled at the Polo Grounds. Vic Willis, the NL workhorse of 1902 (27–20, 410 innings) toed the slab for Boston. In the third frame he started the winning rally with a double and soon scored. It was the first of 5 runs leading to an 8-3 win over Chick Fraser (12–17) before a crowd of 8,250 on a cool, clear afternoon at the Huntingdon Grounds (later Baker Bowl). Willis (12–18) had two hits as did his catcher, Mal Kittridge (.213, two RBI, and a run that day). Left fielder Duff Cooley (.289) had three singles and knocked in the first run. Manager Al Buckenberger's Beaneater star 1B, Fred Tenney (.313), scored twice. Phils' LF Bill "Wagon Tongue" Keister (.320), playing in his last of seven seasons, drove out two hits and got two RBI. Strangely, Bill never played for the same team in consecutive years but also never played for a different ML team other than the one he started with in any year. Rookie lefty Fred Burchell (0–3) relieved Fraser and got the Quakers' third RBI. He played most of his short (13-15) career later with the Red Sox. In 1903 Chief Zimmer caught his final 37 games (.220) as the Phils' skipper.

A clear and mild day brought out 20,000 Polo Grounds spectators, who were treated to an offensive explosion as both the Giants and Brooklyn scored four runs in the first inning, but the Superbas prevailed, 9-7. The wife of Giants president John T. Brush threw out the first pitch, and from the grandstand the Seventh Regiment Band entertained the throng. In attendance was "the father of baseball" and first scorekeeper, Henry Chadwick. Yells of "Harrah for Muggsey" came from everywhere for New York manager John McGraw, who some papers had listed as a possible Opening Day starter. In reality, retired legend McGraw played only a handful of games from 1903 to 1906, mostly necessitated by player injuries. Umpire Hank O'Day shouted, "Play ball" at 4:05 p.m.

A century's worth of hindsight shows the pitching matchup to have been an odd classic. Christy Mathewson (30–13), who would have a 17-year Hall of Fame career, faced Texan Henry Schmidt (22-13), in what was Henry's only ML campaign. Ned Hanlon's men got nine hits off Christy, but Mathewson's five walks, two wild pitches, and six Giant errors really sealed the home club's tomb that day. Much traveled veteran 1B "Dirty" Jack Doyle (.313) had three of Brooklyn's hits. Left fielder Jimmy Sheckard (.332, NL leader with nine home runs) had two singles, scored three runs, and swiped three bases. Playing in his only ML season, RF Walt McCreedie (.324 in 56 games) also touched home thrice. Sub CF Ed Householder, who played just 12 ML games (.209), had a hit and scored twice.

For New York, city native 3B Billy Lauder (.281) began his final of five ML campaigns with three hits of the Giants 11 and had three RBI. Schmidt first faced

RF/leadoff man George Browne, who immediately smashed his first of 18 career home runs over the right-field fence. Star CF George Van Haltren (.257) tripled, doubled, and scored twice. Van Haltren would end his 17-year career (.316) in 1903, and his first hit on Opening Day was the last of his 162 three-baggers. Sam Mertes (.280), a vet of both Chicago franchises, belted the first of his NL-top 32 doubles, but didn't drive home any of his NL-high 104 RBI. Sam did score twice. Rookie SS Charlie Babb (.248) had two singles and scored for the losers. Babb played his other two years for Brooklyn. 1B Dan McGann smacked a double, had an RBI, scored once, and swiped two pillows. Playing in his first full Giants season, Roger Bresnahan (.350) sat out the Opener. He patrolled the pastures mostly in 1903, catching only 11 times.

When Brooklyn opened at its Washington Park home four days later, Matty and Henry dueled again. Some 17,000 roaring fans saw Schmidt pitch much better, but this time Christy had his Cooperstown stuff, winning 2-1, on a three-hitter. Crack pistol shot 3B Sammy Strang walked and scored in the first inning off Matty, but then "Big Six" slammed the run door shut. Browne and McGann (two hits) later toured the basepaths for the Giants to nip Schmidt's eight-hit effort.

Thirty-year-old rookie Schmidt is one of the most interesting characters of 1903. The Brownsville-born righty remains the lone hurler to win 20-plus games in the only season he ever pitched in the majors. In 1902, Henry (35–20) was in the outlaw Independent California League with the pennant-winning Oakland Clamdiggers (108 wins). Only Los Angeles workhorse Oscar Jones (36–25) had more decisions and wins. Batters hit less than .200 against both of the two pitchers. Brooklyn also signed Jones for the 1903 campaign (19–14) to make up for the loss of moundsmen Frank Kitson (19–13 in 1902) and Wild Bill Donovan (17–15) to AL Detroit.

After his battles with Mathewson, Schmidt shut out Philadelphia, Boston, and Philly again (on 17 total hits) before losing to Boston. Henry ended his campaign with a great flourish, going 7–0–1 in mid-August/September. Matty beat him 3-1 on August 10, on a five-hitter and George Browne scoring twice. Then Henry began his streak. After one win he defeated rookie Cub Weimer 6-2 as each gave up seven hits and scored a run. Chicago's six errors and four walks by Tornado Jake gave host Brooklyn the win on the day super horse "Dan Patch" set a world pacing record at nearby Brighton Beach track. Schmidt did get whacked around once, but the Superbas won 11-10 anyway. In September Henry erased Boston 5-0 on two hits, beat New York ace Joe McGinnity, 3-0 at the Polo Grounds behind Sheckard's bat, edged Colt (aka Cub) Currie 3-2 in Chi-town, tied St. Louis and nipped pennant winner Pittsburgh, 5-4 in 10 innings after blowing a lead in the ninth. Opposing Cardinal pitcher Jim Hackett (1–7 career, usually a 1B) ruined Schmidt's perfect month with three hits (2 runs, 2 RBI) in their 5-5 tie. Pittsburgh manager Clarke came off the bench to pinch hit a home run to tie Schmidt in the ninth. If another Pirate had been on base or Brooklyn had scored one less run, Clarke's blast would have ended the game and Henry's season the way it started, by serving up a rare round tripper. Unknown to anyone, that was the last of Schmidt in the majors. Though the Texan's arm kept the mediocre Superbas above .500, Schmidt returned his 1904 contract unsigned, saying he simply did not like living in the East. Henry toiled in the reorganized Pacific Coast League through 1908, going 26–28 for Oakland in 1904.

Giant McGinnity (born McGinty), arguably baseball's best flinger from 1899 to 1904, topped the NL in wins with a tireless 31-20 record (434 innings) in 1903. McGraw's "Iron Man" ace won his first and second starts by beating Brooklyn, 6-1 and 7-2, on April 19 and 22. He left the NL his calling card on April 19, gaining the first Giant win with a one-hitter. Dirty Doyle managed the hit while LF Sheckard toured the bags on an E-wp-E sandwich for Brooklyn. Catcher Bresnahan singled and homered (2 RBI, 2 runs) to beat vagabond hurler Roy Evans (4–12), who had been arrested in February in Butte, MT, for passing bad checks. Joe was the pennant-winning Superbas' big winner in 1900 at 29-9. He then moved to AL Baltimore with McGraw for that town's 1901 inaugural campaign where he was 26–20.

BAN JOHNSON'S BOYS COMMENCE HOSTILITIES

It was not until Monday, April 20, that the American League got under way in 1903, and it did so with a huge bang. It was Patriots' Day in Boston and New England's Hub was in a sports and holiday frenzy. There were home doubleheaders slated for both the AL's Huntington Avenue Grounds and the South End Grounds of the NL, located just across some railroad tracks. But those events had to share a grand spring day with the seventh annual Boston Athletic Association marathon (31 of 56 runners finished), a major horse show, a boxing match, the city of Revere and Charles River Park cycle races, an auto hill-climbing contest, Tufts College facing the "strong" amateur Wellington club (6-4 Tufts) in baseball, the city's North End Park athletic games, and the area's annual Revolutionary War hoopla at Lexington Green and Concord's famed Old North Bridge, "where embattled farmers stood." Another veterans event was also held in nearby Arlington. Tuesday's Boston *Globe* newspaper estimated that more than 360,000 persons attended all these events, with 200,000 of them lining the 26-mile marathon route.

The AL's morning and afternoon contests drew 27,660 persons to the NL's 5,700. As baseball sometimes goes, however, the marquee pitchers in both games were shelled like British redcoats. Connie Mack's 1902 AL champs split with manager/3B Jimmy Collins' 1903 pennant winners. Visiting Athletics' lefty ace, Rube Waddell (21–16, 302 K) lost the morning tilt, 9-4 to George Winter (9–8), while Cy Young (AL win high 28–9) blew an apparent easy win over Eddie Plank (23–16, 336 innings), by losing 10-7 in the afternoon. Waddell fanned the first four Pilgrims he faced, but when ahead 2-0 gave up doubles to 1B Candy LaChance (2 RBI, 2 runs) and mound foe Winter (2 RBI) in the five-run fourth frame. Second baseman Hobe Ferris had two hits, scored twice, and knocked one home for Winter. Right fielder Buck Freeman singled and scored (AL tops with 13 home runs and 104 RBI). For Philly, SS Monte Cross, CF Ollie Pickering, and 2B Danny Murphy (run) each had two hits. Seventeen-year veteran, 3B Lave Cross, doubled and scored, as did gentleman 1B Harry Davis. Newspapers reported that fans lustily booed each foul strike call by the umpire.

In the afternoon encore the script was reversed. When the A's seventh inning began they were hitless, and Boston had pounded Plank for a 6-0 lead. Of 16 Pilgrim safeties, both Freeman and SS Fred Parent (.304) had accumulated a single, double, and triple each (2 runs and an RBI for Buck and 2 RBI for Fred). LaChance scored twice and Young had an RBI. But it all evaporated in the seventh when Philadelphia clobbered Cy's suddenly docile throws for 6 runs. Pickering's 2-RBI triple and run were key. Ollie had another RBI in the eighth and Lave finished the job with his own two-run triple in the ninth. Right fielder "Socks" Seybold, Lave, and Davis each scored twice for Philly. Shortstop Monte had an RBI single and scored. Mack's boys smashed 12 hits over their final three frames. "Long Tom" Hughes (20–7) relieved Young in the ninth and allowed the last three Philly scores. Boston managed only a lone tally in their final turn at the dish.

Albert Charles Bender, half Chippewa and a Carlisle Indian School star, took over for "Gettysburg Eddie" in the fifth. It was the Minnesota reservation-born rookie's first ML game. SABR folks elected Mack's celebrated Chief as the AL's top 1903 freshman. Bender (17–13) swatted his first hit and scored, helping his own cause in the Opening Day comeback victory.

Also of note in the second game was the Pilgrims' touching tribute to 16-year catcher Charley "Duke" Farrell. In the second inning he was presented with an expensive diamond ring by his baseball buddies. Bay State native Farrell played only one year for any Boston club before 1903 (17 games, .404). It was for the 1891 Boston Reds, winners of the final American Association pennant. Duke (3B-C) hit .302 and led the circuit with 12 home runs and 110 RBI. Farrell caught both '03 Opening Day games, collected three hits, scored, and knocked home a couple of mates. A week later Farrell broke his leg trying to steal against Washington. He hit .212 in 1904 and retired after seven games in 1905.

Across the tracks the NL Boston-Philadelphia matchup was also a split decision, Boston winning the morning game 4-3, as Togie Pittinger (top NL loser at 19–23) tasted victory. In the afternoon the Phillies defeated their host Beantowners 10-7, behind Fred Mitchell (11–15). Willis, Boston's Opening Day victor, took the loss despite getting three hits off Mitchell, who made two himself and scored twice.

It wasn't until April 22 that the other AL teams played their first games of 1903. In Detroit, a record crowd of 16,482 piled into Corktown's Bennett Park on a cold, raw day to see the Tigers edge Cleveland 4-2. It was an early matchup between (then sophomore) phenoms George Mullin (19–15) and Addie Joss (18–13), a twosome worth seeing even in bad weather. Five hundred Elks were on hand and the mayor made the first ceremonial toss. Leadoff/CF Harry "Deerfoot" Bay singled (.292, 45 steals) and scored on 1B Charlie "Piano Legs" Hickman's (.330, 12 homers, 97 RBI) two-out base hit in the initial frame. In the third inning 3B Bill Bradley reached on a Mullin bobble and scored on a double play attempt after a Nap Lajoie single ('03 batting title champ with .355). Hickman and star RF Elmer Flick (.299) each had two hits. Detroit tied the score in the fifth, when ex-NL Clevelander, Lewis "Sport" McAllister (C), playing in his final season, doubled. With one out Bay dropped CF Jimmy Barrett's fly (.315), and both came home on 2B George "Heinie" Smith's double. Joss lost the game to Ed Barrow's boys in the eighth as AL newcomer and triples leader (25), LF Sam Crawford (.335) walked, SS Norm "Tabasco Kid" Elberfeld singled, and rookie RF Harry "Doc" Gessler doubled into the crowd. Bill Armour's Naps had no rally left in them. Smith, in his final season, Elberfeld and Gessler each had two hits of Detroit's seven. Mullin was a happy victor, since it was only two and half months since he surrendered to the Wayne County, IN, sheriff because he was wanted for perjury in a case concerning his finances.

Win Mercer, who was 15–18 for Detroit in 1902, was supposed to manage this Bengal edition, but he committed suicide by inhaling gas in San Francisco in mid-January.

At Sportsman's Park, 3,800 Brownie fans in overcoats and earmuffs saw their team pummeled by Charles Comiskey's White Sox, 14-4. Left fielder Bill H. Hallman scored four times with only one hit. Manager Nixey Callahan started Patsy Flaherty (11–25) for Chicago. Jimmy McAleer countered with Francis "Red" Donahue (15–16, 8–7 with the Browns), who gave up 16 hits. For Chicago, CF Fielder Jones, 3B Frank Isbell (two doubles, usually played 1B), and C Ed McFarland (.209) each had three hits. Four Sox scored twice and only hurler Flaherty didn't make a hit. For St. Louis, star leadoff/LF Jesse Burkett had two hits (including a home run) as did SS Bobby Wallace. First baseman/cleanup hitter John Anderson stroked three (one triple) and scored once. Browns captain/2B Dick Padden (.202/29 games) was injured, so outfielder Bill Friel played in his spot and made three early, costly errors. It was Friel's last of three ML seasons. At campaign's end, however, St. Louis had five more wins than Chicago, and Flaherty topped the AL in defeats.

Not in the Comiskey-Callahan Chicago lineup was primo club jumper (SS) George Davis, who hit .299 in 1902. His checkerboard leaps from the NL Giants to AL Chicago and back were daily headlines, while ongoing judicial rulings fell like rain. Except for a handful of games with New York, George missed the entire season. The courts gave him back to Comiskey for 1904.

Ban Johnson's popular circuit dumped Baltimore in exchange for New York before its third season. The new "Highlanders" were managed by Clark Griffith, who bossed Chicago in 1902. A bleak, raw day greeted 12,000 onlookers packed in at Washington's National Park, leaving several thousand more latecomers at vantage points outside the ballyard. Al Orth (10–22) pitched for Tom Loftus's hosts while NL jumper from Pittsburgh, Jack Chesbro (21–15), hurled for New

NATIONAL BASEBALL HALL OF FAME LIBRARY, COOPERSTOWN, NY

Cy Young (far left) and Candy LaChance (far right) flank the 1903 Boston Pilgrims team.

York. The New York *Daily Tribune* sometimes referred to the club as the New York Americans, but usually called them the "Invaders." Though RF Willie Keeler scored in the first frame, "Curveless Wonder" Orth took the contest, 3-1, for the cellar-ending Senators. His 22 defeats tied mate Casey Patten for the league's high.

Keeler, from NL Brooklyn (1902), walked with one out and CF Dave Fultz (from AL '02 Philly) singled him to third. Second baseman (from 1902 Baltimore) Jimmy Williams got Willie home on a grounder. Washington tied it in the fourth when 1902's top AL hitter, LF Ed Delahanty (.376) walked and was sacrificed to second. George "Scoops" Carey (.202) singled him to third, but out-of-condition Ed was nailed in a rundown when the next batter grounded back to Chesbro. Carey scored when 2B Gene DeMontreville doubled. "DeMont" only played 12 games (and four in 1904) in ending his career. In the fifth, Senator rookie SS Bill "Rabbit" Robinson singled, as did RF Kip Selbach. Delahanty sent Robinson home with a third single off Chesbro. Selbach then scored on Carey's muffed grounder to SS Herman Long, 13-year Boston vet playing in his final season, except for a solo 1904 game. Though Robinson made two errors (and Orth one), he also had seven assists and dazzled the crowd with his basepath sprints. Each team got six safeties, and Fultz was the only player with two. For New York, 3B William "Wid" Conroy (from Pittsburgh) had a single while Senator CF Jimmy Ryan, a 2,000-hit getter with NL Chicago, went hitless in what would be his last ML Opening Day. He had played more than 100 games in 15 of his 18 solid seasons. Orth and Chesbro became New York teammates in July 1904, the season Jack would set the franchise and AL record for most wins with 41.

New York won 7-2 the next day as their ballpark in Manhattan was still being readied for their arrival. Soon known as just Hilltop Park, the New York *Times* on the day of the inaugural game said it would be called "the American League Park at Washington Heights." Chesbro beat Senator Jack Townsend (2–11), 6-2 on April 30.

As May 1 dawned Delahanty was still swinging mightily. His decision to jump the Washington club while traveling home from Detroit by train and subsequent mysterious fatal plunge at Niagara Falls on July 2, the most notable tragedy of 1903, was still two months away. But for now, every team still had a sporting chance at the pennant.

WHICH PLAYER HAD MORE HALL OF FAMERS AS TEAMMATES THAN ANY OTHER PLAYER? *In January 1996, on the occasion of Milt Gaston's 100th birthday, Ben Walker of the Associated Press listed 17 Hall of Famers who were either teammates or managers of Gaston's. He stated that Gaston holds the record.*

The list included (alphabetically): Luke Appling, Earle Combs, Jocko Conlan, Joe Cronin, Red Faber, Lou Gehrig, Goose Goslin, Waite Hoyt, Ted Lyons, Herb Pennock, Sam Rice, Red Ruffing, Babe Ruth, Al Simmons, George Sisler, and managers Bucky Harris and Miller Huggins. —BILL NOWLIN

Nine Baseball Scrapbooks

by Bill Swank

My father used to say, "Son, you were talkin' when you should have been listenin' ... "

When I looked inside the large, heavy cardboard suitcase from the 1930s and saw that it was crammed with undated newspaper clippings, my old man's wisdom slammed home like a fastball in the ribs.

In 1994, I was asked to write an article about the Lane Field Padres for *The Journal of San Diego History* to complement the Pacific Coast League exhibition, "Runs, Hits and an Era," that would open at the San Diego Historical Society Museum in April 1995. Along with fellow SABR member James D. Smith III, we resolved to search and interview original Padres for our journal article.

Jack Graham was on a pace to hit 80 home runs for the Padres in 1948. By July 25th, he had already launched 46 round trippers. But Jack was beaned that day when he lost sight of a pitch thrown by Angels hurler Red Adams in the late afternoon shadows of Wrigley Field in Los Angeles. Graham returned from the head injury late in the season, added two more homers to his total, and was selected as the Most Valuable Player of the Pacific Coast League.

When I interviewed Jack in January 1995, he gave me a battered box from his garage that contained a stack of yellowed newspapers. He said, "You can have these. This stuff should help with your project." Although Graham was a famous minor league slugger, he didn't have a scrapbook. His filing system was simple. Toss everything in a box.

I made copy negatives from photographs that he had nonchalantly piled in another neglected box. I cut out the newspaper articles and glued them into a scrapbook. After making copies for my records, I gave the new scrapbook to Jack. He loved it. Henceforth, when people would ask about his baseball career, it was much easier for him to show them the scrapbook. Jack would just laugh because, admittedly, he was starting to forget some of the details of his storied past.

Pete Coscarart learned about Jack's scrapbook and asked if I would be willing to make a scrapbook for him. "Of course," was the answer of the fool who is still haunted by the sight of Pete's large cardboard suitcase from the 1930s. It took exactly one second to realize that I had made a huge mistake by volunteering to tackle this project.

Coscarart's professional career started in 1934 with the PCL Portland Beavers and St. Joseph (Missouri) Saints of the Western League. His nine years in the big leagues began with the Brooklyn Dodgers in 1938. By this time he was married. His wife, June, was too busy caring for her young family to work on a scrapbook. Besides, Pete just wasn't the kind of guy to gather stories about himself. That the cardboard luggage and clippings survived after all these years is a miracle.

My Big Apple buddies, Bronx native Bob Dreher

Bill Swank is the author of Echoes from Lane Field, A History of the San Diego Padres, 1936–1957. *His scale model of Lane Field is on display at the San Diego Hall of Champions. Swank also makes baseball scrapbooks in his spare time.*

and Brooklyn-born Bill Dunne, offered to help "date" the clippings. Armed with copies of the *Baseball Encyclopedia*, it took us three full days just to separate them by year. We soon realized that if Zeke Bonura appeared in a New York Giants box score, the year was 1939. Vito Tamulis, Johnny Hudson, and Van Lingle Mungo soon became key indicators for dating the numerous Dodger articles. (One of our favorites had nothing to do with Pete. It was titled "The Ballplayer and the Ladies" and dealt with Van Lingle Mungo's escapades during the Dodgers spring training trip to Havana in 1941. I would love to make his scrapbooks.)

Eventually the piles of clippings were fine-tuned and placed in chronological order. In the end, it took four months of cut and paste to complete the 277 double-sided pages that became the Coscarart scrapbook.

Among the highlights of Pete's career was Johnny Vander Meer's second consecutive no-hit game pitched on June 15, 1938. Early in the game, Coscarart almost spoiled the historic perfecto when he pressed Reds outfielder Wally Berger against the wall to catch a ball that seemed headed for the seats. The suitcase produced a ticket stub from that game, which also happened to be the first major league night game at Ebbets Field.

An article by Tommy Holmes stated, "Coscarart, incidentally, is winning recognition as the outstanding second baseman in the league. Bill Terry called him that after his great all-around performance at the Polo Grounds last Sunday. In Cincinnati, Bill McKechnie seconded the motion."

Pete's three-run home run was all the offense Tex Carleton needed on April 30, 1940 to no-hit the National League champion Cincinnati Reds, 3-0. Later that summer, the "Bounding Basque" was named to the National League All-Star team. How many ballplayers can say they were struck out by Bob Feller in an All-Star game?

A picture of Pete sleeping in his bed, mouth agape (snoring, too?), was used in an advertisement headlined, "Early to Bed, Early to Rise and He Eats Wheaties ... Pete Coscarart is Wise!" Other pictures in the ad show wife June selecting a box of Wheaties off the grocery shelf and Pete eating a spoonful of "the Breakfast of Champions" with baby daughter Carol at the family table in Flatbush.

Nineteen double-sided pages of the scrapbooks are devoted to articles from nine New York dailies about the 1941 Dodgers cinching their first pennant in 21 years. The jubilant Brooklyn celebration was front-page headlines for eight of the city's major newspapers, but the staid New York *Times* carried only a brief story sans photos about "Gaffers and Urchins Set Up Din" in "Pennant Victory Paean." (Now, how many feckless Dodgertown gaffers and urchins would know the difference between a paean and a paeon?) "... men and women stared vacantly at each other in sheer happiness. They walked into traffic stanchions and head-on at trolley cars (as opposed to dodging them). Urchins raced in roadways, screeching the victory cry, and oldsters hoarsely echoed it.... Brooklyn, in short, went nuts."

Game four of the '41 World Series would provide one of baseball's indelible memories. Brooklyn took a 4-3 lead into the ninth inning and, with two outs, Hugh Casey slipped strike three past Tommy Henrich. The plate umpire raised his right arm and the Bums had seemingly tied the Series. But the ball bounced off dependable Mickey Owen's catcher's mitt and started to roll. Coscarart went to back up Dolph Camilli at first base as Henrich raced down the line. The ball rolled...and rolled...and rolled. Henrich was safe at first. The Yankees rallied to win, 7-4. They claimed the next two games to capture an anticlimatic world championship from the shell-shocked Dodgers.

According to Pete and June, nothing was comparable to being part of the Brooklyn Dodgers. Notwithstanding, Coscarart was traded during that off-season to Pittsburgh where he played until 1946. Following an abortive attempt by labor lawyer Bob Murphy to unionize the Pirates, Coscarart, an outspoken Baseball Guild supporter, was sold to the PCL Padres. He contemplated jumping to the Mexican League, but decided to report to San Diego, which is near his hometown of Escondido. Three years later, Coscarart was traded to Sacramento. He hung up his glove for the last time following the 1950 season with Yakima of the Western International League.

After reading his completed scrapbooks, in typical Coscarart understatement, Pete said, "I guess I was a pretty good player." We joked about the day he first showed me his suitcase. At last count, I think I have made over twenty Xerox copies of the scrapbooks for his friends and family members.

Dolores Glynn made scrapbooks for her husband, Cleveland first baseman Bill Glynn, back in the late 1940s and early 1950s. With the passage of time, the books began to fall apart. Dolores wanted to rework the contents into a larger, modern scrapbook. This didn't seem like a big job (always a stupid assessment).

As luck would have it, I found an Indians fan at a local commercial lamination plant who agreed to seal the oversized pages for a very reasonable fee.

The transfer and lamination of the 14"x17" pages proceeded with relative ease, but the difficulty was punching 34 uniform holes for proper alignment with the fancy 34 spine clamps. To make matters worse, not all of the clamps shut properly. My friend Rich Nelson spent several evenings forcing surgical "IV" tubing over each clamp so the pages would turn smoothly.

Glynn came up through the Philadelphia Phillies farm system that produced the 1950 "Whiz Kids." In 1946, his first year in organized baseball, Bill hit .328 to lead Americus to a Georgia-Florida League pennant. This headline from an early clipping was a confidence boost: "Rookie is Compared to Gehrig in His Early Days." There was a story of young Glynn sitting on first base eating his sandwich and drinking milk during lunch because he did not want to relinquish the sack to any challengers.

Moving up to the Class A Eastern League with Utica in 1947, Billy Glynn joined Richie Ashburn, Granny Hamner, and Stan Lopata as the Blue Sox claimed the league championship. Glynn continued to develop as a power hitter and advanced to the International League with Toronto and Baltimore.

In 1952, he was traded to the Sacramento Solons in the Pacific Coast League. Manager Joe Gordon insisted on two changes for his young slugger: "He was working out for two or three hours and then stopping off at a corner drive-in and drinking not only one milkshake but two." Gordon also taught Glynn to hit through the pitcher's mound and run like hell: "Anyone with Bill's speed and his natural ability to bunt and drag the ball should never settle for a batting average under .290."

Glynn was soon leading the PCL in hitting, and the Cleveland Indians purchased him to back up Luke Easter at first base. They liked his defense and speed. He stuck with the Tribe and was featured in their 1953 Home Schedule sliding past a diving Yogi Berra.

Lou "The Clocker" Miller was one of the pioneers in the use of a stopwatch to time runners out of the batters box to first base. In his February 4, 1953, *Sporting News* article, Mickey Mantle was proclaimed the fastest man in baseball. He covered the distance in 3.1 seconds. Bobby Thomson of the New York Giants led the National League at 3.3 seconds. Washington Senators outfielders Gil Coan and Jim Busby were tied for second in the AL at 3.4 seconds. In a seven-way

TOP: *Memories from Bill Glynn's scrapbook.*
BOTTOM: *Ruth, Gehrig, and Cedric Durst article, and a Christmas card from Babe Ruth.*

TOP: *Al Olsen's uniform went to the majors in 1943; alas, Al was not in it.* BOTTOM: *Jack Graham was on pace to hit 80 home runs in 1948 when he was felled by a bean ball in July.*

tied for fourth at 3.6 seconds were Mantle's New York teammates Phil Rizzuto, Gil McDougal, Irv Noren and Gene Woodling along with Philadelphia's Dave Philley and Cleveland's Larry Doby and Bill Glynn.

Bill mistakenly confided to a Cleveland sportswriter that he wished he was as good as Philadelphia Athletics first baseman Ferris Fain. The story came out as, "I'm another Ferris Fain, don't you think?" A fan wrote Glynn a letter: "Ferris Fain, my ass! You couldn't hit an elephant in the ass with an oar paddle!" Injured by the misunderstanding, Bill turned to Bob Feller. The future Hall of Famer, who was nearing the end of his career, shared one of his letters: "I'm a mechanic and if I fixed cars like you pitched, I'd be out of business.

One of Bill's favorite articles is from the August 30, 1986, Toronto *Star*: "(Joe) Carter, who also singled twice, drove in four runs. He became the first Cleveland player to hit three home runs in a game since George Hendrick on June 19, 1973 and first to accomplish the feat on the road since Bill Glynn on July 5, 1954." He remembers his teammates greeted him after his first two home runs, but they acted like nothing had happened after the third. "Then, about 30 seconds later, they all jumped up and cheered. They were all in on it and, you know, ballplayers have a sense of humor."

One favorite page in the Glynn scrapbook is a bright yellow flyer announcing the grand opening of a Cleveland Gulf Service station on May 22nd and 23rd, 1953. To entice customers, the station was offering premiums with the purchase of seven gallons of gasoline: "Your choice of 6 glasses or a whisk broom autographed by Bill Glynn." Bill can't remember if the motorists preferred the personalized whisk broom to a set of glasses.

In 1948, a year after Jackie Robinson broke the color barrier in major league baseball, Johnny Ritchey became the first African-American player in the Pacific Coast League. While Robinson was making history in Brooklyn, John Ritchey was leading the Negro American League with a .381 average for the Chicago American Giants in 1947. His reward was a contract with the San Diego Padres, where he was already a high school, American Legion, and college baseball legend.

When San Diego Post 6 won the American Legion Junior World Series in 1938, Johnny Ritchey was a 15-year-old substitute. Two years later, he was the star of the team that again made the finals from a field of over

1,300 teams. However, Post 6 would be facing an all-white team from Albemarle, North Carolina—in Albemarle. John and Nelson Manuel were not allowed to participate in the games, and San Diego lost the series.

The team returned to a heroes welcome and this excerpt from Tom Akers' column: "Let us honor John Ritchey and Nelson Manuel for the manly grit they have shown and help them, if we can, to forget their degradation, their humiliation and suffering. At least we can do that much toward these two members of a race which has been downtrodden, abused and discriminated against down through the years since a presidential proclamation freed them from bondage and declared them 'free and equal' of all men."

Johnny's scrapbook was a classic woodshop project with a folding plywood cover and leather thong holding the pages inside. Like many old scrapbooks, the pages were breaking up and falling out. Fixing the pages required a double backing for the left edge and new holes. New hinges were added and the leather was replaced with album screws. This was the easiest of all the scrapbooks that I repaired. It was also one of the most historically significant.

Clippings about the Negro Leagues are few. John was busy playing baseball and not collecting articles. It is puzzling to see all the various averages posted in different newspapers after Ritchey won the batting crown. The range is .369 to "better than .400." Best known of the black sportswriters was Wendell Smith, sports editor of the Pittsburgh *Courier*, who credited Johnny with a .386 average. Nat Low, a surprisingly well-informed sportswriter for the American Communist Party's *Daily Worker*, wrote glowingly of Ritchey's .378 batting average. The Chicago papers listed his league best as .369 and .382. San Diego papers also used the .369 figure and Low's .378. Interestingly, it appears .381 was the most likely batting average that Johnny achieved in 1947.

As an aside, Smith reported that after winning the batting title, Ritchey "worked out at Wrigley Field today before a group of Cub officials and scouts." A rumor that the White Sox were interested in the young catcher prompted the Padres to quickly sign him to a contract. J. B. Martin, owner of the American Giants, immediately sent a protest to baseball commissioner A. B. "Happy" Chandler. Wendell Smith described Negro baseball business operations as "slip-shod." "When Brooklyn signed Jackie Robinson and sent him to Montreal, J. L. Wilkinson of the Kansas City Monarchs hollered 'robber,' too. But like Martin, he was unable to produce a bonafide contract with Robinson's name on it. That, too, we'll call a slight oversight. In fact, that's all you can call it. But in each instance that 'slight oversight' cost the respective owners many a good dollar."

Bucky Walter of the San Francisco *Examiner* wrote, "It doesn't take many minutes to capsule Ritchey. He's a shy, gentlemanly and intelligent youngster who only asks to be considered as 'another ball player.' 'That's impossible right now, I realize,' he rationalizes. 'I'm unique and for that reason it's only natural you fellows want to interview me. But the newness should wear off in time. I'll be grateful for that, because honestly, I don't want any publicity except that I'm able to earn on the ballfield."

At the end of the '48 season, Herman Hill was complementary: "Ritchey is the first athlete of his race to play in the Coast League. He has proven himself to be a brilliant prospect, a gentleman both on and off the field, popular with his teammates and a great competitor. He batted .323 in his first year in organized baseball and drove in a flock of runs. John was especially formidable at the plate with men on base."

It was always Johnny's dream to make the big leagues, but that was not to be. In addition to San Diego, he played with Coast League teams in Sacramento, Portland, and San Francisco, where he finished his career in 1955.

Rudy Regalado asked if I could get his scrapbooks laminated. His mother and wife had done a fine job filling several scrapbooks with baseball and basketball articles going back to his days as a high school star in Glendale, California. As a youth, Regalado narrowly missed being selected as the first team All-California Interscholastic Federation shortstop for three consecutive years from 1945 through 1947.

Rudy's wife, Marilyn, employed a favorite scrapbook technique perfected by my mother. If there is a blank space on a page, glue a contemporary item alongside the old articles. For example, on the same page with a clipping from the late 1940s about the All-CIF team beating the Los Angeles All-City team, 2-1, the results of a recent Saint Patrick's Day Twilight golf tournament, won by Rudy and Marilyn Regalado, was glued into place.

He played in a schoolboy series at the Polo Grounds billed as the U. S. Stars vs. N. Y. Stars. One of his U. S. teammates was a kid from Chicago named Bill Skowron. Rudy was a freshman when his USC team won the NCAA baseball championship in 1948. A teammate was Bill Sharman, who was also a pretty fair basketball player and coach. Regalado would go on to lead the Trojans in batting and sign with the Cleveland Indians in 1953.

Although unlisted on the Indians 1954 spring training roster, he was an instant success. "Regalado, an infielder who was with Reading in the Eastern League and Indianapolis in the American Association last season, has smashed nine home runs in Cleveland's 17 exhibition games to steal the thunder from such established home-hitters as Ed Matthews, Duke Snider, Al Rosen and Ted Kluszewski. In addition to his nine home runs, Regalado has hit three triples and ranks behind (Don) Lenhardt and (Jim) Findley with a .481 Grapefruit League batting average."

L.A. sportswriter Braven Dyer opined, "If Cleveland doesn't open the season with their rookie slugging sensation, ex-Trojan Rudy Regalado, in the lineup it'll prove what a lot of die-hard Indians fans have long suspected — that the club is run by numbskulls."

When Rudy got his chance, it set off a bizarre chain of events. On April 24, 1954, Cleveland first baseman Bill Glynn was second among American League hitters with a .419 average. Despite this, manager Al Lopez benched Glynn, switched 1953 AL Most Valuable Player Al Rosen from third to first and had Regalado assume the hot corner. "Lopez said he was making the switch in an effort to shake the Indians from the doldrums. The Tribe is in last place."

Although the experiment proved temporary, Cleveland emerged from the doldrums to register a record 111 victories to pry the pennant from the five-time consecutive world champion New York Yankees. Regalado was percolating at .321 in June, but slumped to finish his rookie season with a .250 batting average.

Like his good friend Bill Glynn, Rudy's scrapbook memories of the 1954 World Series are bittersweet. The Indians and New York Giants knew each other well. Both teams scrimmaged in Arizona and did, in effect, conclude their spring training barnstorming by rail as they zigzagged back into the Midwest. Willie Mays, Dusty Rhodes, and the Giants would stun Cleveland with a four-game sweep.

Whereas the unknown Regalado had been a surprise slugger in March, an unheralded Dusty Rhodes would become one of October's most unlikely heroes. And 1954, of course, is remembered for Willie Mays's signature catch of Vic Wertz's drive into the depths of the Polo Ground.

Rudy would primarily spend the next two years on the Cleveland bench. In 1957, he was farmed out to the Padres. He responded with a fine season that earned him an appearance on *The Ed Sullivan Show* as the Outstanding Third Baseman in the minor leagues. Regalado longed to return to the majors, but it did not happen. He was outstanding for San Diego, but there are only two Padre articles in his scrapbook. The final pages are devoted to reunions, golf, and old friends.

Cedric Durst called himself "Babe Ruth's caddy." An original Lane Field Padre and later the most successful manager in Padre history, Durst's major league career was spent in the shadow of two Hall of Famers, George Sisler in St. Louis and Babe Ruth in New York. Babe was known to imbibe and would sometimes "take ill." At such time Durst would fill in. What are you suppose to do when subbing for the Sultan of Swat? On June 2, 1929, Durst hit a home run.

In the fourth and final game of the Yankees' sweep of the St. Louis Cardinals in the 1928 World Series, Babe Ruth hit three home runs while Lou Gehrig and Cedric Durst each added one for a single-game team record five home runs. This records stands today.

Ced Durst was born in Austin, Texas, on August 23, 1896. Around that time his family started a scrapbook by pasting news articles over handwritten entries in an ancient business ledger. By the 1910s, most of the clippings were about young Cedric's prowess on the baseball diamond. When Durst died in 1971, the book was full and falling apart. By the 1990s, his daughter, Autumn Keltner, was keeping it in a plastic bag. Whenever the book was removed for the grand kids to view, tiny bits of paper covered the kitchen table and floor like snowflakes. Autumn was concerned that the old scrapbook was beyond repair.

My first step was to remove all of the pages and reinforce the left edges with carefully measured strips made from blank ledger pages. The lamination company was understandably reluctant to accept the job and required a statement that they would not be held liable for any resulting damage from handling the brittle pages. They did a beautiful job of sealing all the old memories for posterity.

There are Christmas cards from Ruth and Gehrig. A cover from the 1927 World Series program featuring oval portraits of rival managers Miller Huggins and Owen J. Bush was pasted onto one page. "When my mother was putting these items in the scrapbook, there was no thought given to their value. She was just chronicling Dad's baseball career," says Autumn, who

CARLETON HURLS NO-HITTER DODGERS WIN NO. 9, 3-0

Story on Page 58

(Associated Press Wirefoto)

(Associated Press Wirefoto)

Hero!

Here's Tex Carleton as he hurled first of two pitches to Goodman, last man up in 9th at Cincinnati yesterday. Goodman lined out to Walker.

↑ Wallop That Won

Pete Coscarart crosses the platter with three-run fifth-inning homer that sewed up the game for Brooklyn. Franks (19) and Vosmik (8) offer congrats. Only 145 games to go, boys!

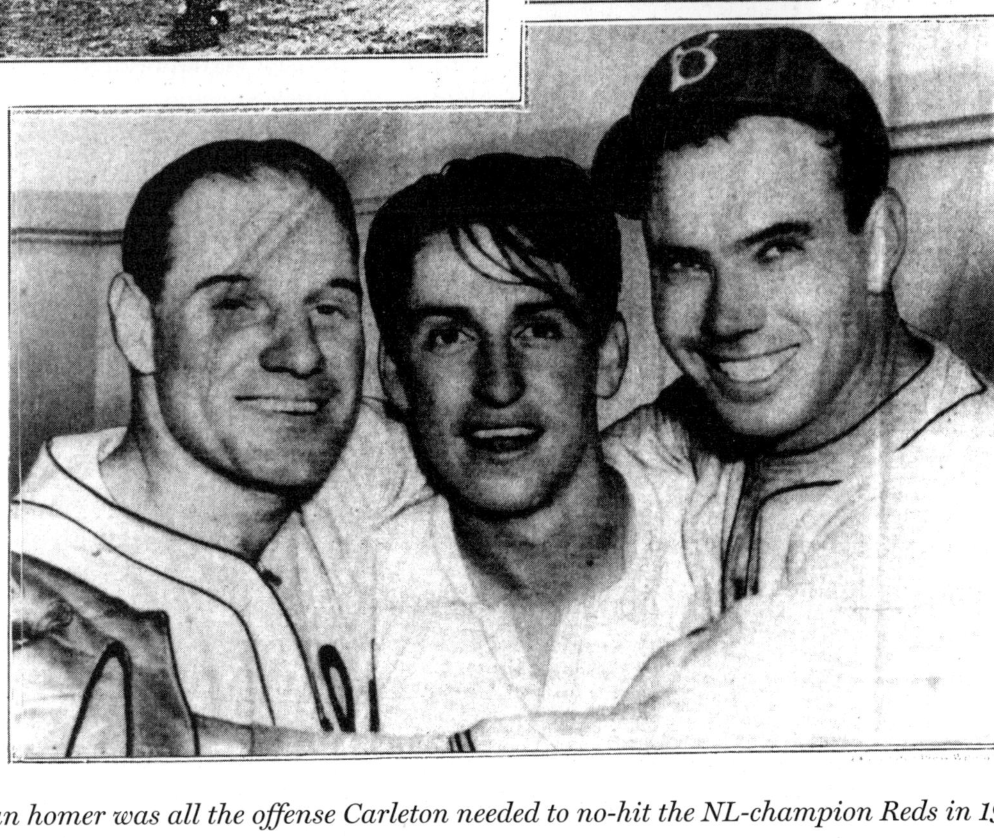

Reasons Why Brooklyn Went Crazy→

From joyous left to jubilant right, Leo (This Is Our Year) Durocher, Pete (Home Run) Coscarart and Tex (No-Hit) Carleton celebrate Dodgers' ninth straight victory in Cincy last night. Score: Brooklyn, three runs, five hits, three cheers; Cincinnati, no runs, no hits, no dice.

Pete Coscarart's three-run homer was all the offense Carleton needed to no-hit the NL-champion Reds in 1940.

is grateful the scrapbook had been saved.

The Durst scrapbook covers San Diego baseball in depth from 1936 through 1943 and include clippings from 1933-35 when the Hollywood Stars were struggling to cover rent at Wrigley Field. The following year, an exasperated Bill "Hardrock" Lane pulled up stakes and moved his beleaguered franchise to San Diego. Many predicted he would go broke in this sleepy border town. The doubters were wrong. The Padres were a solid hit, and Durst would play a prominent role during the team's formative years. Although he turned 40 during the first year in San Diego, Ced Durst would play and later manage for six seasons with the Padres and accumulate a .297 composite batting average.

An article from The Los Angeles *Examiner* is highly complementary of the former Hollywood MVP. "It's a pity that every baseball fan in San Diego doesn't know Cedric Durst, Padre centerfielder, personally. One thing which specially recommends Durst to me is his attitude toward the youngsters, the 'rookies.' He does everything he can to help them, to show them their faults and how to remedy them. I honestly believe that he would help a young player better his game even if he knew the kid was in line for his job. A great guy."

The Padres won the league playoff championship in 1937. Ted Williams batted .291 and hit 23 home runs. Four San Diego pitchers (Manuel Salvo, Wally Hebert, Dick Ward, and Tiny Chaplin) each hurled a pair of complete games as the Padres swept Sacramento and Portland in the Shaughnessey playoffs.

Venerable Bay Area sportswriter Jack McDonald writing in the San Francisco *News Call Bulletin* on March 4, 1965, about Giants pitching coach and original San Diego Padres skipper Frank Shellenback stated, "As manager of the Padres, he started Ted Williams on his career. 'Ted came to us out of a San Diego high school as a pitcher,' he was saying. 'His arm wasn't strong, but he looked like a natural hitter to me, if a pitcher can judge such things. I turned him over to Cedric Durst, to convert Ted into an outfielder."

After San Diego failed to qualify for the playoffs in 1938, Durst replaced Shellenback as manager of the Padres. During his 4½ year tenure, San Diego would record a .506 winning percentage. Alex Shults, writing for the Seattle *Times* in 1942, noted, "Durst has had amazing success with recent Padre teams, battling for the lead with aggregations the experts tabbed for the cellar." After Durst was forced to resign in 1943, respected PCL scribe Morton Moss wrote, "The fact is that Durst, who by some strange magical miracle landed out of the first division once during his tenure, ranked in many minds as the most able skipper in the Coast League. Time after time, he refuted the axiom which asserts that you can't make a silk purse out of a sow's ear. Cedric did it with the Padres. He was a magician."

Nobody wore the Padre flannels longer than Al Olsen, a San Diego native who in 1939 joined the Padres upon graduation from San Diego High School and was immediately hailed as "another Freddie Hutchinson."

Although Olsen did not make it to the majors, his uniform did. For years the *Baseball Encyclopedia* credited him with a walk and stolen base for the Boston Red Sox during the 1943 season. Subsequent research revealed that an unknown base thief was wearing the same uniform assigned to Olsen during spring training that year.

In his Nevada *State Journal* column, "Inside Stuff," Ty Cobb wrote, "Al 'Lefty' Olsen, who used to pitch for Smith Valley in the Sierra Nevada League, thence to San Diego Padres and Boston Red Sox, is still mowing them down. He's on the mound staff of Red Ruffing's Sixth Ferrying Group and Friday stuck out 12 U.S.C. batters ... " This was during World War II, when Airman Olsen pitched his Army Air Forces team to the Far West Championship. His teammates included Nanny Fernandez, Max West, Harry Danning, and Chuck Stevens.

On June 15, 1946, in response to "irate subscriber" requests for appreciation of out-of-town players, San Francisco *Examiner* sportswriter Will Connolly wrote, "...they waited a decent interval of two or three days after Al Olsen, San Diego pitcher, lost a 16-inning heartbreaker to the Seals last Friday night and still nothing in the paper about Hero Olsen." Connolly penned a tongue-in-cheek biography that included Al's favorite movie stars from a team questionnaire and described the lanky six foot one, 175-pound southpaw as "slatty." He concluded his masterpiece with "He is a competent, consistent and conscientious workman, as scions of Scandinavian blood almost invariably are."

Following baseball, Olsen went into coaching and eventually became athletic director at San Diego State College. He is remembered for hiring an unknown football coach named Don Coryell who led the Aztecs to national gridiron prominence. Al died in 1994. His wife and high school sweetheart, Mary, asked me to fix and laminate their scrapbooks. One of the best was made by 11-year-old Al Olsen, Jr., while his father was wrapping up his pitching career for Oklahoma City in 1953 after eleven seasons with the Padres.

My last baseball project involved the repair, update, and lamination of scrapbooks for the family of Wally "Preacher" Hebert, who died in December 1999 at age 92. As one might expect from a collection which starts during the 1920s, many of these books were falling apart. The earliest scrapbooks were made by Bobbie Hebert, Preacher's wife of 67 years, who as a young teenager began pasting clippings about her beau over her schoolwork in sturdy composition folders.

It was important to the family that the originals be laminated, but I had lost my source for doing large page lamination. I suggested completely redoing the scrapbooks by removing the old articles and gluing them onto 8½x11 pages. I had to steam several articles glued on back pages to preserve them. My friend Chris Schuehle lended his lamination machine to seal 127 double-sided pages. This project took over two months to complete.

In 1932, the "19-year-old southpaw rookie from Lake Charles, La." made his first major league start against the powerful Philadelphia Athletics. The reigning American League champs "got near worst beating at the hands of 'Preacher' Hebert." Although the rookie was actually 24 years old, he limited the heart of the A's batting order (Jimmy Dykes, Mule Haas, Al Simmons, Jimmie Foxx) to a feeble single by Jimmie Foxx as the lowly St. Louis Browns triumphed, 8-2.

Hebert followed this with a 4-2 victory over Red Ruffing, Babe Ruth, Lou Gehrig, and the New York Yankees. It was Preacher's "trenchant if not especially powerful bat" that drove in two runs which would prove to be the margin of victory. The game was attended by "various inmates of the Passaic Orphanage in New Jersey," who were rewarded by an audience with Babe Ruth after they had heroically "flagged an express train with 500 passengers aboard just before it neared a probably tragic disaster in the form of a washout."

The heart of the Hebert scrapbooks highlight his seven wonderful years with the Padres from 1936 through 1942. During that period he was a 20-game winner three times and posted a 126-95 record. According to a 1937 article, "The second game saw Wally Hebert, brilliant Padre southpaw hurler, and Ted Williams combine their talents to embarrass the (Portland) Beavers no little. Hebert held them to six scattered hits and no earned runs while Williams drove in four runs, three of them with another homer over the right field wall, making it five for the series."

Mickey Haslin listens in 1941 as manager Durst suggests that the PCL umpire visit an optometrist.

"Wally Hebert Day" was celebrated at Lane Field on September 19, 1941. Teammates took up a collection and gave the lanky Cajun a dollar ($104) to represent every victory he had hurled since the old Hollywood Stars moved to San Diego in 1936. Fans presented Hebert with a live chicken and a Louisiana catfish, since Mrs. Hebert's Southern cooking and hospitality were widely known and appreciated.

On August 16, 1998, the New Orleans *Times-Picayune* carried a feature story, "The Babe in The Big Easy." The article commemorated the fiftieth anniversary of Ruth's death and recalled his visit to New Orleans on March 10, 1922. "When the motorman of a Tulane belt streetcar passed Heinemann Park yesterday around high noon, and saw a baseball come floating over the center field fence, he remarked, 'Gee, nobody but Babe could have sloughed that ball."

Ninety-one-year-old Preacher Hebert was contacted

by the reporter and asked to recall his memories of pitching to the Babe. " ... he was swinging with everything he had. I threw him a slow curve, and he hit a little squibber to second base. Grounded into a double play. As he was running back to the dugout, he looked at me and yelled, 'You can stick that slow curve right up your ass'."

Whitey Wietelmann celebrated his 83rd birthday on March 15, 2002. He died on March 26, 2002. Whitey played for the Pacific Coast League Lane Field Padres from 1949 until 1953 and coached for the PCL Westgate Padres from 1960 to 1966. When San Diego became a National League expansion team in 1969, Wietelmann returned as a member of manager Preston Gomez's coaching staff and remained in that capacity through a series of managerial changes until the 1980 season. Over the next fourteen years he served the team in a variety of functions and is remembered for his chili, his acerbic humor, and his cherubic grin. Whitey was known by the fans as "Mr. San Diego Baseball." The Padres simply called him "Mr. Indispensable."

Not many people outside baseball realize that Whitey created a series of scrapbooks which contained every Padres box score for twenty-five years, from 1969 through the 1993 season. I doubt that any major league team has every box score of every game they ever played. Although the scrapbooks were Whitey's prize possession, he stopped making them after his retirement from the Padres. They were boxed up in his garage and would fall apart when opened. Years ago, I had offered to laminate the pages, but Whitey only growled, "Nobody cares. They just collect dust."

Following his death, the family offered the collection to the San Diego Padres, but they declined to accept it. The San Diego Hall of Champions did not have space for a large box of unmatched binders and loose papers. Though I had previously vowed to never make another baseball scrapbook, I volunteered to preserve this legacy. As of August 2002, I have survived the mold, laminated over 1,000 pages and made twenty-eight matching binders with covers.

All of the baseball groups and organizations in San Diego were invited to participate in the completion of this project, which became focused on locating the missing Padres box scores from 1994 through 2001.

The San Diego Ted Williams SABR chapter has been the most responsive. Thanks are extended to Bob Dreher, Tom Larwin, Bob Diaz, Andy Aguinaldo, Art Kaliel, Tim Scheidt, Tom Maggard, Chris Schuehle, Phil White, Jon Wietelmann (Whitey's nephew), and Doc Mattei. Special recognition is given to Bob Boynton, who made photocopies of all the box scores for the 1994, 1996, and 1997 seasons.

It has primarily been through the generous contributions of individuals and former Padres players like John Curtis and Randy Jones that the restoration process began in earnest. Both of these pitchers remember watching Whitey in the clubhouse cutting and taping box scores onto the pages of his scrapbooks.

I am making the 2002 box score scrapbook and hope to find an organization that will continue to maintain the "Wietelmann Scrapbooks" in the future as a part of the Padres living history. When completed, the collection will be donated to the San Diego SABR Baseball Research Center at the downtown San Diego Library.

Interestingly, the only reference that I found about Whitey himself is a handwritten caption beneath a newspaper photograph of beloved Padres owner Ray Kroc throwing the first pitch at the 1978 All-Star game in San Diego. Whitey wrote, "I caught it."

Just Someone's Old Worn Out Pasture

by Jack Keeley

1874 had been a banner year for "Base Ball" in the small river town of Saugerties, New York. The local newspaper accounts told of ten ball clubs from the central village and surrounding rural hamlets, playing "matches" among themselves and against opponents from as far distant as 70 miles. That excursion, a significant trip in those times, was undertaken by the Sunny Sides of Sing Sing, who made the day worthwhile by playing (and losing) a split double-header against two different local teams. Lost in the mists of time is whether the Sunny Sides was a team of guards from Sing Sing Prison, whose warden was from Saugerties, or simply represented the town, that being its name rather than the present Ossining.

Indeed, since The Game had tested the Knickerbocker Rules at Hoboken's Elysian Field in 1846, it had quickly spread the 100 miles up the Hudson, and by 1860 Saugerties was rooting for its first organized baseball club, the Ulsters. Yet despite having a history here, the intense diamond activity in the Summer of '74 was such as to inspire Edward Jernegan, editor of the Saugerties *Telegraph*, to pen an editorial in the September 18, 1874, issue which cloaked the diamond sport with a virtual quasi-religious aura. The emotional prose went like this:

The game of base ball has been a rage in Saugerties during the past season as, indeed, it has been throughout the country. During the day time, in the fierce July and August suns, our middle-aged men, our young men and boys of tender years have practiced the manly game; and at even-tide when, in a village like ours, the laboring man, the man of business and the professor assemble in sociable knots on the streets, the favorite subject for discussion has been the base ball game. It is a grand old sport, savoring of the athletic games of Ancient Greece. It does a good thing for our middle-aged men, bringing back fresh to their memories the days of youth, making them young again and lifting for a time, if not permanently, the cares which necessarily attend their business or profession. It does a better thing for our young men, making them strong and manly, and taking from them the desire to practice other games which, with their associations, tend to weaken their intellects, destroy their bodies and waste their souls.

It took, however, little time to become quite clear that the editor's view of "the grand old game" (of 28 years' vintage?) was not shared by all of the township's residents. That revelation came about when a group came together in October of '74 to organize a new and superior ball club to represent the town. These were obviously baseball purists who preferred quality to quantity, their goal being a "first class ball club" in the tradition of teams of the past which had been recognized as "Champions of the Hudson River" by no less than the baseball Bible of the time, the New York *Clipper*. It would seem implicit in their planning that

Jack Keeley, a retired parole supervisor, is one of three Cub fans in Saugerties, New York. He dotes on local baseball history and those bygone years when the Cubs won games.

they were not at all impressed with the past summer's "quantity" of ten ball teams in town, the best of which being endowed with dubious diamond skills.

The innovators christened their creation with the storied name of past glories, that of both the 1860 Ulsters and a later organization of the same name that came into existence in 1869, filling the baseball void brought about by the Civil War. The new group agreed at their very first meeting that a "first class base ball club" required "a ground suitable for playing on." Thus, a committee of three was appointed for the purpose of solving this need and went about their assignment with both speed and vigor. It was, however, the contacts made in this pursuit that brought to light the fact that not everyone embraced The Game with the same ardor as the newspaper editor. The committee's report was published in the *Telegraph*'s December 4, 1874, issue and, permeated with chagrin, read:

> *To the Chairman, Saugerties B.B.C.:*
>
> *Sir, Having been appointed a committee to procure suitable grounds for the use of a Base Ball Club, we submit the following report, viz: We have applied to different persons with unvarying (lack of) success. We found a number of suitable grounds but no disposition on the part of the owners to hire them on any consideration whatsoever, although they were offered more than their land was worth to them for farming purposes. We were told that base ball playing was wicked!, hence we conclude that the spirit of the age is too moral for the game, or that when men grow old they out-grow an appreciation for the manly games of their youth, when they are no longer able to participate in them. Although our efforts have been in part a failure, we think our wants might be laid before the public by advertising, as it is not generally known that we boys have been trying for more than ten years to beg the privilege of playing ball on somebody's old worn out pasture field and paying well for it at that; we therefore suggest that the Association advertise in the Saugerties* Telegraph *for a man with public spirit enough to furnish the five hundred ball players of Saugerties with a ball ground at a reasonable price.*
>
> *s. Mynderse Freligh*
> *Frank Pidgeon, Jr.*
> *John C. Davis*

Despite the committee's discouraging experience, the playing field problem was solved by the spring of 1875. Ironically, that was largely due to the apparent failure of a harness racing facility on the southeast edge of town named the Glasco Driving Park. Newly constructed and commencing business with its Fall Meeting on October 10, 1874, after this initial competition, racing results never again gained mention in the *Telegraph*. Instead, for the next couple years the Ulsters and other local ball clubs were reported as playing their matches on the site. It appears likely, however, that by 1877 the driving park owner had put his land to another use, as for the next eight years the ballgames were reported as taking place at a variety of locations, all of which seemed to be makeshift.

But at long last the problem with which the 1874 Ulsters committee had wrestled, and which they bemoaned had existed for a decade prior, was solved in the fall of 1884. The September 11, 1884, issue of the *Telegraph* reported an enthusiastic organizational meeting at which the Saugerties Driving Park Association was founded with the goal of securing grounds for a "trotting course, base ball park, fair grounds, etc." The very next edition told of speedy progress, namely the leasing of a 15-acre "piece of ground from Captain Finger" on the northeast edge of town. Just a week later came news of the "dire speed" with which the half-mile track was being constructed, and by the second week in November the *Telegraph* announced that "people are pleasure-driving" on the track.

In the midst of the construction a prophetic line appeared in the newspaper which stated, "The owners anticipate a great deal of pleasure to our people in different ways on their park in the next season." By the spring of 1885, the old committee of Freligh, Pidgeon, and Davis must have been wearing broad smiles as the first baseball game took place on the site.

As the years passed by, trotting races disappeared, the plot underwent changes of ownership, and its name evolved from the Driving Park to Shults' Park to the Athletic Field, but the ball games continued and newer sports utilized the grounds. There was even professional baseball on the site from 1903 thru 1905 as Saugerties had an entry in the Class C Hudson River League. By 1934 it was owned by the father and son duo of Martin and Holley Cantine. Both had been catchers in their youth, and Martin had played on the very first ball club to use the grounds. Their paper mill was a major employer in the town, and as early as 1911

Martin had been described in a publication as "one of the most public-spirited men of our village." This reputation was surely reinforced when, in impressive ceremonies in November 1934, they deeded and donated to the town what was then officially called Cantine Memorial Field.

There were ceremonies also on May 8, 1938, to celebrate considerable improvements to the facility resulting from a WPA project. In 1967 the town purchased a large field adjoining it on the west, thereby doubling the park's size. As time went on and athletic programs multiplied, dedicated volunteers added additional facilities, and yet another ceremony was held on May 13, 1979, to mark further enhancements to the grounds, accomplished by $200,000 in government grants. In 1991 the town took out of its checkbook once again and acquired a sizable plot adjoining it on the north. The result was another doubling of the park's acreage.

One cannot view the present facilities without thinking of the Messieurs Freligh, Pidgeon and Davis and their search for just "somebody's old worn out pasture" in order to allow Saugerties' 500 ballplayers to do their thing. The trio would now be viewing a complex that could and often does accommodate 500 athletes all cavorting at the same time. And then there was the Driving Park Association's thought that their venture would afford "great pleasure to our people in different ways." The ways in which the people of Saugerties now derive pleasure at the expanded grounds of the Driving Park are via eleven baseball, softball, and Little League diamonds (five lighted), four soccer fields (one lighted), four lighted tennis courts, three basketball courts, four pavilions, three playgrounds with a children's pool at one, a band stage, two sets of horseshoe pits, and the latest addition, an indoor ice arena that accommodates both youth and adult hockey leagues as well as open periods for public use. Nor has the "fair grounds" aspect vanished. Thousands visit the grounds for the annual 4th of July celebration, and some 30,000 attend the Annual Garlic Festival on the last weekend in September.

It would indeed appear that the negative attitude toward sports encountered by the 1874 Ulsters ballfield committee has mellowed with the passage of the decades. It might, in fact, be near impossible to find a soul in Saugerties these days who would assert "that base ball playing was wicked."

MR. ROGERS, MR. JACKSON AND THAT AWESOME MR. BECK

by Jim Healey

When the starter starts to struggle
So you think he may be hexed
Just replace him with the trio
That makes batters nervous wrecks
That set of fearsome firemen
Will have those hitters vexed
Mr. Rogers, Mr. Jackson and
that awesome Mr. Beck

When we lead by just a run
And the game's been neck and neck
We can call on those three-stoppers
Those three aces in our deck
Those Giant mow-em-downers
Loved a bushel and a peck
Mr. Rogers, Mr. Jackson and
that awesome Mr. Beck

If our starters never finish
Might we say, "Oh, what the heck?"
Who cares who gets the victory
When all four have thrown that spec
We'll rejoice in having hurlers
Whose arms are so high-tech
Mr. Rogers, Mr. Jackson and
that awesome Mr. Beck

A Very Special Evening

by Tommy Manville

In the spring of 1953 I was a nine-year-old Boston Red Sox fan. I played stick ball in my schoolyard at Saint Mary's in Fall River, Massachusetts. I collected old newspapers, sold them for scrap, and used a portion of the proceeds to buy bubble gum baseball cards. My parents had recently bought our first television, and now I could watch the Red Sox play. Television was still in its infancy at that time. There were not many channels or programs to choose from. One of the weekly shows aired on the ABC network was a prime time half-hour game show, *The Name's The Same*. A celebrity panel tried to guess the identities of guest contestants who had the same name as famous people, famous places, or famous objects. Each panelist could ask up to ten yes or no questions of the guests. All panelist who could not identify the guest had to pay him or her twenty-five dollars. Each week the show featured a celebrity guest in a segment called, "I'd Like to Be." If that celebrity guest could be anyone else other than himself, that name was revealed to the audience and the panel would try to guess that name. The celebrity guest would donate their winnings to their favorite charity.

The panel consisted of Merideth Wilson, an author, conductor, and composer of *The Music Man*. Joan Alexander was a radio and television actress. Carl Reiner was a comedian on the popular television program *Show of Shows*. The host and moderator was Robert Q. Lewis. I was invited to appear on this program as a contestant because I had what was then a famous name, Tommy Manville.

The famous bearer of this name was a multi-millionaire playboy who was heir to the Johns Manville asbestos fortune. He was married thirteen times to eleven women. He described himself as "a retired business man." After one of his frequent divorces he was quoted as saying, "she cried and the judge wiped her tears with my check-book." Although we shared the same name, we were not related.

My dad drove my mom, my older brother Bill, and myself to New York City. We had never been there, nor had I ever been that far from home. I was going to appear on a national television program and meet some famous people. It would prove to be a very special evening for a young baseball fan.

When we arrived at the television studio, my dad and brother were seated in the audience. My mom was seated backstage with me. All of the contestants with famous names were introduced to each other except for the celebrity guest, who had not yet arrived. I met Dorothy Lamour, A.(rlene) Stork, and Henry Clay. The show was about to begin, and we were asked to be as quiet as possible. This was live television and a monitor was placed in front of us to view the show.

Dorothy Lamour, a New York City housewife, was the first contestant. While she was being questioned by the panel, a young man arrived backstage and was

---

Tommy Manville lives in Tiverton, Rhode Island, and is a life-long Boston Red Sox fan.

seated next to my mom. He looked familiar to me. I really could not concentrate on him because I was thinking that soon I would be seen by millions of viewers. After a series of questions by Carl Reiner and Joan Alexander, Dorothy Lamour's name was correctly guessed by Meredith Wilson.

The next contestant was a 15-year-old high school student from Brigatine, New Jersey, A. Stork. After determining that her namesake delivered something, the panelist asked her if it involved a mailbox, a coal chute, or something with a ladder, a long hose, and painted red. Meredith Wilson asked, "Does it haul away garbage?" Joan Alexander finally guessed the name of A. Stork. Now it was time for the celebrity guest to appear in the "I'd Like to Be" segment.

The young man next to my mom rose from his chair and walked toward the stage. Robert Q. Lewis introduced him with these words; "Here is one of the greatest young guys in organized baseball that I ever had the pleasure of meeting, Mr. Mickey Mantle." To say that I was surprised would be an understatement. This was not someone with the same name as Mickey Mantle. This was the real Mickey Mantle. The Mick! The television monitor now had my complete undivided attention.

Evidently the Yankees had played an extra-inning game the previous night. Mr. Lewis remarked to Mickey, "I had a very pleasant twelve hours watching you play last night. Do you guys get paid for a doubleheader?" Mickey replied, "No, but next year they are going to sign us by the hour." Now it was time to reveal, to the audience, the name of the person that Mickey Mantle would want to be. It was Prince Philip of England. (I had hoped that Mickey, now in his third year as a Yankee, would want to be my hero, Ted Williams of the Boston Red Sox.) Mr. Lewis reminded everyone that all of Mickey's winnings would be donated to his favorite charity. Joan Alexander evoked some laughter when she said that Mickey's favorite charity was the Dodgers, no doubt.

The questioning began with Meredith Wilson, who wanted to know the distance of the long home run that Mickey had recently hit. That home run is generally regarded as the longest ever hit in the major leagues. He hit it off the Washington Senators' Chuck Stobbs, on April 17, 1953, at Griffith Stadium. Mr. Wilson wanted to know if it was 562 or 563 feet. Mickey modestly replied, "562 feet, I think." Through a series of questions by Mr. Wilson, the panel learned that the person Mickey would want to be was a living man and not an American.

It was now Carl Reiner's turn to ask questions. Mr. Reiner immediately commented, "Most people want to be Mickey Mantle. Why you want to be anyone else, I don't know." Mickey's answers to Mr, Reiner's questions determined that the person was a European who spoke English and not a sports figure.

An amusing verbal exchange was started by Joan Alexander. She asked if the person was from England or in England now. Mickey answered yes. She then asked if he is a young and handsome man. Mr. Lewis asked her to clarify what she considered "young." Her reply was, "Oh, about Meredith's age." This response prompted Merideth Wilson to kiss Joan Alexander on the cheek. Mr. Lewis then looked at his fingernails, brushed his hair, smiled, and asked, "What do you mean by...handsome?" Miss Alexander immediately replied, "Someone who looks like Mickey Mantle."

With a few more questions it was established that the person was indirectly involved in politics, connected with royalty, and originally from Greece. Referring to Princess Elizabeth, Miss Alexander asked Mickey, "Is he married to a very beautiful lady who will be a star in a ceremony very soon?" Mickey said, "Yes." Her final question was, "Would you like to be Prince Philip?" Again, Mickey replied, "Yes." Mr. Lewis thanked Mickey for being a contestant, and in parting, commented, "Mickey, you don't have to be anybody in the whole world except one of the best Yankees there has ever been." Mickey walked over to the panelists, said good night, and collected his winnings to give to his favorite charity. Presumably, the Brooklyn Dodgers were fifty dollars richer.

It was now my turn to be a contestant. I was led to one end of the stage while Mickey exited at the other end. I did not want to appear nervous, and was hoping to get through this as quickly as possible. I wanted to return backstage and talk to Mickey about baseball. I walked onto the stage, and Mr. Lewis placed a Manhattan telephone directory on my chair so that I could see over the desk. It was a thrill to be on this television stage with these famous people. I was asked a series of questions by the panel in an attempt to determine the occupation of my namesake, Tommy Manville. He really did not have an occupation. After the panel discovered he was wealthy, and had inherited his fortune, Joan Alexander asked me if he had been married many times. I answered, "Yes." Her final question to me was, "Are you Tommy Manville?" Again, I replied, "Yes." The audience applauded and Mr. Lewis thanked me for being a contestant. I walked over to the panel, shook hands, and collected two twenty-five dollar checks. I returned backstage, sat down, and looked around for Mickey Mantle.

The final contestant was Henry Clay, a service technician from Long Island, New York. Upon questioning Mr. Clay, the panel learned that his namesake was not living and was involved in politics. Joan Alexander was trying to pinpoint the time frame that the person was in politics. Mr. Lewis had to stop the questioning at that point because time was running out for the show. Mr. Clay collected his winnings, and the host and panelists said good night to the audience.

Henry Clay rejoined his fellow contestants backstage and we were invited to return to the stage to have our photographs taken with Robert Q. Lewis. I had to stand on a chair for my photo because Mr. Lewis was tall and I was not. After the photo, I asked one of the stage personnel if Mickey Mantle was still in the theater, and he said Mickey had to leave because of another engagement. I was a little disappointed that I did not get to talk to Mickey about baseball.

On the very bright side, I did get to go to New York City. I did appear on a national television show and meet some famous people. As a contestant, I was in the same lineup as Mickey Mantle. I now have a video of that program and I am able to relive my wonderful experience. For a nine-year-old baseball fan, it was, indeed, a very special evening.

May of '27

A Bizarre Month for the Cubs

by Art Ahrens

In May of 1927 the Model T Ford was in its final year of production. Movies were silent but would soon learn how to talk. Home radios were becoming so popular that supply could not keep up with demand. Calvin Coolidge was in the White House.

In a Europe that seemed far away to most Americans, ominous events were already in the making. Still a little-known soapbox agitator, Adolf Hitler was haranguing small gatherings in Germany, drawing more flies than people. Inside the dark labyrinths of the Soviet Union, Joseph Stalin was checkmating his hated rival, Leon Trotsky, at every move.

The month in question was hardly the most successful in Chicago Cubs annals—that had occurred in August of 1906, when they went 26-3. By contrast, they finished 15-10 in May of '27, good but hardly earth-shattering. Yet the latter month was easily the most unusual in the team's history. It was weird, exciting, historic, and at times hilarious. A brief review of the events that transpired will explain why.

On May 1, a crowd of 33,000 squeezed into Wrigley Field to watch the Cubs draw swords with the Pirates. In the seventh inning, Chuck Tolson, a second-string utility man, connected off Ray Kramer for the first pinch-hit grand slam home run in Cub history. Pittsburgh won the game, however, 7-6.

After a rainout the following day, the Cubs took the Reds 4-3 on May 3 and 13-9 the next afternoon. The May 4 contest witnessed an eight-run Cub uprising in the third inning, highlighted by right fielder Earl Webb's double and three-run homer. Four years later, as a member of the Red Sox, Webb would set the major league record for doubles in one season with 67.

There was no game May 5, as the Cubs took a train to New York for a series with the Giants. What was supposed to be a four-game set ended up as two, thanks to rain on May 6 and 9. In between cloudbursts, the Cubs beat the Giants, 6-4, after which New York edged Chicago, 5-4, in contests that saw nothing out of the ordinary.

By May 10, Chicago's North Side heroes were in Philadelphia for another four-game series. The Cubs took the first match, 6-3, on four baggers by Riggs Stephenson, Hack Wilson, and Gabby Hartnett. Hardly intimidated, the Phillies came back to kick the Cubs, 5-2, the next day.

On May 12 a drunken fan was ejected from the staid Baker Bowl bleachers while Phillie catcher Jimmy Wilson was tossed from the game for protesting a close safe call at home plate. The Cubs won, 4-1, but the undaunted Philadelphians bounced back to win by the same score on the 13th.

Saturday, May 14, saw the Cubs in Boston to play the hapless Braves. It would turn out to be a long day, as after 17 innings the score was knotted up at two apiece. Finally, in the top of the 18th, Chicago broke loose for five runs, going on to win, 7-2. Cub starter

A SABR member since 1971, Art Ahrens has co-authored five books on Cubs history with fellow SABR member Eddie Gold, and has written many articles on baseball history.

Guy Bush went the distance for a well-earned victory. Charlie Roberston, who five years earlier had pitched a perfect game for the Chicago White Sox, hurled the first 17⅓ innings for the Braves.

Due to Boston's Sunday blue laws, no baseball was performed the following day, giving both teams a much needed rest. On Monday, Mother Nature rather than the Boston Brahmins intervened, awarding them another day of recuperation.

But baseball is a game of unbelievable oddities, and never was this more evident than on May 17. This time the Braves Field fans—such as they were, after a while—sat through 22 innings, only to see their favorites fall, 4-3, when Cub first baseman Charlie Grimm drove home Hack Wilson in the top of the last frame for the eventual winning run. Despite the modest score, Chicago had collected 20 hits during the game while Boston amassed 15. Loser Bob Smith, later a Cub, pitched the entire game for Beantown while winner Bob Osborn threw the last 14 for Al Capone's turf. This was the longest game, inning-wise, in Cub history, yet the clock time was "only" four hours and 13 minutes. Today, many a nine-inning contest will take almost as long. Moreover, it had taken Chicago and Boston a whole 40 innings to play two games. This remains the record for most innings played by the same teams in two successive matches.

After the Boston marathons, the Cubs were on their way to Brooklyn, always an adventure. On May 18, the Cubs took the Dodgers, or Robins as they were then more commonly called, 7-4. This was followed by—you guessed it—another rainout.

By the time the showers ceased on May 20, the natives of Ebbets Field were restless as they heaved several pop bottles and one whiskey bottle at plate umpire Peter McLaughlin over one of his calls. Ignoring the soda containers, McLaughlin picked up the whiskey bottle but discarded it when he discovered that it was empty. In the meantime the Cubs outlasted the Robins, 7-5, despite two home runs by Brooklyn idol/clown Floyd "Babe" Herman, a fun-loving character whose personality was a cross between that of Babe Ruth and Dizzy Dean.

On May 21, Charles Lindbergh landed in Paris before a crowd that was so frenzied he was not sure whether he was being welcomed or lynched. Back in Brooklyn the locals had lost the morning game of a doubleheader, 6-4, but held a 6-2 lead over the Cubs in game two as the top of the ninth began. It looked as if the Dodgers would at last salvage a game.

Darkness was already encroaching the ballpark as bleacherites poured onto the field, angry at plate ump Frank Wilson for not calling the game. But Wilson ignored them, ordering that the contest be continued. Batting for catcher Mike Gonzales, Cub flychaser Cliff Heathcote led off with a walk off Dodger starter Bill Doak. Floyd Scott then pinch hit for third baseman Clyde Beck, beating out an infield hit. Up came the third consecutive Chicago pinch hitter, Chuck Tolson, in place of pitcher Sheriff Blake. Tolson doubled down the right-field line, and Heathcote and Scott crossed the plate to make it 6-4.

At that point Dodger manager Wilbert Robinson yanked Doak and replaced him with Rube Ehrhardt. With Woody English pinch-running for pinch-hitter Tolson, Earl "Sparky" Adams grounded to Robin third baseman Johnny Butler for the first out. Then Jimmy Cooney singled and Earl Webb walked, filling the bases for the most dreaded man in the Cub lineup, Hack Wilson. Normally a slow runner, Wilson this time legged out a bases-clearing triple to give his teammates a 7-6 lead.

When Riggs Stephenson walked, Jumbo Elliott replaced the befuddled Ehrhardt on the mound. Proving no more effective than his predecessor, Elliott walked Charlie Grimm to fill the bags once more. Gabby Hartnett then batted for previous pinch-hitter Heathcote, running out an infield single as Wilson scored for an 8-6 margin. Floyd Scott, making his second pinch appearance of the inning, sent the ball bouncing into the left-field stands for a ground-rule double. Stephenson and Grimm were allowed to score, but Hartnett was held at third as the Bruins expanded their lead to 10-6.

Jumbo Elliott was then sent to the dugout as Guy Cantrell came in to pitch. Howie Freigau, the fifth and final Cub pinch-hitter of the inning, drew a walk to fill the bases again. This led to Cantrell's immediate replacement by Norman Plitt, the fifth Brooklyn pitcher of this dream that had become a nightmare. Plitt promptly gave Sparky Adams a base on balls, forcing Hartnett home to put the Cubs further ahead, 11-6. Mercifully, Jimmy Cooney hit into a double play to end the carnage. In collecting four pinch hits and two pinch walks in the same inning, the Cubs had set a unique record that stands to this day.

Pitching in relief, Charlie Root put down the humiliated Robins in order, turning defeat into victory for Sheriff Blake. In time-honored Flatbush tradition, Dodger coach Otto Miller led an angry mob of fans after umpire Wilson. The police, however, escorted him to safety.

Having made bums out of the Dodgers in four straight, the Cubs met their match in Cincinnati when the Reds clipped them, 8-4, during a one-day stand on May 22. The following afternoon was an off day as the Cubs headed back to Chicago for a two-game set with the defending world champion Cardinals.

But on the 24th, the Cubs sat through their sixth rainout of the month (whether or not this is a record is for a more ambitious researcher than the present one to determine), necessitating a twin bill the following day. Former Cub Grover Alexander bested his ex-teammates, 8-5, in the opener, but Chicago came back to take the nightcap, 8-4. In game one Earl Webb hit an inside-the-park home run—getting rare since the advent of the lively ball seven years earlier—in a losing cause.

NATIONAL BASEBALL HALL OF FAME LIBRARY, COOPERSTOWN, NY

Current and future Cubs managers, Joe McCarthy and Charlie Grimm.

The Reds were in town on May 26 as the Cubs won their easiest game of the month. Buoyed by a six-run fifth, they coasted to an 11-2 laugher. The next day they again beat Cincinnati, but this time it took them 11 innings to do it. Charlie Root, who had gone the distance only 24 hours before, came on in relief to get his second victory in as many days. To make it even more satisfying, Root drove in Gabby Hartnett with the winning run in a 3-2 thriller. For Charlie, it was his ninth career win over the Reds against only one loss. However, the Reds got even the following day with an 8-0 shellacking.

Sunday, May 29, saw the Pirates sail into Lake Michigan to clip the Cubs, 8-5, for their 11th consecutive victory despite Hack Wilson's eighth home run of the season. As soon as the game was completed, both teams packed their bags to travel to the Steel City for the remainder of the series. The reason for this was that Pennsylvania, like Massachussetts, still banned Sunday baseball at that time.

The morning game of the Memorial Day doubleheader at Pittsburgh's Forbes Field began inauspiciously enough. In the bottom of the fourth, the Pirates had Lloyd Waner on second base and Clyde Barnhart on first as Lloyd's brother Paul came to bat. At shortstop for the Cubs was Jimmy Cooney.

With the hit-and-run on, Cooney snagged the elder Waner's line drive, stepped on second to double Lloyd, then tagged Barnhart coming down the line for an unassisted triple play. It was all over in seconds. The Cubs went on to win the game, 7-6, in 10 innings, snapping the Bucs' winning streak. Not disheartened, the Pirates won the afternoon contest, 6-5, also in 10.

Cooney had become one of only ten players in history (including those since) to pull off an unassisted triple killing. To make the story even more unbelievable, Johnny Neun of the Tigers did it against the Indians the very next day!

After that, the feat was not duplicated until July 20, 1968, when the Senators' Ron Hansen scalped three Indians again. Cooney's remained the last in the National League until Mickey Morandini of the Phillies tripled up the Pirates on September 20, 1992. For a touch of irony, Cooney while a member of the Cardinals in 1925 had been one of the victims of an unassisted triple play himself when Pittsburgh's Glenn Wright had turned the trick.

As for the Cubs on May 31, they fell to Pittsburgh again, 10-9, blowing leads of 4-0, 6-1, 7-5, and 9-6. The month had ended in embarrassment.

Just eight days after his history making feat, Jimmy Cooney was traded to the Phillies for pitcher Hal Carlson. The Cubs had 20-year-old Woody English waiting in the wings for the shortstop job, so the 33-

year-old Cooney was an unneeded commodity. Thanks largely to a 12-game winning streak in June, the Cubs Soared into first place, a position they held as late as September 1. Unfortunately, a 12-18 log during the final month dropped them to fourth place as the Pirates copped the flag. So who says the "September swoon" started in 1969? It was already a long-standing Cub tradition!

THERE ARE NOW FOUR PLAYERS *with 600 career home runs, as Barry Bonds joined the club in August. When Babe Ruth established the club in 1931, Rogers Hornsby was second on the all-time career home run list with 293 dingers. The Babe had three hits in the game (he was ejected in the seventh inning) and paid a young fan $10 for his home run ball. Ruth was the only member of the 300, 400, 500, and 600 home run clubs at the time.*

Willie Mays pinch hit his 600th homer in 1969 before a small crowd in San Diego that gave the slugger a five-minute standing ovation. Mays was joined 19 months later by Hank Aaron, thus forming the only active 600-homer duo ever until Mays retired at the end of the 1973 season. Ironically, Mays won that 1971 game in the 10th inning with his fourth hit of the contest.

Ruth was the youngest of the four sluggers to reach the mark and took far fewer at-bats to hit 600 home runs. He is also the only American Leaguer on the list. All of the National League blasts involve the San Francisco Giants. Two of the players were members of the Giants when they struck their historic blows, and a Giants' hurler surrendered Aaron's clout. —DAVID VINCENT

HOME RUN #600 (AB: career at-bat for #600)

PLAYER	TM	LG	DATE	PITCHER	TM	SITE	AGE	ON	AB	AB/HR
Babe Ruth	NYY	AL	08/21/1931	George Blaeholder	SLA	SLA	36	1	6921	11.54
Willie Mays	SFN	NL	09/22/1969	Mike Corkins	SDN	SDN	38	1	9514	15.86
Hank Aaron	ATL	NL	04/27/1971	Gaylord Perry	SFN	ATL	37	1	10014	16.69
Barry Bonds	SFN	NL	08/09/2002	Kip Wells	PIT	SFN	38	0	8211	13.69

Late in the Game

The Integration of the Washington Senators

by David A. Evans

On September 6, 1954, more than seven years after Jackie Robinson stepped onto the diamond at Ebbets Field for the Brooklyn Dodgers, Carlos Paula trotted out to left field at Griffith Stadium in Washington, D.C. He was the first black to appear in a regular season lineup of the Washington Senators. This event, while long a matter of speculation since the Robinson signing, barely rated a mention in the mainstream newspapers, and wasn't covered in any great depth among the black media. The continued poor performance of the bottom-dwelling Senators, plus Paula's status as a Cuban national, contributed to the lack of coverage, as the Senators had a long history of using Latin American players. Still, the integration of the national pastime in the nation's capital deserves study. In order to understand the historic significance of this event, I will argue that the debut of Paula with the Washington Senators, while symbolically an act of integration, was in fact consistent with the team's long-standing tradition of using Latin American players. Furthermore, this act of integration was lost in the long period of time between Jackie Robinson's 1947 appearance and the Red Sox 1959 integration and by Paula's mediocre talents and the halfhearted manner in which his debut took place.

The history of the integration of major league baseball up until 1954 shows that the hiring of black ballplayers by individual teams was largely a matter of the personality and the philosophy of the individual owners. These owners obviously responded to larger shifts in the league and in society in regards to integration. Major league clubs sharing the same city often had very different patterns of hiring black players. In New York, for example, the Brooklyn Dodgers were the first and most aggressive in signing blacks, while the vaunted Yankees were one of the last teams to integrate. The Senators had a poor record in the long process of integration. Clark Calvin Griffith dominated the history of the original Washington Senators that played in the nation's capital from 1901-1960. Born in Clear Creek, Missouri, in 1869, Griffith was a first-rate pitcher who won 240 games as a major league hurler and won 24 games in the inaugural American League season of 1901 as a member of the Chicago White Sox. Griffith came to the Senators in 1912 as a player-manager and in 1920 bought a controlling interest in the team. He stayed with the Senators until his death in 1955 and was succeeded by his adopted son Calvin Griffith. Under Clark Griffith's tutelage, the Washington Senators earned the most famous epithet in baseball history: "Washington—first in war, first in peace and last in the American League." With the possible exception of Connie Mack of the Philadelphia Athletics, no team in baseball more clearly reflected the image of one man than that of the Senators and Clark Griffith. He was certainly not alone in keeping blacks off his team in the first

David Evans was born in Washington, DC and attended Senators games at RFK Stadium with his father. He now lives in Charlestown, West Virginia.

decades of the twentieth century, but he did play the paramount part in keeping blacks off the Senators after the Brooklyn Dodgers had integrated. However, the history of the racial makeup of the Washington Senators is decidedly not an all-white affair. Part of the problem in dealing with the Senators' late acceptance of black ballplayers was their long history of association with Latinos. This characteristic of the Senators served as an irritant to both black and white sportswriters who followed the team, and was also part of the reason why Carlos Paula's premiere brought so little attention.

The Senators were among the first teams to mine the untapped talent pool of the Caribbean and Central and South America. There was no gentlemen's agreement about barring these players, and as long as they were considered white, they were able to ply their trade in the big leagues. In 1935, a full twelve years before Jackie Robinson's debut with the Dodgers, the Senators put Bobby Estalella, a Cuban national, in the outfield at Griffith Stadium. Indeed, many D.C. fans of the time viewed Estalella as black. Next in line was Mel Almada, a Mexican, who was a full-time center fielder and batted .309 in 1937 in 100 games with the Senators. A Venezuelan Alex Carrasquel, also widely perceived as being black, joined the Senators pitching staff in 1939. There were other notable Latino players during the 1940s and 1950s. Cuba produced pitcher Rene Monteagudo and infielders Gil Torres, Pedro Gomez and Mike Guerra. Two Cuban brothers roamed the outfield for the Senators: Roberto Ortiz and Baby Ortiz. Mexico sent infielder Chile Gomez. Clearly, not all the Washington Senators players hailed from the breadbasket of the U.S.A.

There were two main reasons for this influx of foreigners, especially during the 1940s and 1950s. The first of these was that non-U.S. citizens could not be drafted. Both before and during the war the appeal to Griffith of these foreigners was obvious: He would not lose the core of his team to the armed forces, while his competitors who relied on native-born talent would. This strategy had mixed results, as the Senators finished last and next to last in 1942 and 1944, but they did manage to finish second twice, in 1943 and 1945. Any Senators finish in the first division was an aberration and was probably due to the fact that other American League teams lost more talented players to the armed forces than the Senators. The second reason for Griffith signing so many foreign-born players was financial. Griffith was always in financial difficulty, and like their black counterparts a few years later, Latino players made less money than whites. In short they were a good source of cheap labor. These immigrant workers also served to point out the glaring absence of American blacks during this time.

Shirley Povich, the longtime sportswriter of the Washington *Post*, declared in 1953, "Mr. Griffith would give Washington fans dark players from other lands, but never an American Negro." Povich was also an outspoken critic of other segregated professional teams in Washington. Writing on the Redskins, Povich declared, "The Redskins colors are burgundy, gold and Caucasian." In a famous piece of Washington lore Povich wrote, "Jim Brown, born ineligible to play for the Redskins, integrated their end zone three times yesterday." Based on Povich's writings, it is clear that most of the Washington, D.C., area's sports fans were aware of the team's exclusion of blacks and the moral and practical problems associated with this. Shirley Povich was no radical rabble-rouser and was writing for a mainstream newspaper. In fairness, Griffith was clearly not a leader in integrating major league baseball, but neither was he all that different from other owners of the time.

Povich was not alone among sportswriters in his condemnation of the racial practices of Clark Griffith. Writing in the Pittsburgh *Courier Journal* in 1943, Wendell Smith declared that Clark Griffith "is one of the big league owners who prefers to go outside of the borders of these United States and bring in players, rather than hire American citizens of color." Both the mainstream and black press were critical of Griffith's refusal to hire black players. As in so many aspects in American history, World War II played a key role in the fight to integrate Major League Baseball. With so many of its players lost to the draft, this era provided the ideal opportunity to hire black players to take their place. The fact that this did not happen speaks volumes about the "gentlemen's agreement" about not hiring blacks. In the aftermath of the war, public protest against this exclusionary policy was evident at Griffith Stadium in Washington, D.C., as well as other ballparks around the country.

According to Jules Tygiel, author of *Baseball's Great Experiment: Jackie Robinson and His Legacy*, protestors showed up sporadically at Senators home games during the early 1950s calling for integration and were dismissed by Griffith as a "committee of Commies." As late as 1953 Griffith was unwilling to put a black player on the field. In April of that year he declared,

"Nobody is going to stampede me into signing Negro players merely for the sake of satisfying certain pressure groups." At this point Paula was playing at the Senators AAA affiliate in Charlotte, North Carolina, and while not tagged as a sure-fire major leaguer, Griffith certainly knew of his existence and the possibility that he would play for the Senators.

According to David Wiggins, Clark Griffith was not shy about letting people know how much he was against black players in the major leagues. There is no doubt that Griffith received much needed income from rent of his stadium to the Homestead Grays, and perhaps the diminishing talent pool of the Negro Leagues and the subsequent loss of income to Griffith were motivating reasons why he elevated Paula to the big leagues late in the 1954 season. Three years before Carlos Paula played for the Senators, owner Clark Griffith said that the first black player on each team, "would have to be a great one." Carlos Paula was a mediocre prospect who put up modest numbers even in the minors. At the time of his call-up in September, 1954, Paula was hitting .290 with the Senators' Sally League affiliate in Charlotte, North Carolina. Why, then, was Paula the pick to become the first black player for the Senators?

Clearly, Griffith did not want a lot of press attention in this matter, for Paula was a late-season call-up for a seventh-place team some forty games out of first. Paula was slipped in during the first game of a meaningless doubleheader between two cellar-dwelling teams. The fact that Paula was not a hot prospect would also lead people to have low expectations of him. This was not a future all-star stepping on the field, but a role player whose shortcomings would soon become apparent. Finally, the fact that Paula was a Cuban is most significant. The Senators had an almost 20-year history of employing Latino ballplayers. Paula would be just one more spice in the Latin flavor of the Washington Senators. Washington's two biggest mainstream newspapers treated this historic event as a footnote in the sports section. The Washington *Post* first mentioned Paula in the third paragraph of an article detailing a doubleheader between the two worst teams in the American League. Commenting on the many new faces brought up from Charlotte, reporter Bob Addie wrote, "Carlos Paula, Jim Lemon, Steve Korcheck and Jesse Levan comprised the Charlotte delegation in the second game and it's sad to report that the quartet didn't get a hit." In dealing with the historic aspect of this game the *Post* reported, "Paula, first Negro ever to play a regular game for the Nats [Senators], played in the first game too, and did contribute two hits including a two-run double." In his column, "The Baseball Beat," sportswriter Burton Hawkins added this bit of perspective: "Add historical notes: Carlos Paula became the first Negro to play in a regular game for Washington in the first game of yesterday's double header." In-depth social or political commentary is not to be expected on reporting of a baseball game; however, the fact that this event didn't merit mention elsewhere in the paper is indicative that the *Post* did not consider it a big story. Washington's other major paper, the Washington *Star*, reported the event in much the same way as its competitor, although it was given slightly greater space. Paula at least rated a mention in the opening paragraph of the story. Again, ignoring *any* social implication whatsoever, the *Star* declared, "The Senators' swarm of Charlotte graduates generally has touched off little whooping and hollering among the most devoted followers of the club, in strong-backed Carlos Paula and towering Jim Lemon they've sensed possible future help." The paper also reported, "Paula, muscular Cuban Negro, whacked a 400-foot double and a single in the first game with the Philadelphia A's." In commenting further on Paula's performance it was reported, "He met three other pitches on the nose, although going hitless in the second game, which the Senators dropped 3-2. He also handles leftfield—a brutal sunfield—adequately." Focusing solely on the baseball significance of Paula's debut, the *Star* continued: "Paula will be tested more thoroughly by more adept pitching than he was stacked against yesterday. Carlos seemingly stands a half block from the plate and would appear to be at a loss against pitches nicking the outside of the plate. He got by in the Sally League with that stance but major league pitchers may force him to alter it."

The reporter, Burt Hawkins, had prescience about Paula's batting style which would become a major cause of the demise of his major league career (along with his fielding), but by ignoring any social ramifications of his appearance, the *Star* was reflecting the unconcern of the mainstream press, and by implication the reading public. Interestingly, the black press, while more complimentary toward Paula, gave the event just slightly more coverage. The Washington *Afro-American* was the only local paper to print a picture of Paula, although they, too, made little of the social significance of his premiere. Under a picture of

Paula in the dugout, the *Afro-American* called his debut "impressive." The paper declared: "The first colored player in history to wear a Washington Senator uniform in a regular season game, Carlos Paula made an auspicious bow in the Labor Day double-header against Philadelphia at Griffith Stadium. The 25-year old, 6-foot, 3-inch Cuban outfielder collected two hits, one a double, and drove in two runs in the nightcap. Defensively, he had six putouts, one a spectacular leaping stab of a drive against the leftfield stands by the A's Jim Finigan."

It is again evident that baseball took precedence over any social significance. While being more complimentary with such words as "auspicious" and "spectacular," and printing a picture of him, even the local black press downplayed the event. The *Afro-American* points out that Paula was a Cuban, and this seems to be a point of contention to many people, particularly American-born blacks. It is impossible to tell what would have happened if the first black Washington Senator had been native-born, but the fact that all papers pointed out that he was Cuban leads one to suspect that an American black may have received more press coverage.

Sam Lacy, writing in the Baltimore *Afro-American*, offered one of the few social criticisms of Paula's debut with the Senators. Lacy was critical of Senators' manager Bucky Harris not playing Paula against the New York Yankees the weekend before his actual premiere. Harris claimed that he was reluctant to play too many rookies against the Yankees for fear of drawing criticism by the league-leading Indians that the Senators were going soft on New York. Lacy wrote, "this department thinks very highly of Bucky and appreciates the explanation . . . otherwise, it might have been tempted to suspect that Paula was being spared the pressure of breaking in against a club so obviously anti [black]." This criticism was obviously a blast first at the New York Yankees and second at Bucky Harris. Both criticisms were unfair. First, while it is true that the Yankees were still an all-white team, they had in fact played against integrated teams with no apparent incidents. Second, the Senators were far out of the pennant race and it is tradition in baseball not to appear to be "giving up" by filling a lineup with rookies. That said, Lacy did have the courage to move beyond the baseball diamond in looking at the barrier the Senators were passing.

Lacy also offered an interesting economic incentive to Paula's appearance. With tongue planted firmly in cheek, Lacy declared that he "wouldn't dare conclude that the tan Cuban was being eyed hopefully by the front office as a sort of a prop for a holiday gate that had the misfortune to draw the bedraggled Philadelphia Athletics as a lure." This criticism was interesting on two fronts. First, the economic argument is hard to accept. While Griffith was always strapped for cash and no doubt would have liked to draw a big holiday crowd, Paula's appearance was not announced in advance. Second, the use of the words "tan Cuban" again reflect the mixed feelings of American blacks toward Paula. Lacy, to be fair, at least was able to view the larger context of the event, even if his criticisms were unfair. Paula played in a total of nine games during the 1954 season. He played a full season in 1955, participating in 115 games and hitting a commendable .299. His shortcomings, however, were becoming apparent. For a man of his size he lacked power, hitting a paltry six home runs, an unacceptable number for an outfielder. Even Shirley Povich, an early supporter of integration, mocked Paula as hitting "destructive singles." Along with his lack of power, it was his fielding that ultimately did in Paula. Baseball historian Peter Bjarkman wrote of Paula that his "abilities to smash a baseball never came near to compensating for his seemingly total inability to field one cleanly in the outfield." Even Povich had to admit that Paula was, "something of a crudity in the field." He led all American League outfielders in errors during the 1955 campaign. Paula played in only 33 games for the Senators in 1956 and was sent to the minors for good at the start of the 1957 season.

George Will has called Jackie Robinson's debut with the Brooklyn Dodgers "the most important event in the emancipation of black Americans since the Civil War." While this may be overstated, it does reflect the drama and importance that many placed on Jackie Robinson. Carlos Paula, by comparison, received little attention or credit. There are a few reasons for this. The first had to do with timing. 1954 was a critical year in the growing civil rights movement. The *Brown* decision had huge ramifications on a very personal level. White Washingtonians were faced with the prospect of integrating their public schools. Carlos Paula took the field the day before most of the area's schools opened. It is easy to see why many people did not pay attention. Second, Paula's nationality was a factor in the limited press coverage he received and the lukewarm fan reaction toward him. Many white writers viewed him as another in a long line of Latino players to wear a Senators uniform. Many black writers were resentful of the fact that a native-born man of color wasn't the first to play for Washington. Finally, the fact that Paula wasn't a top prospect probably played the key role in the lack of attention given his debut. A .290 hitter in the minors, who lacked power and was a mediocre fielder at best, was not going to rivet the attention of even hard-core fans. The overall history of the original Washington Senators was largely one of mediocrity. One World Series triumph and three pennants in sixty years are testimony to this fact. The Senators continually displayed substandard performances; it is not surprising that their first dip into the interracial pool had similar results.

THE BLUE HAZE

by Everett Parker

In those bygone days
Field gates would be thrown open
With the game's last out.
Fans streamed onto the field.

Players running heads down
For those distant clubhouse stairs
Past the Captain Eddie Grant monument,
Almost five hundred feet away.

Some overly aggressive fans
Would try to touch or impede idols.
Getting an elbow or a snarl,
"Get out of the way pal."

Leisurely walking across the field
Where living legends just trod.
Clubhouse boys collecting equipment
In littered dugouts.

"The Gashouse Gang,"
Champion tobacco chewers.
Torn and empty Beechnut wrappers
Ankle high on the floor of their dugout.

Fans stood in the bare patch
Where Mel Ott pawed his mark forever.
Others ran the bases,
Headfirst slides in their Sunday best.

I'd walk to deepest center field,
Look back at the closed end
Of the old horseshoe-shaped ballpark.
Coogan's Bluff its silent sentinel.

Gazing into that blue haze
Of a sultry 1930s late afternoon.
Haze from 20,000 cigars and cigarettes
of Giant fans and smokers long dead.

Once dreaming of a day
When I'd track down a ball out there.
When the haze settles in these vineyards,
It all comes back.

His [Danforth's] work on the pitching mound has been more carefully scrutinized and more universally criticized than that of any pitcher on record, not excepting the ill-omened [Carl] Mays.
Why Dave Danforth Has Been a Storm Center *by F.C. Lane,* Baseball Magazine, *July 1924*

It is doubtful if ever a professional athlete has encountered circumstances so discouraging as those which Dave Danforth has had to hurdle in the course of his baseball career.
— J. Roy Stockton, St. Louis Post-Dispatch, *August 19, 1923*

Dave Danforth: Baseball's Forrest Gump

by Steve L. Steinberg

Dave Danforth (1890-1970) is one of the most fascinating pitchers in the history of baseball, though he won only 71 games in the big leagues. Controversy swirled around him for years, and he was a part of a number of key baseball events during a playing career that spanned more than twenty years. Who was this mystery man who kept popping up in interesting places, and why was he such an enigma? Even his assorted nicknames convey a certain impenetrability: *Dashing Dave, Dandy Dave, Daring Dave, Dauntless Dave, Demon Dave.*

In 1911 Dave caught the eye of one of Connie Mack's informal scouts, a grocer from Palestine, Texas, named Hyman Pearlstone. But he refused to sign a pro contract until he finished college. That year Dave won all his games and pitched Baylor University to the Texas state championship. He then joined Mack's great Philadelphia Athletics late in the season and relieved starters Bender, Plank, and Coombs a number of times. At the age of 21, Dave was a full-share member of the world champion A's.

The following year, Connie Mack wanted to strengthen his position players and felt he had an excess of good pitching. So he traded Dave to the Baltimore Orioles of the International League. (A year later, Connie would let another fine young pitcher, Stan Coveleski, get away.)

Steve L. Steinberg is writing a book about baseball in the 1920s, Urban Shocker: Silent History of Baseball's Golden Age. *He lives in Seattle with his wife and three children.*

Dave became a workhorse for the Orioles. He appeared in 90 games his first two years in Baltimore and pitched more than 300 innings in 1913. In 1914, Dave opened the Orioles season by tossing a shutout against Buffalo. The next day, a teammate of his made his pro debut and tossed another shutout. His name was Babe Ruth. Another teammate was former Athletic and future Yankee pitching great, Bob Shawkey.

While with the Orioles, Dave attended the University of Maryland dental school. Orioles owner Jack Dunn even let Dave have his own room, so he could focus on his studies. Dave got his dentistry degree there in 1914, though he would not actively practice until 1933.

Later in the 1914 season, as the Orioles faced competition from the new Federal League's Baltimore Terrapins, owner Jack Dunn sold Dave to the Louisville Colonels of the American Association. During his stay there he invented the shine ball, quite by accident. The dusty field in Louisville was regularly sprayed with oil. Dave used to rub the ball on his trousers to get the oil off. He discovered that a ball shined on one spot gained an unpredictable hop as it was thrown.

Late in the 1915 season he set an American Association record with 18 strikeouts against Kansas City, breaking the record of 17 set by Marty O'Toole with St. Paul in 1911. He went on to strike out 49 men in three games. The current record of 20 strikeouts was set by another Louisviller, Maurice McDermott, in 1949 against St. Paul (per Marshall Wright).

The shine ball became Dave's second ticket to the majors, when he was drafted by the Chicago White Sox after the 1915 season. It was here that he taught the shine ball to Eddie Cicotte, who became more famous and proficient with it. Cicotte was a decent pitcher before 1916, with a record of 103-94. He was a great pitcher after 1915, with a record of 105-55, until he was banned from the game for his role in the 1919 Black Sox scandal.

Dave quickly became a lightning rod of controversy. Tigers manager Hughie Jennings accused him of throwing the emery ball. Tiger Ty Cobb, who had a running battle with Dave for years, accused the pitcher of throwing a paraffin ball, slitting the seams with a razor blade and then loading and pressing them back in place with the wax.

In 1917 Dave became one of the game's first relief pitchers, relieving in forty-one games for the world champions of that year. This was a number of years before Firpo Marberry of the Senators and Wilcy Moore of the Yankees made that role important. For the second time in his young career, he gained a winner's World Series share.

But Dave was not as effective as the man he taught the shine ball to. He occasionally had trouble controlling it. Late in the 1917 season, one of those pitches sailed into the head of Tris Speaker and knocked him unconscious.

By 1919 Dave had lost his effectiveness. But before the White Sox cut him loose, he gave up the first home run Babe Ruth hit in Comiskey Park in July of that year. In late August, the White Sox traded him to Columbus of the American Association. When the White Sox went on to the World Series, Dave filed a claim with the National Commission for a World Series share. Considering his poor numbers that year, it is not surprising he was unsuccessful with the claim.

Rather than reporting to Columbus, Dave pitched for the semi-pro Baltimore Dry Docks at the end of the 1919 season. The Dry Docks stunned the powerful Baltimore Orioles, Dave's former team, four games to three, with Dave and his shine ball playing a key role. He was able to pitch in this series only after manager Joe Tinker of Columbus gave his approval "under duress."

By 1921 Dave was the star of the American Association and one of the best pitchers in the high minors. He won 25 games for a last-place Columbus team that won only 67 times. He also led the league in strikeouts and earned run average. He was united here with one of his biggest boosters, manager Clarence Rowland, who led the White Sox in 1917.

Before the start of the 1922 season, the improving St. Louis Browns acquired Dave in exchange for 11 men, three of whom were to be named later. This may have been the most men ever traded for one player, at least in a deal involving a major league team. Dave did not report right away, instead insisting on 10 percent of the value of the players, which was estimated at $75,000-$90,000. Eventually he settled, though just how much he was paid was not announced.

In Mobile, Alabama, where the Browns were holding spring training, Dave was thought by many to be the missing piece in the Browns' pennant drive. He would supplement Urban Shocker on a team laden with strong hitting. The *Register* of Mobile wrote of Dave, "If he flashes, it means the flag." But a very different opinion came from his 1919 White Sox manager, Kid Gleason: "The three most dangerous things in the world are a 4-flush, an unloaded shotgun, and a left-handed pitcher."

Dave brought his reputation of doctoring the ball with him in his third trip to the majors. He also brought an incredible and controversial pick-off move to first base. Umpires and opposing players were constantly checking the balls he threw for signs of one illegal pitch or another, but he was not caught. Then on July 27, 1922, in a game against the Yankees, umpire Brick Owens tossed Dave for pitching a ball with "loaded seams" of dirt or mud. A 10-game suspension followed. While the Browns were in a fierce pennant race with the Yankees and needed pitching, Browns manager Lee Fohl and business manager Bob Quinn did not feel comfortable with Dave. Quite frankly, they did not believe his claims of innocence.

> *If there is anything illegal in rubbing the hands on the ball, on one side or all sides, then I am guilty of illegal pitching and every other pitcher in baseball is equally guilty. But I have never rubbed dirt or any foreign substance on the ball and I never have loaded a seam.*
>
> — Dave Danforth interview,
> St. Louis *Post-Dispatch*, August 13, 1922

Dave was reputed to have a nail on his left thumb that was as sharp and abrasive as a metal nail. He also was said to have large and powerful hands that could scuff or loosen the cover of a ball. One report said he slept with his pitching hand in a tray of pickle brine, to make it as coarse and callous as a piece of emery paper. But Dave always kept his hand out of sight, explaining that he suffered from embarrassing eczema.

> *Whether Dave could do all these things nobody knew for sure but Dave and he wasn't telling. It seemed that Danforth was not only a pitcher but a practical psychologist as well. Nobody ever saw the left hand which was supposed to be so ruinous to the surface of a baseball...Batters who are always seeking to detect some sign of chicanery on a pitcher's part sometimes become so engrossed in looking for illegal pitches that they forget to hit the legal ones.*
> — Tom Meany, *Baseball Greatest Teams*

The Browns sent Dave down to Tulsa in mid-August, with an option for recall. He cleared waivers, as not one major league team took an interest in him. This indicated that:

> *Dave was either unanimously voted of little value, or a tacit agreement to "railroad" him for the good of the game had taken effect.*
> — John Wray,
> St. Louis *Post-Dispatch*, August 12, 1922

Dave's absence probably cost the Browns the pennant, which they lost by one game to the Yankees. One wonders what different course St. Louis baseball would have taken had the Browns won the city's first flag and cemented the stronger loyalties with the fans and higher attendance they had than the Cardinals had. Interestingly, Dave's Tulsa Oilers won the Western League pennant that year.

In 1923, Browns owner Phil Ball insisted the team bring Dave back for what would be his fourth trip up to the big leagues. By June, Bob Quinn resigned in frustration over Ball's meddling and began to put together the group that bought the Boston Red Sox from Harry Frazee. On August 1, umpire George Moriarty threw Dave out of a game with the Athletics for throwing a doctored ball with rough spots. Once again, the automatic 10-day suspension followed. It was known that Moriarty and Danforth, who were teammates on the 1916 White Sox, did not get along. Their feud was said to be the most bitter in baseball. But it wasn't just Moriarty, though the accusations were always vague:

> *I have talked with almost every umpire in the American League on the charge against Danforth. The report from them is unanimous — that Dave applies a foreign substance or otherwise tampers with the ball.*
> — Sid Keener,
> St. Louis *Times*, August 3, 1923

Many of the Browns players wanted to sign a petition supporting Dave's innocence. George Sisler, as decent a player as there was in the game and Dave's manager in 1924 and 1925, had this to say about Dave:

> *In all the time he has played with us, I have never known Dave Danforth to use any illegal delivery...If he does things with a ball that other pitchers can't do, that is no proof of illegal delivery... Danforth is a high grade fellow in every way and he deserves the right to work at his profession without being molested.*
> — "Why Dave Danforth Has Been a Storm Center," *Baseball Magazine*, July 1924

But the Browns' quiet and unassuming manager, Lee Fohl, did not agree. Once again he did not support his pitcher, and this time the Dave Danforth controversy cost him his job. Phil Ball fired him in early August.

> *I know the character of Lee Fohl. He would give a friend the last dime he had in the world. . . If Lee wouldn't sign [the petition] there must be some black smoke in the air.*
> — Sid Keener,
> St. Louis *Times*, August 3, 1923

Lee later met with Sid Keener and showed the sports editor a number of new balls Dave had thrown that all had a rough spot of at least two inches in length. Sid featured the story in the St. Louis *Times* on August 22.

In the meantime, on August 16, 1923, Dave returned to pitch under the watchful eyes of both Commissioner Landis and AL President Johnson. Dave knew his career was on the line. Veteran umpire Billy Evans was behind the plate. An incredible total of 58 balls were used in the game. Dave himself even asked for a new ball a number of times. While Dave lost 3-1 to Herb Pennock and the New York Yankees, he threw a brilliant three-hitter and gained grudging respect from even his biggest critics. J. Roy Stockton called Dave "the gamest man in baseball" (*Post-Dispatch*, August 19), and Sid Keener was impressed:

> *It was a game that only a steel heart and a concrete spine could have pitched. Considering all events in the case I have never seen its equal on the ball field.*
>
> — St. Louis *Times*, August 17, 1923

Frank O'Neill of the *Sun* of New York tried to analyze the Brown pitcher. Before this closely scrutinized game, he wrote, "Danforth is shaving the rules. He does not give them a close shave either." After Dave's bravura performance, Frank referred to an unnamed "baseball critic" who compared Dave to a shoplifter who doesn't have to steal, but is compelled to do illegal things by uncontrollable urges. (*Sun*, August 17, 1923)

Dave managed to stay in the majors for two more rather uneventful years, winning 22 games for the Browns in 1924-1925. He then began another remarkable minor league career.

He helped his 1926 Milwaukee Brewers set the all-time American Association win streak of 21 games in late June. His 16-4 record in 1927 led his New Orleans Pelicans to the Southern Association title. In Eugene Murdock's oral history, *Baseball Between the Wars*, Ed Wells said that Dave threw the spitter with New Orleans.

On July 3, 1930, in the first night game with arc lighting in the International League, 40-year-old Dave Danforth started for Buffalo in a 5-4 loss to Montreal. Just a few weeks later, on September 20, he set a new International League record by striking out 20 Rochester Red Wings. Once again Dave was accused of throwing a doctored ball. Wings player-manager Billy Southworth, who rarely struck out, whiffed five times in this game. The current record of 22 strikeouts was set by Bob Veale of Columbus in 1962 (per Marshall Wright).

In 1932 Dave ended his professional baseball career in Buffalo and finally Scranton. His Scranton manager was his former Baltimore teammate of almost 20 years earlier, Bob Shawkey. In Buffalo a teammate said he had a little locked black bag that perhaps hid the secret to his pitching success.

After his baseball career Dave practiced dentistry in Baltimore for many years. SABR member Tim Newman is married to Dave's granddaughter. He brought to my attention the 1927 controversy that Commissioner Landis investigated over whether the White Sox paid the Detroit Tigers to lose to them late in the 1917 season. Payments were indeed made to the Tigers by the Sox, including a straight arrow like Eddie Collins. Landis found the White Sox of 1917 innocent and agreed with their explanation that the payments were "thank you" gifts for the Tigers' sweeping the White Sox's closest rivals for the pennant, the Boston Red Sox, in a key series. Interestingly, only three White Sox had no knowledge of the gifts and were not connected to them in any way. Dave Danforth was one of the three.

While Dave would be 112 years old today, I was able to talk to one of his teammates about the controversial pitcher. In 1932, when Dave was near the end of his career in Buffalo, one of his teammates was Billy Werber, a former Yankee and later a key member of the pennant-winning Cincinnati Reds of 1939 and 1940. The 93-year-old Werber remembered Dave instantly:

> *Danforth, he was a lefty. A gentlemanly type . . . a quiet fellow. Never had a hell of a lot to say . . . Dave didn't have the disposition to do anything illegal with the ball.*
>
> — Telephone interview, July 11, 2001

Billy remembered Dave's pleasant personality, which only added to the mystery of his pitching repertoire. He was not a rough character, but rather a well-educated, clean-cut man. He simply didn't fit the mold of a ruthless or tricky person. But as the editor of *Baseball Magazine* F.C. Lane recognized, "Danforth was originally the apostle of the freak delivery." Dave himself admitted as much in that July 1924 article in *Baseball Magazine:*

> *I will admit that in my time I have used every delivery that I ever heard of. If I had known of any others I should have used them.*

After the controversy of the 1923 season, an editorial in *Baseball Magazine* gave Dave his due, but still did not make a clear endorsement of the pitcher:

> *Danforth doesn't mutter incantations over the*

baseball in the dark of the moon near a convenient grave yard with the accompaniment of bats' wings and rabbits' feet. What he does, if anything, he does in the full view of lynx-eyed umpires and ball players and the ball itself that he handles is evidence pro or con. Why not clear up the Danforth mystery once and for all?
— *Baseball Magazine*, October 1923

Perhaps a column a few years later in *The Sporting News* said it best:

One of the unwritten rules of baseball is that murder is all right if you can get away with it . . . Any ordinary pitcher facing the abuse and suspicion and steady scrutiny he has faced would certainly break down and reveal his method in self defense. It requires a good deal of courage to take all the persecution Danforth has taken without weakening. Whether he is a cheater or a wizard we are willing to admit Dave has won his point. More power to him.
— "Scribbled by Scribes,"
The Sporting News, July 15, 1926

DANFORTH, DAVID CHARLES (DAVE)

BORN: March 7, 1890, Granger, TX DIED: Sept.19, 1970, Baltimore, MD BAT:L THROW: L Height, 6.00. Weight, 175.
Attended Baylor College. He played on their team in 1910 and 1911. Played in the 1917 World Series.

YR.	CLUB	LEAGUE	G	CG	IP	W	L	PCT	H	BB	SO	R	ER	ERA
1911	Philadelphia	American	14	1	36	4	1	.800	27	26	37	15	14	3.71
1912	Philadelphia	American	3	0	20	0	0	.000	26	12	8	13	9	4.05
	Baltimore	International	37		221	12	10	.545	197	59	116	100		
1913	Baltimore	International	53*		304	16	14	.533	288	96	150	146		
1914	Baltimore	International	32		184	12	15	.444	147	75	68	79		
	Louisville	American Assoc.	13		89	6	5	.545	80	48	74	42	38	3.84
1915	Louisville	American Assoc.	33	11	189	12	8	.600	150	91	172	83	63	3.00
1916	Chicago	American	28	1	94	5	5	.500	87	37	49	43	34	3.27
1917	Chicago	American	50*	1	173	11	6	.647	155	74	79	56	51	2.66
1918	Chicago	American	38	5	138	6	15	.286	148	40	48	73	53	3.46
1919	Chicago	American	15	0	42	1	3	.250	58	20	17	44	36	7.71
1920	Columbus	American Assoc.	29		228	13	12	.520	198	68	188	94	65	2.57
1921	Columbus	American Assoc.	44		329	25*	16	.610	292	114	204*	136	97	2.66*
1922	Tulsa	Western	10	10	90	6	4	.600	96	15	86	46		
	St. Louis	American	20	3	80	5	2	.714	93	38	48	37	29	3.27
1923	St. Louis	American	38	16	226	16	14	.533	221	87	96	111	99	3.94
1924	St. Louis	American	41	12	220	15	12	.556	246	69	65	126	110	4.50
1925	St. Louis	American	38	5	159	7	9	.438	172	61	53		77	4.36
1926	Milwaukee	American Assoc.	43		273	17	15	.531	294	74	123	145	119	3.92
1927	Milwaukee	American Assoc.	6		19	1	1	.500	31	11	4	18	17	8.05
	New Orleans	Southern Assoc.	26		181	16	4	.800	159	28	59	51	45	2.25
1928	New Orleans	Southern Assoc.	37		212	10	11	.476	253	62	78	114	111	4.71
1929	New Orleans	Southern Assoc.	32		162	8	7	.533	136	48	87	79	61	3.39
1930	Dallas	Texas	13	3	74	2	5	.286	92	25	43	50	47	5.76
	Buffalo	International	24	11	161	12	8	.600	158	45	161	80	75	4.19
1931	Buffalo	International	14	1	60	3	6	.333	81	17	37	48	43	6.45
	Chattanooga	Southern Assoc.	16		73	4	6	.400	85	21	26	37	33	4.13
1932	Buffalo	International	4	0	5	0	1	.000	11	4	2	8	7	12.60
	Scranton	NY-Penn.	6		40	2	2	.500	53	12	11	26	23	5.18

Statistics courtesy of Ray Nemec/Baseball Research and Statistics

Don Lee and Thornton Lee

by Bill Nowlin

There's a well-known baseball trivia question: What father-and-son pitching combination both gave up a home run to the same batter? The batter was Ted Williams and the pitchers were Thornton Lee and his son Don Lee. Thornton Lee surrendered Ted's 28th home run on September 17, 1939 and Don yielded home run #517 on September 2, 1960—right near the tail end of Ted's last year.

Wouldn't it have been something if Don, in turn, had a son and he'd faced Ted sometime in batting practice or a spring training workout? Or gone up against Ted's son John Henry, when the younger Williams was giving baseball a shot? Well, Don did have a son—and his name was Bill Lee!

No, not *the* Bill Lee who pitched for Boston. Wouldn't *that* have been a story itself! This Bill Lee played ball one year when he was 14, was clocked by a radar gun at 82-83 miles an hour, and had a "great curve and a great changeup," according to his dad. But he didn't want to do what his granddaddy and his daddy did, and they didn't push him. Bill owns his own auto mechanics shop today in Tucson, Bill's Toy Shop (it specializes in Toyotas).

Thornton Lee debuted for the Indians on September 19 late in the 1933 season. He had two starts and threw 17⅓ innings that year and then served three more years with the Indians. Don Lee had already been conceived by the time of his dad's debut; he was born February 26, 1934—just 160 days later.

Thornton then pitched for the White Sox for 11 years (1937-1947, and a record of 104 wins and 104 losses), before wrapping up his career with one final year (1948) with the New York Giants. He finished with a 117-124 mark, a career 3.56 ERA, appearing in 374 major league games.

Don Lee debuted on April 23, 1957, pitching for the Detroit Tigers seven years after his father retired. Don Lee saw duty for six teams—the Tigers, Senators, Twins, Angels (both the Los Angeles Angels and the California Angels), Houston (just the Astros, having arrived midseason the year they shed the Colt .45s name and became the Astros), and the Cubs. Don's record was 40-44, with a 3.61 ERA. He appeared in 244 games. Between them, the father-son combination yielded 202 home runs (Ted's two plus 200 others) over 3,159⅔ innings.

Don remembers the time he got touched up by Ted: "Daddy told me that Ted Williams was the best left-handed hitter that he'd ever faced. I talked to Ted on numerous occasions my first year in the big leagues. I remember one time when I was in Detroit. We got rained out and I was in the parking lot and we were both waiting for cabs and I talked to him for a good half hour. He was very nice and he was also very complimentary of Daddy. I've read a couple of articles where he said that Daddy was the best left-handed

Bill Nowlin is the co-author (with Jim Prime) of several books on Ted Williams and the Red Sox, most recently Ted Williams: The Pursuit of Perfection.

pitcher he ever faced. Of course, he said that about a lot of pitchers. My dad told me, 'When you pitch to Ted Williams, you never throw him the same pitch twice.' I said, 'Well, I'll remember that.'

"But one time I threw him three changeups in a row, and he broke his bat on home plate after the third one because he stood and took it. He looked at me and I thought to myself, 'Don't you ever throw him another one!'

"Ted had a bit of a temper and he would throw a few choice words out and throw the bat and all this kind of stuff. There was just something about him—when he got into the batter's box he never took his eyes off you.

"I pitched against him in Washington when I was a Senator in 1960. The first game that year, he hit four balls so hard right at our second baseman, the last time up the kid was in the outfield grass. That home run. If memory serves me, that was the only hit he ever got off me. It was in Fenway Park over the bullpen and it was a slider. I didn't get it in far enough. Two balls and no strikes. You know what Ted Williams said when he rounded first base after hitting the home run off me? He'd hit this home run and, boy, it was a blast. He rounded first base and he said to me as he rounded the bag—I was looking right at him—he says, 'Take that, you son-of-a-bitch! One off your old man and one off you, and I'm gonna quit.' That's what he said. He ran around the bases and I never forgot that."

Between the two of them, Thornton Lee and Don Lee faced quite a number of Hall of Fame ballplayers—68 in all. "Dad pitched against a lot of great ballplayers. And so did I, which is one of the things I hold very high. Not too many families get to pitch against so many great Hall of Fame ballplayers. I would like to own that lineup if I could put it on the field today." I asked Don Lee to list the Hall of Famers that either he or his dad had pitched against.

It is an impressive list. Thornton Lee pitched to: Luke Appling, Earl Averill, Jim Bottomley, Lou Boudreau, Mickey Cochrane, Earle Combs, Dizzy Dean, Bill Dickey, Joe DiMaggio, Bobby Doerr, Red Faber, Bob Feller, Jimmie Foxx, Lou Gehrig, Charlie Gehringer, Lefty Gomez, Goose Goslin, Hank Greenberg, Burleigh Grimes, Lefty Grove, Gabby Hartnett, Rogers Hornsby, Carl Hubbell, Ted Lyons, Stan Musial, Mel Ott, Herb Pennock, Phil Rizzuto, Red Ruffing, Babe Ruth, Joe Sewell, Al Simmons, Dazzy Vance, Arky Vaughan, Lloyd Waner, Paul Waner, Ted Williams, and Early Wynn. Don Lee pitched to: Hank Aaron, Luis Aparicio, Richie Ashburn, Ernie Banks, Yogi Berra, Lou Brock, Jim Bunning, Steve Carlton, Orlando Cepeda, Roberto Clemente, Larry Doby, Don Drysdale, Whitey Ford, Nellie Fox, Bob Gibson, Al Kaline, Harmon Killebrew, Mickey Mantle, Willie McCovey, Willie Mays, Tony Perez, Robin Roberts, Brooks Robinson, Duke Snider, Warren Spahn, Willie Stargell, Hoyt Wilhelm, Billy Williams, Ted Williams, Early Wynn, and Carl Yastrzemski.

Don talks a bit more about another Ted, Ted Lyons. "One of Daddy's teammates that he was very fond of was Ted Lyons. I went to see Ted Lyons when I was doing my baseball work and my dad told me, if you ever get down there in Vinton, Louisiana, call Ted Lyons. Well, I had an extra day so I did, and I called him from a convenience store. Ted answered the phone and I introduced myself and I told him I was in town traveling to Shreveport and he said, 'Well, you step outside and look across the railroad tracks and that's my home.' He said, 'Please come over.' So I spent about an hour and a half with him.

"I can remember as a little boy, my dad would always send him a Christmas card and he would address it to: 1 2 3 4 5 6 7 8 9 10, Vinton, Louisiana. That was his address, because he had the only place in town. Ted made lots of tapes with stories about baseball and told me that he left all his baseball memorabilia to Baylor University. I just enjoyed the conversation so much and I was glad to do that. Gee, the place was old-fashioned and dark. He was a bachelor, you know. I told my dad I spent an hour and a half with him. He got sick taking care of his sister. He passed away not long after that from pneumonia."

The father/son team of "Lefty" (Thornton) and Don actually combined in another baseball activity as well. Both served as scouts for the St. Louis Cardinals. Thornton Lee was on salary; Don Lee worked as an "information scout" from 1975-1983. It was a system under which if Don recommended a player out of school and he made it to the majors for the Cardinals, he'd get $500.

Starting in 1983 until 1991, Don worked for the commissioner's office of the National Baseball Association, the West Coast representative in the minor league system. "When I was scouting, my dad was also scouting for the Cardinals and he signed John Denny, the Cy Young winner. A little after that, Curt Schilling came along. He was up at Yavupai Junior College. I was not scouting at that time, but he was signed out of Yavupai College.

"At the beginning, when I was helping Daddy with the Cardinals, I got credit for Tom Pagnozzi. I tried to get the Cardinals to take Jack Howell, but they wouldn't listen to me. The area supervisor told me later, 'I could never see him, and I made a mistake.' I also tried my damnedest to sign Gil Heredia out of Nogales High School. I talked like a Dutch uncle for him.

"Daddy was up in years and I would take the southern part of the state, while he would take the Phoenix area and north. If I saw somebody worthwhile, I would call him and he would come down and take a look. One of my former teammates with the Cubs was my area supervisor, Marty Keough. [Keough was a former teammate of Ted Williams, too, having broken in with the Red Sox in 1956 and playing there until midseason 1960, when he was traded to Cleveland. Keough thus was not in Boston when Ted homered off Don Lee.] "I scouted for the Phillies for a few years, up until 1995, maybe 1996. I couldn't see eye to eye with their area supervisor, so I didn't get anybody. I put in some names, but they're playing with other organizations and I didn't get any of those.

"I scouted everybody [position players and pitchers]. You have to look into the future—how big a kid is going to be and how much stronger he is going to be. When I first saw John Denny, he was 6'0" and 160 pounds. I told Daddy to come look at him. I said the guy can throw. The ball just wouldn't go straight. Now when he finished up, what was he? About 6'3", 6'4" and about 225-230. "I took a liking to pitchers. On the report I sent in on Pagnozzi—he was a third baseman in high school—I said this guy should be made a catcher and, lo and behold, that's the way it worked out even though I had nothing to do with that. He was not fleet of foot at all. He had very little range and I said to myself, this is the only place he's got a chance. He had a wonderful arm and wonderful hands, though—oh, a couple of pillows for hands.

"That's the way we worked. Daddy's judgment in baseball was very sound, and he had some very little quirks that he told me about that almost always proved to be when you're looking at a ballplayer—different little things that they should have or possess. We had just a real good time."

EARL RAPP WAS A DETERMINED MAN *despite hitting only .262 over parts of three big league seasons. A minor league slugger of note, Rapp drove in 145 runs for Chuck Dressen's champion Oakland Oaks in 1950, then knocked in more than 100 runs in 1953-55 with San Diego. He led the PCL in RBI in 1955 with 133.*

Rapp's determination for baseball came from a horror-filled night in the Colmar pocket on the French-German border in World War II. His story was told in the May 28, 1946, issue of The Sporting News. *Rapp's 48-man platoon was cut off by a German infantry unit and forced to dig in for the night. Sgt. Rapp was in command after his lieutenant was picked off by a sniper. The plan was to break through to the American lines at dawn.*

"The only way we had a chance," recalled Rapp, "was to jump out of our holes, one man at a time, run like mad for ten yards, then hit the ground before the SS sharpshooters got the range." As each man made a break for it, his mates laid down covering fire. The last man to leave was Rapp. Only seven of the men survived. For his actions that day Rapp was awarded a Silver Star.

"Strange, what thoughts run through your mind when you're hugging the ground and waiting for the hour. I thought about baseball, and how hard I'd work and go all-out if I had the opportunity to go back to spring training. 'Rapper,' I told myself, 'if you ever get through this, you'll play baseball like you never played it.'"

—DICK THOMPSON

Reminiscing with Ray Hayworth

by J. Ronald Oakley

When Ray Hayworth died at the age of 98 on September 25, 2002, he was the oldest living major league player and the last surviving teammate of the legendary Ty Cobb. I feel very fortunate to have had the chance to spend a pleasant afternoon talking baseball with him in the Spring of 2001 before he became critically ill.

Hayworth was not a great major league player, but he was a very good one, and few men have enjoyed a longer career or had a deeper love of the game. Born in High Point, North Carolina, on January 29, 1904, Hayworth was still a student at nearby Oak Ridge Military Academy when he signed as a catcher with the Detroit Tigers in 1925. He played 12 games for the Tigers in 1926, spent the next two years in the minors, then returned to the Tigers in 1929 to resume a big league playing career that spanned 699 games with four teams before he retired in 1945 to work on the administrative side of the game.

At six feet, 180 pounds, Hayworth was one of the best defensive catchers in the majors and would have played more if he could have provided the offensive punch expected of catchers. But he had a weak bat, compiling a lifetime batting average of .265 and collecting only five homers and 238 RBIs in fifteen major league seasons.

J. Ronald Oakley has been a history instructor at Davidson County Community College in Lexington, North Carolina for 36 years and is the author of Baseball's Last Golden Age, 1946-1960 *(McFarland, 1994)*

His prime years fell between 1930 and 1936. He was the Tigers' starting catcher for four years, but in December of 1933, the Tigers acquired future Hall of Famer Mickey Cochrane, widely regarded as one of the best catchers in the game, from the Philadelphia Athletics for $100,000 and catcher Johnny Pasek. The two catchers were platooned, with player-manager Cochrane taking the field against right-handed pitchers and Hayworth going against lefties.

Detroit had not won a pennant since 1909 or finished in the first division since 1927, but with Cochrane at the helm, Schoolboy Rowe and Tommy Bridges combining for 46 wins, and seven regulars hitting .300 or better, the 1934 Tigers ran away with the pennant, winning 101 games and leading the league in batting average, stolen bases, and runs. Hayworth's playing time dropped from a career-high of 134 games in 1933 to only 54, but in his new role he hit .293, well above his lifetime average. Still, he played in only one game (with no at bats) in a dramatic World Series captured in seven games by Dizzy and Paul Dean and the rest of the Gashouse Gang.

In 1935 Hayworth hit a career-high .309 in 51 games, second among American League catchers only to Cochrane's .319, as the Tigers won their second consecutive pennant and went on to defeat the Chicago Cubs four games to two to claim their first world championship. Hayworth watched the Series from the dugout, but he finally got the championship ring that he would wear so proudly for over 60 years.

The Tigers fell to second place in 1936 and 1937 and to fourth in 1938, and when Cochrane suffered a fractured skull in 1937 from a pitched ball that shortened his career, it was rookie slugger Rudy York (.307, 35 homers, 103 RBIs), not Hayworth, who took over the main catching duties. Hayworth now had to learn to keep his bags packed. Traded to the Brooklyn Dodgers in 1938, he saw limited action with them, the New York Giants, St. Louis Browns, and then the Dodgers again before hanging up his catcher's mitt in July of 1945.

As Hayworth's playing time fizzled during the war years, Dodger owner Branch Rickey kept him on the payroll, sometimes on the inactive list, using him more on the management side of the game than behind the plate. Always grateful for any opportunity to stay in baseball, Hayworth embarked on a nearly 30-year career as a coach, scout, minor league manager, and director of player development for the Dodgers, Chicago Cubs, Milwaukee and Atlanta Braves, and Montreal Expos. He retired in 1973, ending a career in organized baseball that began fifty years earlier when he played in the Coalfield League in West Virginia while he was still a student at Oak Ridge.

I visited Hayworth in May of 2001 in the assisted living unit at the Piedmont Retirement Center in Thomasville, North Carolina, just a few miles from where he had grown up and developed his skills on the diamond. In the past few years he had had a pacemaker installed and undergone gall bladder and prostate surgery, and he had trouble walking and hearing. But his sense of humor remained unimpaired, his mind was quick, and his memory was still amazingly good. When I asked him a question, he usually responded immediately, though he had to search for a word now and then and occasionally had trouble recalling names.

During our interview, he sat in an easy chair by his bed dressed in blue slacks, a plaid shirt, and yellow cardigan sweater. He didn't really look and act like a man who was born just three years after the debut of the American League. I placed the tape recorder on a table near him and settled back to listen to this courteous, kind, soft-spoken gentleman talk about his years in baseball and his passion for the game.

I began by asking him how he broke into the majors, and that question quickly brought him to one of his favorite subjects, Ty Cobb. The Georgia Peach was player-manager at Detroit from 1921 through 1926 and was instrumental in bringing Hayworth up to the big leagues. "In 1926, Cobb had seen me play in spring training when I was with Toronto [the Tigers' franchise], and he took a liking to me. When catcher Johnny Bassler broke his leg in May, Cobb said, 'Bring that Hayworth kid up. We need him.' When I joined the club, he said, 'Well, you've made it to the big leagues, kid.' We struck up a friendship. From then on, whenever I was on the field and he was in the coaching box, he'd say 'How ya doing, kid?'"

He still remembered his first day in the majors in 1926. "It was a dream come true. I joined the Tigers in Chicago. I was 22, and had never even seen a major league game. When I walked out on the field for the first time, I looked down at my Tiger uniform, and looked around the diamond and the bleachers, and said to myself, 'Boy, I really made it. I'm here. I'm in the big leagues.' On Sunday we got back to Detroit. I was put in during the middle of the game. I walked up to home plate. It seemed like a mile up there. I didn't even have a bat—had to borrow someone else's. I hit the ball pretty good, but straight to the shortstop, who threw me out. We shut out the White Sox 1-0."

I asked him if any one game besides that first one stands out above the others in his career. "I remember especially one day in Yankee Stadium when we were playing the Yankees and Lefty Gomez was pitching for them. There were about 75,000 people in the stands. I came up in the seventh or eighth inning. Gomez let one

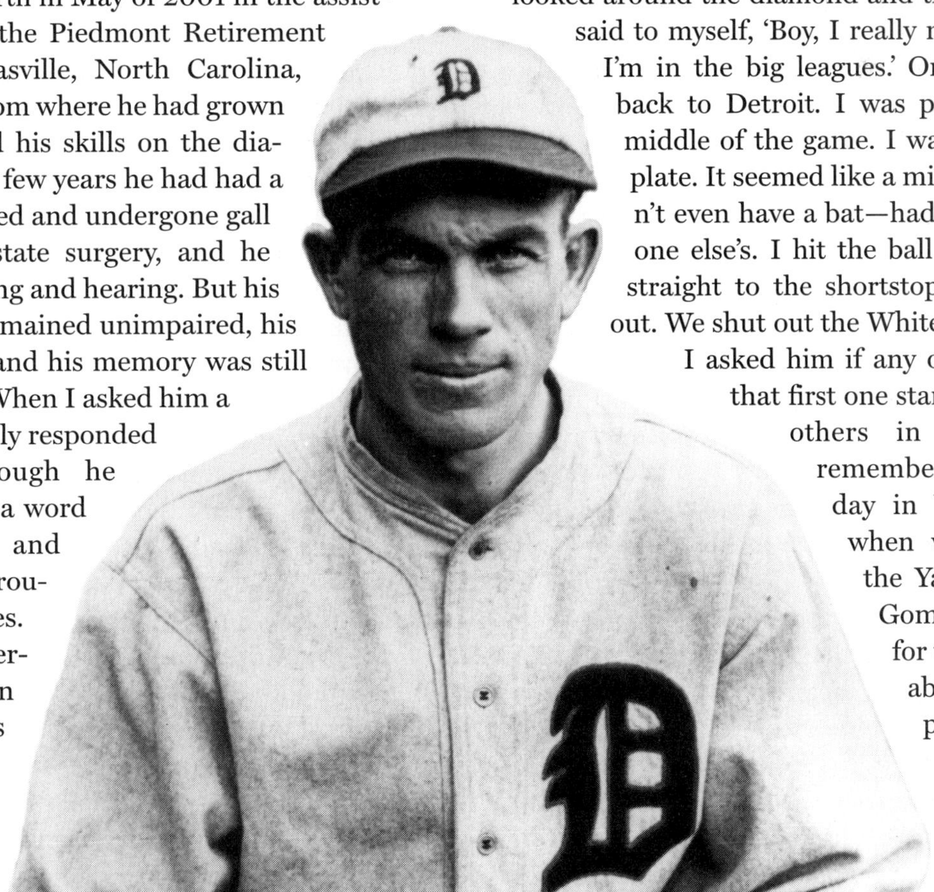

slip just a little bit, a low inside curve ball that hung just a little, and I hit it into the left-field bleachers. As I rounded the bases I said to myself, 'What a thrill this is to trot around the same base paths Babe Ruth did. I wonder how many times he made this same trip around the bases I'm making now.' I felt like a bird flying. It was a great feeling."

That was just one of the many exciting games of his career. "It's kinda like Charlie Gehringer said one time when he was asked this same question: 'Well, you have a great play today, and you think that's it. Tomorrow, you could have one that might even be a little better. They just keep building and building and building. As long as you play, they'll keep doing that.' And they will."

He played with and against some of the greatest in the game, but he was reluctant to name the best player he had ever seen. "There were so many," he said, "that you can't just single out one," but he quickly called off the names of Babe Ruth, Lou Gehrig, Walter Johnson, Cochrane, Hank Greenberg, Joe DiMaggio, Mickey Mantle, Willie Mays, Tris Speaker, Bob Feller, Ted Williams, and, of course, Cobb. When he talked about these and other great players, it was obvious from the passion in his voice that he was as much in awe of them as the fans have been. He was always generous in his comments about other players, including Cochrane, who bumped him from his starting role in 1934. "I knew that Cochrane was the best catcher in the league and could help our team. I always said that I'd rather be backup catcher on a winning team than a starter on a last-place club. He and I got along good."

I asked him if Cobb was really as mean and ornery as he has been portrayed to be. He quickly replied, "No. That's not true. He was a fierce competitor on the field. He looked at opposing players as his enemies, and he would do anything to win. But off the field he was as nice and friendly as any guy you'd ever meet. He was always good to me. Ty was a great character. A great hitter, and thorough in everything he did in baseball. He gave everything on the field his entire attention."

He handed me a copy of a 1926 photo of him and Cobb, autographed by both. "I'm the last living person who played with Cobb," he said, with a sparkle in his eyes and pride in his voice. Although he and Cobb had played together only one season, Hayworth never forgot that Cobb had befriended him and given him the chance to play in the big leagues. He obviously revered his benefactor, and I knew I would get no anti-Cobb stories in this interview.

He also showed me a 1934 photo of him spread-eagled across home plate tagging Ruth on the leg while batter Lou Gehrig looked on and umpire Brick Owens called Ruth out. "That photo has created more interest than any picture I have. It has so much action in it. That's one of the best sports pictures I ever saw." I had to agree with him.

I asked him if Ruth ever talked when he came to the plate. "Not much. He might look down at me and say, 'That ball was inside,' or 'That ball was low.' But he never argued. I talked with him more when he was coach over at Brooklyn in 1938 when I went over there from Detroit. I didn't play much, and the Babe and I did a lot of talking as we sat on the bench. I got to know him better then than in the whole six years I played against him. Babe was a remarkable fellow. He and Cobb were two of the greatest, no doubt about that. I saw some great characters over all those years. Some made it big, some didn't."

Hayworth hit against Walter Johnson, Lefty Gomez, Red Ruffing, Wes Ferrell, and many other star pitchers of his day, but he regarded Bob Feller as the best he ever saw or hit against. "I was a pull hitter, usually hitting down the third base line. But when I hit against Feller, I hit mainly down the first base line. That's how fast he was. And he had so much deception. During his whole delivery, he was looking out in right field until the very last second. Then he'd pick you up at the plate, and the ball would come whizzing in. I hated to hit against him. I had a wife and two kids to support, and I used to think that one of these days he was going to kill me at home plate."

I reminded him that in the 125 years of major league history, millions of young males had dreamed of playing in the big leagues, but only some 15,400 had ever made it.

"Is that right?" he said. "Well, I was most fortunate to get to play. I wasn't all that great. I could move around good behind the plate. In 1931, I set a record for catchers by handling 439 chances in a row without an error. The streak came to an end in Philadelphia when I called for a curve ball and [Earl] Whitehill crossed me up with a high inside fast ball. It got by me, and the umpire had to charge me with an error. And nature gave me a good arm. I could throw that ball hard to any base, and I was accurate, too." He certainly was. He routinely threw out some of the top base stealers of the day, once cutting down Yankee Ben Chapman, the American League's leading base stealer in the early 1930s, three times in one game.

He was modest about his hitting. "I had a .265 lifetime batting average, and I guess that's not too bad. I didn't have a lot of power, but I did hit a lot of doubles [92] and triples [16]. I could hit left handers pretty well." Then he laughed and said, "If they'd all been left handers, I expect I'd be in the Hall of Fame. I know I'd have played a lot more. But I had a good career in baseball. It was a good life, and it was a real privilege to get to play in the big leagues. I loved every minute of it."

Who were the best managers you played for? "Well, there were several. I liked Cobb, I played several years under Bucky Harris, and of course Casey Stengel over at Brooklyn in 1938."

During his years in off-the-field jobs he worked for several club owners, but his favorite was Branch Rickey, one of the most innovative men in the history of the game. "Rickey is the one who started me. I worked closely with him. George Sisler and me scouted all the colored clubs. One Saturday night they sent George and me up to Springfield, Mass to look at Don Newcombe. We watched him throw, and the next day we had a meeting in the office with Rickey. He looked down over his glasses and said, 'What do you think, Ray?' 'Mr. Rickey,' I said, 'I'll explain it in just a few words. Don Newcombe can throw harder right now than anyone you have on your Brooklyn staff.' Two weeks later we bought him and signed him, and what a pickup that was!"

In 2001, Hayworth proudly holds a 1926 photo of himself and Cobb, signed by both.

Warming to the subject of his scouting, he said "When I was in Chicago we got a tip on a boy who was a Kansas City Monarch, named Ernie Banks. I went out to Davenport, Iowa, to see him. He was just a young kid who had just come back from the Army. Out in Davenport, there were trees behind the fence and a big water tank. Dang if he didn't come up and hit one right over the top of the water tank. I knew that a boy who can hit a ball that far one time could do it anytime. The next day I had a meeting with Mr. Wrigley and others, and we bought Banks for $22,500."

During our conversation, Hayworth often brought up his family. He was especially proud of the fact that all but one of his four brothers played professional baseball, all as catchers. His youngest brother, Red, was the only one to make it to the majors, playing a total of 145 games with the St. Louis Browns in 1944 and 1945 and catching all six games of the 1944 World Series between the Browns and Cardinals. "Red's in his eighties," he told me, "and still plays golf and drives his car everywhere. He did real well. He had a good long career in baseball. Didn't play too much, was on the other side of it like me. He became a scout like I did."

He showed me framed photos of his children, grandchildren, and great-grandchildren. His wife had died a few years earlier when they were living in the independent living quarters of the retirement center. One of their sons, Ray Jr., lives in Salisbury, and the other, Johnny, lives nearby in High Point.

During his career Hayworth collected a wealth of memorabilia associated with his career—photographs, newspaper clippings, baseballs signed by Babe Ruth and other stars of his time, gloves, bats, spikes, championship rings, programs—that he used to enjoy showing to visitors to his apartment in the retirement center. Now that he lived in just one room in the assisted-living unit, he had passed some of these treasures on to his family and stored the rest in bank safety deposit boxes and in a warehouse.

Over the years he had gotten a lot of mail from fans all across the world, much of it asking him to autograph books, photographs, bats, balls and other memorabilia they had enclosed and telling him, "I saw you play when I was a little boy" or "My father saw you play" or "My grandfather saw you play." He always signed these items and mailed them back to the sender. Sometimes visitors he didn't even know just dropped in unannounced to speak to him, even at night. He seemed a little puzzled at all the attention. "I'm not all that great, but they just come in, they just want to see me. I'm surprised sometimes at how they find out about me, as old as I am and as young as they are." Understandably, Hayworth's health and thoughtless or potentially unscrupulous memorabilia seekers forced the Piedmont Center staff and Hayworth's family to carefully screen his visitors, and his son Johnny now handled all his business, including requests for autographed memorabilia.

I asked him what he thought of baseball today. His eyes lit up and he said, "I think baseball hasn't peaked. It's even more popular than ever before. The fans love all these homers today's players are hitting. If you've got something the kids really love to see—and I know kids love to see the home run, and they love to have autographed balls, and they like to come to the ball park and eat hot dogs—they'll come out to the park. As long as 20 million kids are happy, baseball is going to survive, not only be where it is today but is going to be more attractive. I know it will be."

He often watched baseball games on television. "People ask me where I see the games, and I tell them I see them right here in my grandfather's chair. I've got the best seat in the house. I've got a lifetime pass, of course, but I wouldn't go to a game today because I couldn't stand to sit there for nine innings. I fell out of the bed a while back and injured my spine a little bit. I have trouble getting up and walking. I can walk with that walker over there, but I couldn't get up and walk out of this room. I'd fall flat on my face. I can't hold my balance."

I hated to bring the interview to a close, but I saw that my host was getting a little tired. He graciously posed for a few photos, and when I shook his hand as I was leaving I said, "It was a real honor to get to talk with you. I'll come back to see you." "Do that," he said. "You do that. It's always a pleasure to talk about baseball."

Baseball was good to Ray Hayworth, and he was good for it. With his passing, the national pastime lost one if its biggest fans and greatest ambassadors.

Photo, p. 59: National Baseball Hall of Fame Library, Cooperstown, New York.

GUY STURDY LED THE AMERICAN LEAGUE IN PINCH-HITS *while playing for Dan Howley and the St. Louis Browns in 1928. Writer Edgar Brands related this interesting anecdote on Sturdy in his column in the October 15, 1931, issue of* The Sporting News*:*

"Rube Walberg had been mowing down the Browns batters all day and Sturdy was riding his teammates about it. Howley turned to Sturdy late in the game and told him to grab a bat.

"You hot dog-eating son-of-a-gun, you've been popping off all during the game about how easy Walberg is to hit. Go in there now and pinch-hit," ordered Howley.

"Well, I went up there," related Sturdy. "Walberg threw me the doggonest curve you ever saw. I pulled away from the plate to make sure I'd dodge the ball, which then accidentally hit my bat and popped over third for a clean single, scoring a couple of runs."

Howley then lifted Sturdy for a runner. "I'm sending in a runner for you," spit out Howley, "because I want you to sit here on the bench and tell me all about that great hit you just got." —DICK THOMPSON

Early Wynn and His Number One Fan

by Elsie H. Gilmore

When my grandmother, May Elizabeth Sanders, was a 53 year-old salesclerk in the handkerchiefs and laces department of Belk Brothers department store in downtown Charlotte, North Carolina, Early Wynn walked into her life. The year was 1937. She was a seasoned widow who had weathered the majority of the Depression by her own wits; Early was a green, wet-behind-the-ears, poor kid from Alabama. Later Early was to tell the reporter Roger Kahn, "They write that when I showed up at a pro tryout I was barefoot. I wasn't, but I was wearing overalls. It's a long way from Hartford, Alabama, to Cooperstown." My grandmother says Early didn't walk into Belk's barefoot either, but he was a country boy. You could tell by his unnatural swagger and his naïve grin. For several years he stocked merchandise at Belk's most of the fall, winter, and spring while he played baseball for Clark Griffith's Charlotte Hornets in the summer.

Even small-time, field-team baseball in the late thirties had its superheroes, and Early Wynn quickly rose to that prized position. He was good-looking and personable; moreover, the first game he batted (in those days Early was a formidable slugger), the girls went crazy. They chased him, telephoned him, and, in my grandmother's words, generally "made fools of themselves." He was a "hunk" (in today's slang), and my grandmother, May, his mentor at Belk's, became his self-assigned protector extraordinaire at home. He was her boy, and she was his Charlotte mama from day one.

May Sanders and Early Wynn's personal relationship progressed by way of food. In May's mind, no boy living alone in a strange city ate right. While watching him pitch and bat, she agonized over how poorly she imagined him eating. Something had to be done, and she was the one to do it. She invited him "home" for Sunday dinner: fried chicken, rice and gravy, green beans, corn, cornbread, ice-cold iced tea, and blackberry cobbler. Who could resist? Who would even try? Soon Early showed up every Sunday, sometimes bringing a friend—sometimes two. Then he began to "drop in" (an admirable Southern custom) at other times as well.

In addition to working for Belk's, May Sanders had an unofficial, semi-boarding house. Since her husband had died in 1926 and she had an eight-year-old daughter to raise, she had divided her one major possession, her house, into a duplex, and she took in renters. The Depression multiplied her clients, both paying and non-paying. Her little house, even her two-bedroom side of it, always brimmed with people sleeping and eating. Early Wynn became just the latest one. He could hide out there. In the tiny breakfast room at the back of May's duplex, he and his cronies could share a beer and swap stories. They could also get away from work, baseball, the girls, and any other uneasiness consuming their lives. May's haven was

Elsie Gilmore attended countless Charlotte Hornet games with the grandmother featured in this article. Today Elsie resides in Baraboo, Wisconsin.

downtown Charlotte (Woodlawn, now Irwin Avenue), easy to get to, always welcoming, and safe.

So it was that May and Early's relationship grew. It was an easy and lasting alliance, based on mutual respect, genuine love, and gentle, home-grown humor. "Have a beer, May," Early would tease. May was a life-long teetotaler, so she would grunt her disapproval. "Aw, May, just one ain't gonna hurt nothin'," Early would retort. "You'd better watch yourself or you'll end up playing for Fort Mill," May would mock sternly, but with a twinkle in her eye. She adored him. "He only drank a few beers," she'd say in his defense if anyone dared to criticize his drinking in her presence.

It was only a short time until one of his fans, a less than hysterical young woman, caught Early Wynn's eye. In 1939 they married. Early was only nineteen years old. May, no judge of Early's drinking, was no critic of this young match either. When a Charlotte fan called such a youthful marriage Early's undoing, May argued, "It's good for him. Marriage will settle him down and keep those hussies away." And immediately she gathered Mabel Allman, the young bride from Morganton, North Carolina, under her wing just as she had adopted Early a year or two before. When Mabel's relatives came to visit, she befriended them, too, and when Mabel and Early had a baby (Joe Early) in March of 1941, May baby-sat. "Young folks don't need to be so tied down" was her theory.

During those beginning years, Early bounced around the minor leagues at Charlotte and Springfield, Massachusetts, with a few promising and not so promising games with the Washington Senators. Already in 1939, at nineteen, Early made three major league appearances with Washington (0-2); then again in 1941, he pitched five more major league games (3-1). When he pitched these games for the Senators before WW II, writers called him "erratic—a burly batch of talent with no clear idea of what to do." Still, after the three wins of '41, Early was in the majors to stay. In the off-season, he worked at the Charlotte Belk's and often hung out at May's.

Tragedy, however, struck swiftly. On a night when May could not baby-sit, Early and Mabel returned home late from a party, and Mabel took the sitter home. Meanwhile Early collapsed into a deep sleep at his apartment with their young toddler. Mabel did not return. In the wee hours of the morning, December 6, 1942, her car collided with a Charlotte city bus, and she died almost immediately from head injuries. Early slept so soundly that even the police at his door did not wake him. He was unaware of her death until 7:00 the next morning.

"They keep questioning me, May," he agonized, "as if Mabel was up to some hanky-panky. I'm the only devil in this family. She was simply taking the sitter home." May tried to restrain his anger with the police, plus she responded to his pain with sympathy and much more. Mostly, she made arrangements: Early would come to live at her own house, not the YMCA; Flossie, Mabel's sister, would keep the baby; and Early's mother could stay in the back of the house next door until more permanent decisions could be made. Enthusiastically, she comforted and fed them all.

So it was that Early Wynn became my roommate. Of course, I was only two years old, and Early was 22. (My mother and I had just returned to Charlotte after my mother's divorce in '41.) During the baseball off-season until he remarried just before entering the military in 1945, Early and I shared a tiny bedroom with twin beds, one small dresser, and a corrugated cardboard, portable wardrobe. For a while he continued to work at Belk's and then at the Charlotte munitions plant, "the shell plant." The time was the height of World War II. In the meantime, Early's mother and Mabel's sister raised young Joe Early, with Early himself trying to be an effective though part-time father.

Some time later, women slowly entered Early's life again. To my grandmother's chagrin, he posted their pictures all over the walls of our small bedroom. Then came the day of his draft notice. Uncle Sam pointed his finger, and Early telephoned my grandmother from the shell plant. "May, take all the pictures down and hide them. I've asked Lorraine to marry me."

"Whew!" was my grandmother's relieved response. She liked LorraineFollin, a Maryland girl Early met on his stints with the Senators, and she definitely did not like the others. The pictures went under the old mattress in the hall closet and never appeared again. Sadly, though, Early departed our little home. He and Lorraine married in September of '44, and soon after Early found himself in the Philippines with the U.S. Army Tank Corps. He missed the '45 baseball season and a great deal of '46. The Army, however, was not baseball-deprived. Early, as appointed manager of the Army team, switched himself to shortstop. "I was a helluva shortstop, too," he winked as he told one reporter. As shortstop he played every game (a privilege pitchers never enjoy). Possibly a few old-timers might recall that he clouted a super long home run in Manila, at Rizal Stadium. Only four other players hit homers over that long outfield: Lou Gehrig, Babe Ruth, Earl Averill, and a young man from Japan.

Early Wynn was not the type to forget old friends. After he was well established with the Washington Senators, he invited my grandmother, my mother, and me to Washington. "See," my grandmother would admonish skeptics, "Early doesn't let fame go to his head." The fact that he invited us not just one summer but two confirmed this hypothesis in May's mind. Our first trip included an excursion on the Potomac in his new cabin cruiser. No matter that it broke down in the middle of the river, and we never did get to Mt. Vernon! The second trip simply included Washington game tickets. Of course, Early pitched—and won. My grandmother could not have been happier. Her boy was a champion.

In my grandmother's eyes, Early was always a champion. Times like the fall of '46, not long after he returned from the military, made her swell with pride. In a game versus Detroit, Early pinch hit a grand slam off Detroit's Johnny Gorsica, then pitched the rest of the way through the game. On the other hand, when Early performed poorly in '48, May defended him mightily. She argued that he had little help from his teammates. When Early denied that pretext saying, "I have no squawk about my support. Remember, they had a lot to do with the 17 I did win, so why talk about those I didn't?" May praised him for his loyalty. In her eyes, he could do no wrong.

Later in '48, when Clark Griffith traded Early to the Cleveland Indians, it was Griffith who, according to May, was "blind and stingy." "Early will be better off, you'll see," she told her baseball friends. "Early will blossom now, and the bloom will be glorious." Of course, she was right. The years 1949-1954 were exceptional years for Early Wynn. He won 11, 18, 20, 23, 17, and 23 games each year respectively. Begrudgingly she did give some credit to Mel Harder, the Cleveland pitching coach, who gave Early's fast ball some class and his pitching repertoire new variety. "Even roses need to be cultivated," she declared. She also credited his "good wife" and their new daughter, Sherry.

Those Cleveland years made lively times in our home, full of arguments, speculations, and lots of laughter. The radio was always playing one game or another during baseball season, and the sports announcers kept us well advised during the off-season. Even Bud Abbot and Lou Costello played a role in the good humor of our duplex. They had produced the immortal *Who's on First?* the same year Washington traded Early to Cleveland. They were also two of the Cleveland Indians' most avid fans. What with Abbot and Costello antics, druggists sitting on flagpoles, and all sorts of other sensational promotional stunts, who could resist baseball mania?

Early was constantly in the newspapers as well. May never thought he got a fair shake. She especially despised descriptions sportswriters used. "Surly" and "burly" she dismissed as cheap rhymes, but portrayals

LEFT: *Early, not long before heading for the Philippines in WW II.* CENTER: *Early Wynn (18)—Pitcher for the Charlotte Hornets.* RIGHT: *May Saunders and Early Wynn in New York for the '54 World Series.*

such as gruff, crusty, fierce, grim, scowling, and intimidating she considered unfair and poor judgment of character. When reporters called him mean, she drew the line and was ready to do battle. "He's just doing his job," she argued. Sometimes she would concede a bit, saying, "Poor people have poor ways," meaning that Early had to, or thought he had to, fight for every inch he progressed.

She made few other concessions. For instance, she never reconciled herself to "Gus," Early's nickname both on and off field. Such a boorish nickname was beyond her comprehension. She refused to acknowledge or use the moniker. With a fine and natural name like Early Wynn, who would want to ruin it with a single non-affirming syllable?

All the hullabaloo and wrangling climaxed when the Cleveland Indians crowned the '54 season by clinching the American League pennant—over the Yankees, no less. May grinned when Early sent her airfare and World Series tickets for the New York games with the Giants. By this time she was a buyer for the handkerchief and lace department at Belk's, and she did not have to use her one-week-per-year vacation to attend. She was in heaven on earth. Even Early's loss (thanks to pinch-hitter Dusty Rhodes) and Cleveland's four straight losses failed to dampen her enthusiasm. The Cleveland Indians was her team and Early Wynn was her man. "What's wrong with second place?" she would ask when fellow employees gave her a wide berth and avoided conversation in the days following her return. "We're talking about the *WORLD* series."

Besides, in her mind and in reality, Early was playing with and against some of baseball's all-time greats. Cleveland's pitchers alone were worthy company: Bob Feller was still effective, and in that series year, Wynn, Mike Garcia, and Bob Lemon combined to win 65 of Cleveland's 111 victories. Baseball historians know it as one of the most outstanding pitching staffs in baseball records.

In spite of all the good times, those Cleveland years between '48 and '54 were not without stress and worry for my grandmother. She agonized over Early's every loss. When he undertook to write a column for the Cleveland *News*, she declared, "That column will be his, but he'll get himself in trouble. He's too honest." She was right. It was his — no ghostwriter for Early Wynn. And he did get himself in trouble. He complained against the "front office big guys," and my grandmother always believed, rightly or wrongly, that those accusations held him back at Hall of Fame choosing time.

To my grandmother, the most gratifying victory for Early in those days came not on the field, but from Cleveland's chapter of the AFL-CIO. For several years that chapter voted Early "Baseball Player of the Year." A resounding "Yes" was May's response. As life-long treasurer of the Women's Auxiliary of the Brotherhood of Railroad Trainmen, she felt she understood the importance of unions. Though her railroad husband had died in the '20s, she was active in the auxiliary until her hospitalization in the '70s. She knew that Early had earned the union honor not only for his working-class personality and baseball skill but also for his active participation in players labor disputes from his early days. He often appeared in the Old-timers Classic Game, where ticket proceeds went for players with "pressing medical expenses or [who were] otherwise down on their luck" He also fought for pension and health care plans. He genuinely cared about those players who spent many years in the minors, not accumulating enough years in the majors to be covered. His concern also spread to players who retired before medical benefits came into the picture at all. The working class of Cleveland recognized a partner and an ally in Early Wynn.

After the 1954 fiasco ("What do you write about a thing like that?" Early Wynn asked when he returned to his Cleveland news column), Early began a downhill slide. In reality, the Indians finished second in '55, trailing the Yankees by just three games, and in '56 they had three 20-game winners, Herb Score, Bob Lemon, and Early Wynn. Still, Early seemed to be slowing. "Don't they know he's sick?" May would ask anyone who dared to discuss baseball with her. "Gout's an ugly, painful disease, and in his case it's not a rich man's worry. Early's ailments come from just plain hard work. He runs too much, he pitches too hard, and he always gives over 100 percent." In May's mind, only outside factors could diminish Early's performance. And gout was the only outside factor she could see. Ironically, those lowly vegetables closer to his Alabama roots had to replace the shrimp cocktails and steak he had become accustomed to. Still, every pitch seemed to encourage gout's sharp protein crystals to lodge in his elbow.

Accordingly, when Cleveland judged Early too old and traded him to the Chicago White Sox in 1957, May was on line to back him up. "It's just the beginning," she declared. "He's not going to leave this business without that final victory." She returned to her blooming imagery: "There are early bloomers and late bloomers, but the flower's just as beautiful." Of course, she always added, "People like Early Wynn bloom both early and late." Few others would ever compare "burly Early" to a flower and even fewer had May's confidence. Nevertheless, his old manager from the Indians, Al Lopez, trusted enough to hire him.

Wynn was unfailing. After 14-17 and 14-16 win/loss records in 1957 and 1958, Early, at the age of 39, pitched the White Sox to the pennant in 1959. He also led the American League with 22 wins and only 10 losses. Along with capturing the first win of the World Series, his success was enough to embarrass those who thought he was over the hill and enough to snare the coveted Cy Young award. May, his constant and confident fan, was elated. Even though she was not well enough to attend the Chicago-L.A. Dodgers series, she basked in his success.

Early Wynn's ability indisputably began to decline after 1959. Even May had to admit that grim fact. Then in 1962, when Chicago released him with 299 wins under his belt, May suffered with him. She would listen intently to the radio when his name came up, and she winced when she heard that he attended spring training without a contract. "They owe him," she said. "They owe him just one more game." She might have been more confident than Early himself when, at length, he signed a contract with his old team, the Cleveland Indians. It took five tries, but finally on July 13, 1963, the 43-year-old Early Wynn ultimately attained the 300 mark. "Some people called [my win] tainted, but I didn't care," Wynn said of his 7-4 victory over the Kansas City Athletics. May agreed. "Sure, that victory was protected by reliever Jerry Walker," she argued, "but Early had saved the skin of lots of previous pitchers, too." There was no denying it. In her eyes, Early "hung the moon."

With a 300-win career record, a 3.54 lifetime ERA, and the Cy Young Award to boot, one would think that Early Wynn was an indisputable entrant into the Hall of Fame. But life was not to be so easy. It took three nominations to finally secure him that coveted honor. After his initial bitter remarks, "Hall of Fame? Hell, it's a Hall of Shame," Early had softer comments. "Look, I'm honored to be in there. . .but any man who wins 300 major league games ought to get voted in as soon as he's eligible." My grandmother echoed Early's sentiments: "Hell, don't they know how much work that is?" That remark was mutinous coming from my grandmother; she never said "hell."

In 1976, just three years after Early made it to the Cooperstown hall, my grandmother died, but not before Early paid her one last tribute. Over the years he had given her ball tickets, taken her on a boat ride, even flown her to Florida twice to be with his family, but in her last weeks he visited her himself. She was in the Hawthorne Lane Nursing Home and had not even recognized my mother, her own daughter, for over two weeks. Still, she heard my mother whisper, "Early's coming, Mama, you better gussy up your hair." Mother could not take off work at the time, but the nurses had prepared May appropriately for the big visit. She had on a new nightgown. Excitedly, the staff, in full awareness of the importance of the occasion, had washed and set her hair. Like a monarch, she sat propped with pillows waiting for her honored guest. I wish I had been a fly on the wall to hear the conversation, but the nurses say that she opened her eyes and talked intelligently with "her boy" for almost an hour. They bantered and joked about life in the "big leagues." Early even taunted, "You should have a beer, May. It would cheer you up."

Just last year I initiated a survey, asking my high school students if they knew the name Early Wynn. Only a few die-hard baseball fanatics answered positively. I would point out the recent *Newsweek* poll that listed him 100 in the top 100 all-time greats. They did not seem too impressed.

When I asked older people the same question, the response was more enthusiastic. More often than not, old fans would respond, "Yeah, I had a bat with his name on it. That bat was as tough as he was." Or they would say, "Now, there was a mean cuss; his scowl alone could knock down a batter." Unlike my grandmother, no one saw Early Wynn as a loyal softie with a big heart. "Yeah, now there was one tough, hard intimidator" was the usual remark.

Nevertheless, one chemistry professor at a conference I was attending added, "You know, Wynn had this saying, 'That mound out there. . .that's my office. It's where I conduct my business and make my living.' I feel the same way: My chemistry room is my office. It's where I'm in charge, to succeed or fail." My grandmother would have concurred. Belk's was her office; baseball was Early's. Both fan and player were intensely loyal to their places of business, their vocations. They were intensely loyal to their friends as well.

The Marathon Masterpiece

by Bob Fulton

Three hours after a teammate interrupted his pregame slumber, Tom Walker still wasn't convinced he was awake. This *had* to be a dream.

The Dallas-Fort Worth Spurs righthander, 14 innings into a Class AA Texas League game at Albuquerque on August 4, 1971, had yet to surrender a hit. If the zeroes on the scoreboard hadn't confirmed the fact, Walker might have assumed he was still napping in the clubhouse, dreaming about the game of a lifetime.

Instead, he was *pitching* the game of a lifetime. A game for the ages, in fact.

"It was raining that night in Albuquerque," recalls Walker, who resides in the Pittsburgh suburb of Gibsonia. "I was in the training room, just relaxing, and I kind of fell asleep on the training table. My roommate, Wayne Garland, came in and he says, 'Walker, aren't you gonna pitch?' There was like an out in the top of the first inning. I said, 'I thought we were rained out.' He says, 'No, you better get your butt out there. The game's going on.' So I threw my pants on, buttoned my shirt, went out and threw a few pitches in the bullpen. Honest to God, I'd only thrown about five or six pitches to get loose before I took the hill."

What should have been a recipe for disaster unaccountably yielded an epic result. After the Spurs pushed across a run in the top of the 15th, Walker retired Albuquerque 1-2-3 in the bottom half of the inning to wrap up a 1-0 victory and the second-longest no-hitter in professional baseball history.

"I had always dreamed of pitching a no-hitter, but I never dreamed it would be like this," the 22-year-old Baltimore Orioles farmhand told reporters following the game. "This is just fantastic. It's the greatest thrill of my life."

Thirty-one years later, Walker regards his marathon masterpiece with awe and disbelief. That night, before 1,017 fans at the Albuquerque Sports Stadium, he was the embodiment of the unhittable hurler, facing a potent Dodgers lineup and suffocating pressure and bowing to neither. Knees turn to jelly during nine-inning no-hitters; Walker endured an additional six innings with his heart lodged in his throat, fearful one wayward pitch could undo his bid for baseball immortality.

"It was like sitting on a volcano," says Walker, who posted an 18-23 record with the Expos, Tigers, Cardinals, and Angels between 1972 and 1977. "The amount of tension was enormous. When the game went into extra innings, you could cut it with a knife. I was thinking, we've got to score a run. But the harder you tried the worse it got, for both teams. On any given night, both of those teams were usually in double digits in hits. But that night offense was not big on the agenda."

Indeed, Albuquerque's Jim Haller scattered nine hits over 14 scoreless innings before Dodgers manager

Bob Fulton is the author of Pirates Treasures: Facts, Feats, Firsts in Pittsburgh History *and* Top Ten Baseball Stats. *He resides in Indiana, Pennsylvania.*

Monty Basgall decided he'd had enough. Haller pitched spectacularly, but he was no match for Walker, who handcuffed batters with a 93 mph fastball and a nasty slider. He struck out 11 and allowed only four base runners.

Walker, then in his fourth professional season, first realized he was flirting with a no-hitter in the seventh inning.

"That ballpark had a great big scoreboard," says Walker, a regional director for the Nemschoff Chair Company of Sheboygan, Wisconsin. "I looked out there and all I could see was zeroes. The seventh came along and I thought, holy cow, we have a chance here."

Walker couldn't have imagined then that his work wasn't even half finished. Nor could he have imagined retiring the Dodgers 1-2-3 in 13 of the 15 innings he pitched. Walker threw six perfect innings before Larry Eckenrode and Lee Lacy drew back-to-back walks in the seventh. Royle Stillman and Gary Moore walked in the eighth, but Walker did not permit another baserunner the rest of the way. He retired the final 22 batters in order, thanks to a pair of superlative defensive plays.

Third baseman Steve Green made a bare-handed pickup of Bob Cummings' slow roller down the line leading off the 11th and gunned him out at first to preserve the gem. Left fielder Mike Reinbach then robbed Cummings in the 14th when he speared his sinking line drive while skidding across the damp grass.

"That was the biggest play of the game," Walker says. "He'd have had an easy chance, really, but he slipped on the wet turf. He had to make a circus catch because he was so far off balance when he slipped."

Moments later, Spurs manager Cal Ripken Sr. approached Walker and told him he could pitch only one more inning. Ripken was reluctant to jeopardize the career of a major league prospect over a single ballgame, extraordinary as it was.

"He came down with two outs in the top of the 15th and he said, 'Tom, I can't let you go anymore. This is it.' I didn't want to hear that," says Walker, "but I kind of understood what he was saying. Just then Mike Reinbach drew a walk. The next guy up was Enos Cabell and he went to a 3-2 count, so Reinbach was running on the pitch. Cabell hit it off the wall for a double and Reinbach scored."

Walker retired the Dodgers in order in the bottom half. With his 176th pitch of the night, he induced Lacy to bounce to second baseman Rich Emard to end the game. The Spurs mobbed Walker as the crowd stood and acknowledged his fabulous feat with a thunderous ovation.

"I just couldn't believe the game was really over," Walker says. "I was stunned. I mean, it had gotten to a point where you almost thought you had to keep pitching. I remember thinking, 15 innings, no hits, has anybody ever done this before?"

Surprisingly, yes. On May 10, 1909, Fred Toney of Winchester tossed a 17-inning no-hitter to beat Lexington 1-0 in a Class D Blue Grass League game. Walker's gem ranks as the second-longest in the history of professional baseball.

"Somebody once asked me, 'How did you celebrate, other than the guys jumping up and down?'" says

A TWIST OF FATE

In the days preceding the high point of his baseball career, Tom Walker contemplated ending it.

Stuck in an organization overloaded with top-flight pitchers and sensing little chance for advancement, Walker considered returning to school. But his 15-inning gem at Albuquerque set in motion a chain of events that drew him away from campus and toward the majors.

"There's no doubt that that game happened for a reason, other than just to set a record, and that was to change my life," Walker says. "I was to a point with Baltimore where I was wondering how I'd ever progress through the system. That was the year the Orioles had four 20-game winners. Plus I had Triple-A pitchers ahead of me. I was on the verge of saying, 'I'll never get to the big leagues if I have to stay here [the Baltimore organization]. I think I'll get my master's degree.'"

Walker, who had graduated from the University of Tampa, actually enrolled at the University of Florida. But one peerless performance in Albuquerque altered his plans. The Montreal Expos wound up drafting Walker following the season, and he made his major league debut with them the following spring.

"That no-hitter created a situation where it opened the eyes of other major league teams, the Expos specifically," Walker says. "It propelled me from Double-A to the big leagues, got me off the ground. It changed my life."

Walker. "I guess our celebration was on the bus with some beers while traveling back to Dallas-Fort Worth."

He resumed his nap on the trip east, but not once did Tom Walker dream of pitching the game of a lifetime. There was no reason to. He'd already thrown it.

DALLAS-FORT WORTH	AB	R	H	RBI	ALBUQUERQUE	AB	R	H	RBI
Brown cf	7	0	0	0	Eckenrode 3b	5	0	0	0
Kennedy ss	7	0	1	0	Lacy 2b	5	0	0	0
Reinbach lf	5	1	1	0	Long lf	5	0	0	0
Cabell 1b	6	0	4	1	Stillman 1b	4	0	0	0
Andino rf	7	0	0	0	Yeager c	5	0	0	0
Green 3b	6	0	1	0	Cummings ss	5	0	0	0
Emard 2b	6	0	2	0	Moore cf	4	0	0	0
Hickey c	6	0	1	0	Robinson rf	5	0	0	0
Walker p	6	0	0	0	Haller p	4	0	0	0
					Johnson ph	1	0	0	0
					Allen p	0	0	0	0
Totals	**56**	**1**	**10**	**1**	**Totals**	**43**	**0**	**0**	**0**

Dallas-Fort Worth	**000**	**000**	**000**	**000**	**001**	**— 1**
Albuquerque	**000**	**000**	**000**	**000**	**000**	**— 0**

E—Lacy. DP—Emard and Cabell; Eckenrode, Lacy and Stillman. LOB—Dallas-Fort Worth 10, Albuquerque 2. 2B— Hickey, Cabell. S—Yeager. T—3:07. A—1,017.

PITCHING

Dallas-Fort Worth	IP	H	R	ER	BB	SO
Walker, W	15	0	0	0	4	11

Albuquerque	IP	H	R	ER	BB	SO
Haller	14	9	0	0	3	3
Allen, L	1	1	1	1	1	0

WHAT DO PITCHERS *Vern Law, Jim Perry, Jim Hunter, Ron Guidry, La Marr Hoyt, Bob Welch, Fernando Valenzuela, Pedro Martinez, and Randy Johnson have in common? Ask the average baseball fan and the answer will come in seconds: All are Cy Young Award winners.*

But the more discerning fans will also note that they alone among Cy Young winners also appeared in at least one big league game at another position. All did so either before or after winning the award, with the exception of Perry, who played one game in the outfield in 1970, the year he won the Cy Young. Being short of position players was, of course, the reason for these pitchers playing in the field. Most were put in the outfield; however, Hunter played first base for the 1967 Kansas City A's; Martinez played third base for the 1993 Dodgers, and Valenzuela played first base for the 1989 Dodgers. Valenzuela, then the NL's reigning Cy Young winner, also played a game in the outfield for LA in 1982; a 21-inning, 2-1 defeat of the Cubs that spread over two days, August 17 and 18. Valenzuela played in the 20th inning, rotating with Dusty Baker between left field and right, depending on the batter. Looking for a faster man on defense, Dodger manager Tommy Lasorda replaced Valenzuela with Welch in the 21st inning, making this the only game that featured two Cy Young Award winners playing the outfield in the same game. —LYLE SPATZ

Images of The National Pastime in The Nation's Capital

by Frank Ceresi, Mark Rucker & Carol McMains

Dubbed "America's Game" by Walt Whitman, baseball has been enjoyed in our nation's capital by everyone from young boys playing street stickball to presidents throwing out the inaugural first pitch of the season. Washington, D.C., would see the game played professionally for well over a century.

The city fans would enjoy witnessing all of the greats of the game play the national pastime through the years. What a glorious parade of major league ballplayers that honed their craft in the capital city! From Babe Ruth and Shoeless Joe Jackson visiting Griffith Stadium with their American League teams, to hometown heroes like Walter Johnson, Goose Goslin, Joe Cronin, and Cecil Travis.

Also, from the late 1930s through the war years, the Homestead Grays, perhaps the greatest Negro League team of them all, thrilled fans of the game. The Grays, of course, for years fielded teams featuring legendary greats such as Josh Gibson and Buck Leonard. Showing their skills at Griffith Stadium, the team won nine Negro League world championships over a 10 year span—a record that may never be equaled in any team sport again.

Modern fans still remember Harmon Killebrew and Frank Howard, two of the premier long ball hitters of all time, and for a short period, even Ted Williams managed the Senators in the late 1960s. Sadly and with little warning, D.C.'s professional baseball roots were ripped from the nation's capital not once but twice. Calvin Griffith was the first to defect. After the death of his father, in 1955, son Calvin lobbied to move the franchise to Minneapolis. With the expansion of the American League in 1961, the Senators became the Twins, and Washington was left without a team.

To placate Congress and to preempt any reconsideration of baseball's exemption from the anti-trust laws, the major leagues put an expansion team in Washington that year. The results were the same as with the former franchise: the team lost 100 games or more in each of the first four seasons. Their one winning season came in 1969 under rookie manager Ted Williams. Williams followed a series of former sluggers-turned-skipper of the Nats, including Eddie Yost, Gil Hodges, and Jim Lemon.

In 1972, owner Bob Short was given permission to move the team to Texas. Major League officials assured Washington politicians that a new franchise would replace the Senators in the near future, a promise that is still unfulfilled thirty years later. These featured photos, many of which have never been publicly seen before, are amongst the nearly 200 rare images and photos in our book, *Images of Baseball in Washington, D.C.* (Arcadia Publishing). Mark collaborated with Peter Bjarkman on *Smoke: the Romance and Lore of Cuban Baseball.*

Mark Rucker is a baseball writer, vintage photography expert and a member of SABR. Frank Ceresi and researcher Carl McMains, whose business PC Associates specializes in museum consulting and sports appraisals, are longtime fans of baseball.

Swampoodle Grounds with Connie Mack, Washington, D.C., c. 1888. This rare photograph shows the Washington Nationals playing the Chicago White Stockings at the old Swampoodle Grounds (where part of Washington's Union Station presently sits). The thin fellow behind the plate is said to be Connie Mack. Before Mack became the dignified manager and owner of the Philadelphia Athletics for several decades in the 20th century, a young and energetic Cornelius McGillicuddy caught for the Nationals from 1886 through 1889. The pitcher hurling the ball to Mack is Hank O'Day, Washington's premier pitcher in the late 1880s. Mack is also featured in one of his "Old Judge" poses.

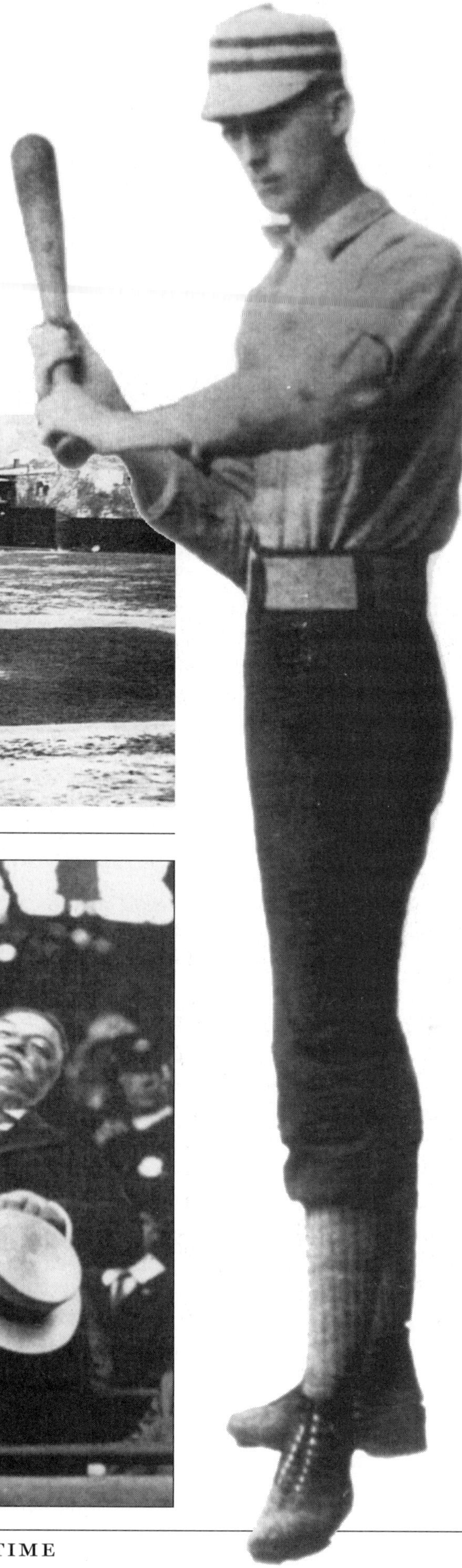

A Tradition Begins. Even though presidents such as Abraham Lincoln, Andrew Johnson, Ulysses S. Grant, and James Buchanan enjoyed watching professional baseball being played in Washington, D.C., during the 19th century, baseball fan President William Howard Taft began the tradition of throwing the ceremonial first pitch of the major league baseball season in 1910.

Walter "The Big Train" Johnson. The 19-year-old Walter Johnson was signed by the Washington Senators to shore up their considerable pitching woes. Johnson played his entire career with the Washington Senators. From 1907 through 1927, he won 416 games with 110 of them by shutout, struck out over 3,500 batters, and led his usually weak hitting team to a world championship in 1924. After his retirement as a player, Johnson managed the Senators for two years and was inducted into the Baseball Hall of Fame in 1936. *The Sporting News* and others voted "The Big Train" amongst the top athletes in the 20th century.

Washington Fans Present Money Cup to Walter Johnson, 1913. Walter Johnson, after winning 36 games for the Senators in 1913, is presented with a silver loving cup filled with money by the appreciative fans from the capital city.

The 1924 World Champion Washington Senators. The entire city was overjoyed in 1924 when the Washington Senators won the American League pennant for the first time in their storied history. They were the underdogs during the World Series because they had to face John McGraw's tough New York Giants National League ball club. However, in the exciting final seventh game of the Series in extra innings with the beloved Walter Johnson pitching, the Senators captured the World's Championship. It would be the first and last major league baseball championship in the capital city.

After the thrilling victory, President Calvin Coolidge hosted the hometown heroes team at the White House. Here President Coolidge is flanked by manager Bucky Harris and a beaming Walter Johnson.

Wartime Baseball, 1941. As the clouds of World War II darkened the skies of our nation, the entire country, including baseball stars of the day like Cecil Travis, prepared for war. Prior to serving with distinction in the United States Army, Cecil had a spectacular season with the Washington Senators in 1941. Not only did he hit an impressive .359 for the year, but his American League buddy and future war veteran Ted Williams would one day recall Cecil's play and say that he was as great an all-around player as he ever played against. Cecil played his entire 12-year career in Washington and posted a .314 lifetime batting average.

The Congressional Game, 1941. As far back as 1909, Republican Congressman John Tener, a former major league pitcher with the Chicago Colts and later president of the National League, organized the first Congressional Game. That game, which pitted the Republicans against the Democrats, continues to be played annually to this day. These ballplayers are members of the "Statesmen" Congressional baseball team. Pictured from left to right are (kneeling) Rep. James Shanley, batboy J. Fishbait, and Rep. Leo Allen; (standing) Rep. John Sparkman, Rep. C.W. Bishop, Rep. Hamilton Fish, Sen. James Mead, Rep. Gordon Canfield and Rep. William Stratton.

The 1944 Homestead Grays. City fans were able to witness the Homestead Grays Negro League team when they played at Griffith Stadium in Washington, D.C., from the late 1930s through 1948. The Grays, originally from Pennsylvania, won an unprecedented nine Negro League championships. How good a team were they? Many baseball historians say the Grays during the 1940s might have been the greatest baseball club ever assembled. Pictured at their dugout in Griffith Stadium from left to right are Jelly Jackson, Ray Battle, Edward Robinson, Sam Bankhead, Josh Gibson, Buck Leonard, Dave Hoskins, Jerry Benjamin, and "Cool Papa" Bell.

Harmon "The Killer" Killebrew, 1959. Although he was signed by the Washington Senators in 1954, it took Harmon Killebrew five years to truly have a breakout season with the team. He certainly did so in 1959, when he began to play regularly batting either cleanup or fifth in the lineup. That year he led the American League with 42 home runs and had 105 RBIs. By the time Harmon ended his career in 1975, he would amass 573 career homers with over 2,000 hits for the Senators, Minnesota Twins, and Kansas City Royals.

Excitement in the Nation's Capital! Ted Williams, "The Splendid Splinter," was a major league ballplayer who can rightfully claim to be the greatest hitter of all time. Despite missing five years to military duty during his prime, Ted's career numbers are astounding: the highest on-base average in history at .483; the second highest slugging average, behind Babe Ruth, at .634; 521 home runs; and a lifetime batting average of .344.

That Washington Senators owner Robert Short would coax Ted Williams out of retirement after nine leisurely years fishing at his home in Florida would be the biggest story in baseball at the end of the 1968 season. Ted knew hitting, agreed to manage the Senators, and smartly surrounded himself with fine coaches like the former great gloveman and future Hall of Famer Nellie Fox. The result? The team won an astounding 86 games in 1969, and "Teddy Ballgame" was named American League Manager of the Year by the A.P.

Major League Baseball Leaves Washington, 1971. The year 1971 and the name Robert Short will live in infamy for Washington baseball fans forever. After manager Ted Williams could not improve the team, who lost 96 games for the year, and fan support continued to dwindle, Short put the team up for sale. There were no takers and major league owners granted Short's wish to move the team to Texas. Washington's last home game, on September 30, 1971, was an eerie and disturbing end to the great professional baseball tradition in the nation's capital. This photo showing Dick Bosman preparing to throw the game's first pitch, perfectly captures all of Washington's displeasure at owner Short's decision. Frank Howard fittingly hit the Senators' last home run in the sixth inning, igniting a rally against the dreaded New York Yankees. However, the game was forfeited in the ninth inning, with two outs and the Senators ahead, 7 to 5. The fans stormed the playing field, and professional baseball ended after over 120 years in the capital city.

Farewell Foutz

by John C. Behlert

MY GREAT-UNCLE, DAVE FOUTZ, was one of the true stars of baseball during the nineteenth century. My research began with the knowledge that he had played major league baseball, but quickly turned into the discovery of a colorful, talented individual. His ambition was to be a major league pitcher. This quest took him from the playing fields of his hometown of Waverly, Maryland, to the silver mines of Leadville, Colorado, to Bay City, Michigan, and finally to St. Louis and Brooklyn.

Dave Foutz was a 27-year-old rookie pitcher with the St. Louis Browns (American Association) when he began his major league career in July of 1884. During his three and a half years with the Browns he won 114 games, lost 48, and helped pitch them to three American Association pennants from 1885 to 1887. His career as a pitcher ended when his thumb was broken after being hit by a line drive off the bat of Cleveland infielder Ed McKean in August of 1887. Browns owner Chris Von der Ahe sold his contract for $5,500 to the Brooklyn Bridegrooms at the end of the 1887 season. With the Bridegrooms he played right field before making the move to first base. Brooklyn won the AA pennant in 1889, and Foutz was voted the best all-around player in the AA by baseball patrons from all over the country (the award was sponsored by the New York *Sporting Times*). The following year (1890) the Bridegrooms won the National League pennant.

Foutz won 147 games and lost 66 during his career. His winning percentage of .690 ties him with Whitey Ford for the best ever. For his career he hit .277 (1,254 hits, 186 doubles, 32 home runs, and 749 RBIs) and appeared in 1,167 games. His major league career lasted twelve and a half seasons, the last four as player-manager of the Brooklyn club, which Brooklyn sports writers dubbed "Foutz Fillies." He died on March 5, 1897, at the age of 40 due to an asthma attack.

On Independence Day 1878, 21-year-old Dave Foutz traveled with a pickup group of ballplayers to Washington, D.C. They had scheduled a doubleheader against the Washington Eagles, a crack semi-professional club. Normally a first baseman, Foutz pitched both games, leading his club to a sweep of the Eagles. When he returned home to Waverly, Maryland, he asked the manager of his Waverly club if he could pitch a few games. Foutz was considered by many to be the premier first baseman in the Baltimore area. His manager told the six-foot-two-inch player that because of his height and sure hands the club needed him more at first base.

The righthander decided in late 1878 to join his older brother John in Leadville, Colorado, where a silver strike was going on. When not mining for or prospecting for silver, he spent his time working on his pitching and mastering the art of curving the ball. John did the catching. After months of work Foutz developed a sizzling curveball that he threw with a sidearm motion.

John Behlert, native of Baltimore, currently resides in Inman, South Carolina with his wife, Kathy. He is in the process of writing a book on the baseball career of his uncle.

In 1879 he traveled to Denver and filled the pitcher's position for the semi-professional Denver Bears. Foutz played ball on the weekends and worked alongside John in the silver mines during the week. By all accounts, John and Dave were successful while mining for silver. They staked various claims that panned out. On one occasion he and his brother lived in a dugout during the winter while protecting one of their claims.

In 1882 Foutz joined the newly formed semi-professional Leadville Blues. Blues captain Juan Hart could take the credit for the pitching success that would come Foutz's way in the future. A club from Salt Lake City challenged the Blues to a three-game series: The winning club would take home a $2,500 prize. Salt Lake won the first game with ease. For the second game Hart decided to give Foutz a shot in the box. The backer of the Leadville club, who had put up half of the $2,500, was upset when he learned that Foutz was to pitch, and after calling Hart a "blockhead" left the grounds. His disgust turned to pride when he heard the results of the game. Foutz pitched the Blues to victory to tie the series. The next day, Foutz once again defeated the Salt Lake club, securing the prize money for Leadville. This same backer then challenged Salt Lake to a six-game series with $5,000 being the prize. The 25-year-old Foutz pitched all six games, winning five and losing one. Once again, Leadville took home the prize money.

Foutz pitched in 41 games during the season, winning 39 and losing 1, and pitching the Blues to the Colorado state championship. Foutz was the toast of the city and the state, and picked up his first nickname "Hunkidori Boy." The cranks bestowed this nickname on him because nothing seemed to upset him while in the box; with Foutz everything was always all right regardless of the score or the situation.

Foutz had done what he set out to do when he left Waverly. He had mastered the art of pitching and curving the ball, and he now realized that it was time to move up in the baseball ranks. In 1883 he ventured to Bay City, Michigan, and signed his first professional contract to pitch and play the outfield for the club. Bay City was a member of the newly formed eight-club Northwestern Minor League.

Foutz lied about his age. He told the Bay City management that he was 22 years old. Foutz was born on September 7, 1856, making him 26. Bay City may not have taken the chance on the slender sidearm twirler if they had known his true age.

No records exist that give an account of his pitching record for the 1883 season. He did appear in 61 of 84 contests, hitting .251 for the season. What is known is that manager/captain William Watkins told *Sporting Life*,"Dave Foutz did some pitching for us in 1883 and was a genuine favorite with the players and cranks."

Even though he was good-natured, quiet, and bashful, Foutz became one of the Bay City team leaders. In a time when facial hair was the norm, he was smooth shaven. He led the club by example. Three words would describe his pitching: "curves, speed, and strategy." His calm demeanor and take-charge attitude inspired confidence.

The Northwestern League expanded to twelve clubs for the 1884 season, with clubs in Indiana, Wisconsin, Minnesota, Illinois, and Michigan. The success of the League would depend on how much crank support the clubs would receive during the 120-game schedule.

Bay City started the season winning 11 straight games. Foutz got the streak started with a May 2 Opening Day 13-inning 4-3 win at Fort Wayne. He struck out 13 batters and allowed nine hits.

Foutz won his first six decisions of the season, limiting his opponents to just 23 runs and 39 hits while striking out 50.

On May 24 he suffered his first loss against Minneapolis and his future teammate Bobby Caruthers, 5-0. Foutz allowed seven hits, but his two errors and three errors by teammates helped Minneapolis to the win.

In a pitching rematch on May 27, Foutz pitched a four-hitter beating Caruthers 10-2. Foutz was working his curveball to perfection as he struck out 13 and had 21 assists.

Bay City ended the month of May in first place with a 16-4 record. Grand Rapids was a close second. Foutz went 8-1 for the month. He pitched a total of 85 innings, allowing 50 hits with 80 strikeouts, and just 32 runs allowed.

On June 3, Foutz and Bob Black hooked up in a scoreless pitchers duel. Bay City scored a run in the top half of the ninth, and Foutz retired the Quincy batters in the bottom of the ninth for the 1-0 win. He limited Quincy to three hits, recorded nine strikeouts, and walked two. Bay City touched Black for six hits. For their efforts in this game *Sporting Life* stated, "Foutz and Black are the best pitchers in the Northwestern League."

Besides pitching, Foutz was seeing playing time at other positions. Watkins felt comfortable playing him at any position except catcher. Through June 17 he was hitting .311. His pitching record stood at 12 wins and just two losses. Bay City was in second place behind Saginaw.

In June reports began to surface that all was not well with the Northwestern League. *Sporting Life* reported, "The directors of the Grand Rapids club are dissatisfied with the light attendance at ball games. The same may be said of this and other cities in the League. Such a bungling job of a schedule was never palmed on a base ball league as the one gotten up for and adopted by the League. There is no city playing in any League, which can contribute crowds everyday for six weeks." (In Bay City the home season started on May 15 and continued for six weeks until July 2. The Bay City club would not return home until mid-August.)

Even with the second best record in the league, and featuring the league's best twirler, Bay City seldom drew crowds of over 500 for a game. The bachelor Foutz, however, did entice more females to the games when he took to the pitcher's box. Some of the other clubs were just hanging on. The club directors were constantly trying to raise money to keep their clubs going.

Foutz won his 14th game of the season against Grand Rapids on June 23. In the 13-3 win he scattered seven hits and only one run was earned. He was red-hot at the plate, going 4-for-5 with two doubles and three runs scored.

At 6 foot 2 inches, and just 167 pounds, Foutz was nicknamed "Scissors."

Bay City played 20 games in June, winning 13 and losing seven. Foutz won seven games and lost two. For the month, he pitched a total of 83 innings, allowing 30 runs, 45 hits, and struck out 51 batters.

Bay City arrived in Stillwater, Minnesota, on July 14, having won seven games in a row. Foutz pitched and won the July 15 game, extending the Bay City winning streak. It was an easy 5-1 win for Foutz as he pitched a three-hitter.

The real baseball news of that day took place back home in Bay City. That evening the stockholders and the board of directors of the club held a business meeting to discuss the team's fate.

The Bay City *Tribune* reported the results of the meeting in its July 17 morning edition: "The Bay City Base Ball Association, like all other members of the Northwestern League, has been cramped for finances. Thus far the players have been paid promptly but the funds have grown beautifully less and it became a serious question whether the club would have to go under for lack of pecuniary assistance. Something has to be done at once and this meeting of the stockholders was held for the purpose of solving the question. The results of the meeting held July 15 was that it was unanimously agreed not to disband but to find ways to continue the operation of the club.

"The presence of Chris Von der Ahe, president of the St. Louis Browns ball club, in Bay City has given rise to rumors in local circles that Dave Foutz was to be released and sold to the Browns. Von der Ahe made an inviting offer of $1,000, but it was rejected, and Foutz will continue to play for Bay City. The directors, after the meeting, resolved not to release Foutz. The Bay City club is as good as the best in the league and will, with a fair portion of luck, bring the pennant to the Third City in October. They are deserving of a large patronage at the games in August, and the public should see that proper encouragement is given them."

After the meeting, club president Fitield, secretary Bennett, and Von der Ahe left to join the club in Quincy. In order to save money, they needed to release one of the players, and Watkins decided to release left fielder Bill McGunnigle. (McGunnigle and Dave Foutz would be reunited in 1888, when McGunnigle would become manager of the Brooklyn Bridegrooms.)

With Von der Ahe in the stands on Friday, July 18, Foutz's 19th win of the season was a thing of beauty. He gave up just two hits and allowed one Quincy run as Bay City won easily, 13-1. Bay City had now won 10 straight games. Foutz didn't realize it at the time, but this would be his last game played with the Bay City club. His ambitions of pitching in the major leagues was about to come true.

Late Friday, the Bay City *Tribune* received the following dispatch from secretary Bennet. "Have released Dave Foutz: He goes to St. Louis for the sale price of $2,000: no other changes made." Bennett also reported, "The club plays in Peoria unless Peoria disbands which she is seriously thinking of doing."

A dispatch from the Detroit *Free Press* had the following to say about the Dave Foutz sale. "The President and Secretary of the Bay City club along with Browns President Chris Von der Ahe have been in Quincy for two days. Bay City has released Dave Foutz, the lightning pitcher, to the Browns for $2,000. Foutz is to get $1,600 from St. Louis for the remainder of the season. The Bay City club will play in Peoria and then in Milwaukee, there they will be disbanded."

Bay City never made it to Milwaukee. On July 22, after a 10-5 loss in Peoria, the plug was pulled on the Bay City club and they disbanded.

Sporting Life reported on the disbanding of the club with the following. "The Bay City club, which was second in the Northwestern League, has received little crank support and was compelled to disband at Peoria, July 22. At the time the club had won forty-one games and lost eighteen. Previous to the collapse Von der Ahe of the Browns paid the extraordinary sum of $2,000 for the release of Dave Foutz, the crack pitcher of the club who will receive $1,600 for the rest of the season. The $2,000 price is believed to be the most money ever spent on the sale of a minor league ball player."

Sporting Life also reported that the $2,000 purchase price enabled the club to pay off all the Bay City players' salaries.

When asked about what kind of pitcher Von der Ahe was getting for his $2,000, all Chris could say was, "Dave Foutz is a bewilder and make no mistake."

Foutz and Von der Ahe arrived in St. Louis on July 20. Foutz would not be available to play with the Browns until July 29. The Association had a 10-day waiting period from the time a player was signed until he could play.

One of the many admirers of Dave Foutz in Bay City, after learning of his release, penned these lines of farewell, published in the Bay City *Tribune* on July 22:

Farewell Foutz By: L.B.
Who will henceforth twirl the sphere at Woodside,
As the great and only Foutz has gone?
Who will ever be for our boys the model,
How to field and catch as he has done?
Diamond fields without him will be barren,
He who covered space as no one ever did,
Who will ever be for our boys the model?
Will the fouls bring in so many kids?
Now, farewell. Seems hard to spare you:
Bereaved is Third like after Hector's dead;
Who will ever be for our girl's the model?
O, how many tears are shed!

(Woodside is the street in Bay City where the ball park was located. Third is a street close to Woodside, where Dave Foutz lived.)

The league lost all but four of its clubs by August 2. On September 3, when Minneapolis disbanded, the league suspended play and went bankrupt.

With Bay City, Foutz appeared in 39 games. He pitched in 22 games and played various field positions in the other 17.

Epilogue—After the 10-day waiting period, Dave Foutz took to the box in Cincinnati against the Reds on Tuesday, July 29.

Sporting Life reported on the game. " Twenty-three-year-old pitcher Dave Foutz pitched his first game for the Browns. The grounds were slippery and barely possible to play. The Reds players and their 2,400 Cranks made fun of the gangly pitcher at first but Foutz proved very puzzling to the Reds batters and to his effective work during the thirteen-inning game St. Louis owes victory.

"From the start, Foutz was cool and collected. He used a combination of curves and changed speed to keep the Reds batters off balance.

"The game was won by the Browns in the bottom of the thirteenth, 6 to 5, after Foutz had held the Reds scoreless to start the inning. In winning his first Major League game, Foutz held Cincinnati to ten hits, two earned runs and struck out thirteen."

BAY CITY 1884 BATTING & PITCHING TOTALS

AB	H	R	EX.BASES	AVG
173	56	33	16	.324

W	L	PCT	IP	H	K	R	SO
18*	4	.818	205	126	151	67	2

*A game pitched on July 18 was won by Bay City and later forfeited to Quincy because Bay City had used an illegal player. If not for this, Foutz would have won 19 games for the season.

America's Earliest Integrated Team?

by Brian Turner

Shortly after the Civil War, a "base ball fever"[1] swept down upon the western Massachusetts mill village of Florence,[2] where from 1865 to 1867 the Florence Eagles made their mark. The Eagles played some 60 games with seven losses, most of which came at the hands of the nation's finest clubs: the Brooklyn Excelsiors and the Brooklyn Atlantics, the Tri-Mountains of Boston, and the Lansingburgh (Troy, NY) Unions.[3] This is not to say that the Eagles' reputation rests on a few celebrated losses, for the "lads" from Florence defeated championship teams from across New England.[4] In most respects the history of the Eagles is consistent with that of other amateur ball clubs of the era and would merit only a brief mention here—except for one extraordinary fact. During its first season and into its second, the Eagles fielded an African American first baseman, Luther B. Askin.[5]

Accounts of the team's history are silent on this subject, for even when Askin is recognized, his race is not. The silence would have remained unbroken if not for Jim Ryan, a semi-pro ballplayer who died at the age of 101 in November, 2000. The two men became acquainted in the 1920s when Askin, then in his 80s, would come into the brush factory where Ryan worked, to pick up bristles to make toothbrushes at home. If Askin had seen Ryan in a recent game, he would seek out the third baseman, and the two of them would talk baseball.[6]

Brian Turner is co-author (with John S. Bowman) of the Hurrah Game: Baseball in Northampton, 1823-1953. He lives in Florence, MA, and teaches writing at Smith College.

"He was a real gentleman, and he loved to talk about the games," recalled Ryan. "I was always surprised by how much he knew about baseball history. I remember him at the games. He lived down the street, and must have walked up to the Smith School, then up through the woods to the field where we played."

Ryan said, "There weren't many blacks around here, so he stood out. Yes, he was light-skinned, but there's no question he was black. And he used to tell me that he was one of the Eagles, though it's funny, I didn't think too much of it at the time."[7]

Were the Florence Eagles America's earliest integrated ball club?

In order to address this question, it might be a good idea to set a few conditions under which the Eagles or any other ball club might qualify. The club should be an association of adults; it should observe the conventions regarding invitation matches, so that the games are more than pickup or split-squad affairs; it should leave a verifiable record, such as box scores, in which the players in question appear regularly, not in isolated instances; and the players must be regarded as black or "colored," even if no one said so at the time.

How often did acts of early integration in baseball go unacknowledged—and for what reasons? Did other amateur ball clubs choose, consciously or unconsciously, not to look too closely at a player whose racial identity was ambiguous? Or did the clubs choose to maintain a discreet silence about such matters even when the answer was evident? After all, it strains credulity to think that, among the thousands of ball games played before 1865, a black player *never* played on a team with whites.[8] Yet game accounts are sketchy, making it difficult, if not impossible, to determine the racial makeup of ball clubs active before the Civil War.

Indeed, if earlier instances of integration did take place, they may have occurred at less formal levels of play. Askin's obituary, for example, states that as early as 1860 he played on a team also calling itself the Eagles. The few references to the "early Florence associations"[9] describe their members as "juveniles,"[10] which aptly describes Askin, who was 15 at the time. Askin's obituary also states that he played for "The Emmetts" in 1864,[11] but few accounts of this team survive, nor does Askin appear in the only known box score. Without confirmation of Askin's presence in the lineup, it would seem wise to set aside the Emmetts for now.

One thing is certain: It would have been highly unusual for a black player to appear in "match games" arranged through invitations by clubs of adult white males. Yet this is precisely what happened when Askin played first base for the Eagles in 1865 and 1866, a period for which there is an abundance of box scores and news accounts for confirmation. A review of the record, as well as the reminiscences of the players, shows that Askin was in the lineup for each of the first 13 matches[12] the Eagles played.

Unlike the early gentlemen's ball clubs of the antebellum period, the Eagles seem not to have turned away applicants based on social class or profession.[13] In this, the Eagles may have been motivated by the limited pool of players available in Florence, a village of only 1,400 people in 1864.[14] Yet the club's willingness to test, however tentatively, the boundaries of class and race closely followed the example set by the community. From the start, Florence was spoken of as "a place of ideas and principles . . . [b]ound by no shackles of party or sect."[15] Sounding the same note decades later, Eagle second baseman John B. O'Donnell remembered Florence as a place where "Protestant, Catholic, Gentile, and Jew, white and black, all were invited, received, and welcomed as members of one common brotherhood."[16] The young O'Donnell had a direct stake in the "common brotherhood," since he was one of a contingent of Eagle players who were "paddies," Irish Catholics, mill workers and manual laborers all. Many of the Eagles came from Protestant roots[17]; some were sons of professional men and, while not averse to manual labor, enjoyed privileges the Irish players did not. Of all the Eagles, however, no one was further from the elite than Luther B. Askin, second son of Sarah Askin, a "jolly good natured colored woman," who had been abandoned by her husband, and who "supported her family by doing washing."[18]

Sarah Askin, Luther Askin's mother, circa 1880-1890.

Eagles captain A. G. Hill remembered Florence as "one of the historical centers of the Anti-Slavery warfare. The workers in the causes were practically the whole village."[19] Florence might have been unusual in this respect, but not unique. Oberlin, Ohio,[20] was also "a hotbed of Abolitionism before and during the Civil War" and, like Florence, "was a stop on the Underground Railroad."[21] Oberlin, it seems, took considerable pride in its tolerance of racial difference, and the same could be said of Florence.[22] It is significant, therefore, that apart from Askin's seasons with the Eagles, the earliest *reported* instance of a black player appearing on a white team was in Oberlin, "in 1869, when the otherwise white Resolute Club . . . featured a black pitcher."[23] If the Oberlin integration is the earliest "reported" instance, then Askin's "unreported" integration of the Florence Eagles, occurring five years before, could be a baseball "first."[24] Other instances of integration may yet be discovered, but finding them could be difficult, especially if, for whatever reason, a veil was drawn over the evidence, as with the Eagles and Askin.

Among African Americans attracted by the nonsectarian, nondiscriminatory ideals that were prevalent in Florence were "Mrs. Askins [sic] . . . and her two sons and four daughters," recalled A. G. Hill.[25] Captain Hill knew perfectly well that his first baseman, Luther B. Askin, was black; it is safe to assume that the rest of the Eagles knew, too, as did most of the folks in Florence, a small, cohesive community. All of which makes the long silence that grew up around the subject of Askin's race even more curious. It would make for heartwarming reading, of course, to claim that Florence was so tolerant that no mention of a person's race was needed, but the picture that emerges from

The Florence Eagles, circa 1867. Askin was no longer a member of the first nine.

the evidence is rather more complicated.

Certainly, Askin's record with the Eagles is intriguing for what it suggests about why he left the team, and whether race had anything to do with it. After a "friendly" tune-up with the second nine in July, 1865, the Eagles were ready for their debut. The club issued a challenge to a team of returning Civil War veterans who called themselves champions of the "Army of the Potomac." On August 1, "[t]o the surprise of nearly everyone, the 'Eagle' was victorious."[26] In this, the Eagles' first official match game, Askin played first base, qualifying him as "one of the original nine," and in most sources thereafter he was recognized as such.

From July to October, 1865, in the seven games for which there are box scores, Askin scored an average of 4.3 runs, a rate of production close to that of O'Donnell, the only other Eagle to appear in every game. (Indeed, Askin surpassed the man who would eventually replace him at first base, Jonas Polmatier, who averaged just 3.0 runs in four games.) Adding up the published final scores during their first season, the Eagles compiled 402 runs, or 4.47 runs per player per game, a rate of production comparable to Askin's. Rudimentary as these statistics are, and even allowing for gaps in the record, the scores suggest that Askin was reasonably productive at the plate.

Askin was valuable enough to play in an "unofficial" match staged in Springfield on November 2 against the champion Hampdens, no less. Rather than stake their unblemished record against the heavily favored rivals downriver, the Eagles announced that they were disbanding. The local newspapers then noted the formation of a "Bay State" club, six of whom were Eagles. The Eagles "resorted to a little stratagem," an anonymous Eagle recalled, "to learn the strength of the Hampden Club." To complete their disguise, the Eagles were "girdled with a 'Bay State' engine company's belt" (not the last time Askin would wear a fireman's uniform[27]). When "Bay State" defeated the Hampdens 26-20, the Springfield papers dismissed their claim to the championship and called the match a "friendly" one, which was how the anonymous Eagle,[28] reminiscing in 1894, described the game. "The result . . . being favorable," he wrote, "a challenge was sent from the Eagle Club for the silver ball championship."[29]

From that day forth the Eagles had one goal, the winning of the silver championship ball; accordingly, their second season took on a different tenor. Baseball had become more than a game; it had become a civic drama meant to display all that was best in a community, and the participation of the Eagles in this drama brought considerable pressure to bear upon the young ballplayers. The games, O'Donnell recalled, "became the occasion of village holidays, and [their] successes and defeats were matters of pride and regret to the whole village."[30] If newspaper estimates are to be believed, crowds larger than the population of Florence turned out: "The crowd assembled was much the largest that has ever attended a base-ball match in western Massachusetts, there being not less than 5,000 people."[31] The *Free Press* described the scene "on the left hand side of the road leading to Leeds and Haydenville past the old Solomon Warner tavern . . . The spectators lined three sides of the large field besides filling neighboring trees and covering the roofs of some buildings nearby."[32]

Local industries were no less eager to lend support. The Florence Sewing Machine Company created the club uniforms, and provided equipment and transportation.[33] If an opponent's ball was suspected of being light, the Sewing Machine Company provided their scales to calibrate its weight.[34] The baseballs came from New York City and cost $3.50 each,[35] a considerable sum, and only a part of the cost of fielding a team. "The club comprised about one hundred members, those who did not play furnishing the expenses of the players, who never were paid a salary."[36] While no salaries were paid, on one occasion an award was offered, as O'Donnell recalled, "when a banquet was tendered us and $100 presented to us as the new champions by the grateful people of our village."[37]

In addition to the occasional cash inducement, another, perhaps subtler form of pressure was placed upon the young men who only the season before had been a "lot of barefooted cotton mill paddies."[38] It was the notion that amateur "Base Ball" ought to have an ennobling, improving effect on all involved. At an Eagles game, the *Free Press* cast its approving eye on those in attendance: "A large number of spectators were present, among whom were many representatives of the beauty and the elite of the village."[39] If anyone disturbed this ideal, the people of Florence were quick to take note: "There were some in the crowd . . . that seemed to take especial delight in standing in front of those who were sitting . . . But there are hogs with the form of men in every large crowd."[40] When good manners were restored the newspapers expressed satisfaction: "There was, we were glad to observe, very little disorder, . . . exhibiting no ill-feeling at the varying fortunes of the game in indulging in the hooting and yelling too frequent on similar occasions."[41]

Public displays of gambling only heightened the intense atmosphere of the matches. "There had also been a large amount of betting on the game, . . . though the friends of the Eagles manifested rather more confidence in the result than did those of the Hampdens."[42] The stakes were surprisingly large: "There was some betting on the result, and it is reported that two of our sporting men won about $700,"[43] a sum more than double the annual wage of a mill hand. And the odds were long: "[W]e hear of instances where parties offered four to one in favor of the Eagles and won." The losers were unlikely to refrain from making pronouncements, as in this letter, entitled, "A Warning to the Eagles"[44]:

> *I should like to have it understood that . . . the friends of Hampden gained an object by wagering a large amount of money on the Florence. They have generally favored the Hampden and do now and are ready to wager two to one on Hampden next time, if they cannot do better. As an outsider I caution them to be on their guard and defeat their object. COM.*[45]

To this the *Free Press* added: "[T]he Eagles will do well to profit by the hint . . . They have won nobly but 'eternal vigilance is the price of'—the silver ball."[46]

Such calls to "eternal vigilance," along with the increasingly high stakes, and the rising expectations that accompanied the success of the Florence club, intensified the pressure to win. Things had changed from the Eagles' first season, when they would "appear on the field barefooted, ununiformed, with one bat, perhaps, and a stick in which to cut notches for tallies."[47] The relatively carefree atmosphere of the early games had given way to the community's baseball "fever" that "their boys" take the championship. It was as if the evolution of the game over the previous decades had been compressed, rapidly evolving in the course of the Eagles' brief seasons from a leisurely recreational activity and social ritual to an all-out drive to win.

Did the drive to win result in the demotion of Askin from the first nine? Certainly, the pressure to take the silver ball and to play against the best clubs contributed to a new attitude on the club, one of vaunting ambition.[48] And yet, based on Askin's reputation, both in contemporary accounts and in reminiscences, his

The Nonotuck Fire Company; 1878; Askin is on the far right. Earliest known image of Luther B. Askin.

disappearance from the first nine appears puzzling. All along Askin had been highly regarded for his fielding. An unsigned letter sent from Middletown, Connecticut, and published in 1886, evaluates Askin as "an excellent first baseman in his day."[49] Moreover, Askin received praise for his hitting: "Askins [sic] . . . excelled in this respect."[50] In the first game of the second season, he scored nine runs, his personal best. Yet, as the championship match drew near, his scoring dropped off. Then, on June 9, 1866, in the showdown for the silver ball Askin had a disastrous day at the plate, scoring no runs.[51]

The 36-10 loss to the Hampdens must have come as a shock, since it was the first defeat that the Eagles had suffered: "The Eagle club did not show nearly as good playing as they usually do," groused the *Free Press.*[52] The disappointment in Florence was matched only by a determination that the boys try again. The Eagles regrouped, retooled, and won the silver ball in August. They defended the ball against all comers until the Hampdens won it back in October (and declined a rematch[53]). For all that time, however, Askin no longer appeared in the Eagle lineup.

Askin wasn't the only Eagle to go scoreless in the June 9, 1866, loss to the Hampdens. Bottum, the center fielder, was also shut out, yet remained in the lineup, even as his slump continued for several more matches; long feared for his power, Bottum had been dubbed, "Battem," by the Greenfield *Gazette.*[54] Askin, too, was recognized for his batting, but for striking, "a much larger number of ground balls,"[55] according to one report. A recently discovered manuscript[56] notes several home runs that Askin hit over his career; in the version of the reminiscence in Sheffeld's *History of Florence* (1894), however, the references to Askin's home runs were edited out. It would seem, therefore, that Askin's true value to the team included his fielding, his scoring, and occasional power.[57]

Askin was not the only player dropped soon after June 9, 1866. Writing years later in 1886, an unnamed player from Middletown praises Askin by name for his fielding, then goes on to praise Mara, the catcher, in almost the same terms, "and who was better than he then." A few sentences later, however, the writer refers to Askin and Mara not by their names but their positions: "[T]he catcher was dropped and . . . the first baseman was dropped."[58] But only Askin's absence would turn out to be permanent.

An odd reticence has accompanied accounts of Askin's time with the Eagles. In the reminiscence of 1894, "one of the players" singles out Askin again for his fielding: "'Old Bushel Basket' was his pet name, for, *until his sickness*, the balls seemed to drop into his fingers and stay there as if a basket had held them"[59] (emphasis added). No explanation is given for the "sickness" said to have reduced Askin's effectiveness. Another five weeks went by before Askin appeared on a ball field again, but this time with the "second" Eagle nine. The "second" Eagles defeated the Torrent Club of Haydenville 40-13 on July 21, 1866, and Askin scored seven runs on that occasion, so it would seem that he wasn't so sick he couldn't play, and play well.[60]

Meanwhile, little notice was taken in the local press of Askin's departure from the Eagles or his reappearance a few weeks later with the second team. Once the Eagles had possession of the silver ball, reporters were quick to declare that the "position and the men on the field had been entirely and advantageously changed, and in batting particularly they showed marked strength and proficiency."[61] With Polmatier taking first base, the Eagles went on a winning streak and kept much the same lineup for the rest of the season. And yet once the winning streak ended, the Eagles did not restore Askin, nor did they bench the players who went scoreless in that loss: Bottum, Polmatier, Robertson, and Whalen.[62] If other factors, such as race,[63] entered into the decision to demote Askin, no documents exist to clarify the matter. Whatever the reason, the baseball career of Luther B. Askin was over.

The Florence Eagles were celebrated for decades as the finest amateur team of the area. Fans nostalgic for the golden age of amateur baseball would cite the Eagles as the ideal, for compared to "the Florence lads," all professional teams fell short. Some of the Eagles were exceptionally well placed to cultivate their legend, prospering as businessmen, journalists, judges, and attorneys, in particular O'Donnell and Hill, who became mayors of Northampton.[64]

The legend of the Florence Eagles was sustained and burnished by the players themselves, including Askin, at the celebrations held in the ballroom of Judge O'Donnell's home in 1915 and 1916, the 50th anniversaries of the club's founding and reign as champions, respectively. These celebrations were amplified by Northampton's two newspapers, the *Gazette* and the *Herald*. On both occasions Askin, then in his mid-70s, spoke on the evolution of baseball to a more "scientific" game. His remarks were reported, but no mention was made of his race, not even to point out the anomaly of his inclusion at the reunion of an all-white team. Nor was Askin included in either of the photographs of the reunited Eagles.

One possible reason for the omission was that Askin, although acknowledged as an "original" Eagle, had not appeared in the matches that earned Florence the silver ball, and so he was denied recognition as "one of the nine that won the championship."[65] But if this is the reason that led to his exclusion, it's odd that James O'Neill was included in the photographs, since he never played an inning, having served as the club's scorekeeper.[66]

A long silence had fallen over the subject of Askin's race, a silence to which Askin may have contributed. What made the silence possible, as Jim Ryan noted, was the fact that Askin was light-skinned. Askin was a founding member of the Nonotuck No. 1 Company in 1870.[67] In a photograph from July 31, 1878,[68] the firemen are resplendent in their uniforms, and all but two form the lines to draw the hose wagon. (One of the "workhorses" is Askin's old teammate and ally, A. G. Hill.) Several in the company are slightly darker, but no one is obviously of African descent. A print of this photograph is in the Florence Association's historical collection, and on its back the firemen are identified. Of the pair of men who stand apart, one is closer to the camera and holds a bouquet, signifying some authority; the other is to the side. The latter is Askin. From his image it is difficult to tell that he is black.

But Askin definitely wasn't white, nor were his relatives, as the municipal records of Pittsfield, Massachusetts, show. The people on his father's side, going back to 1743, were "colored" servants to the "old families" of Pittsfield. Sarah, his mother, came from the Lloyds, one of the "colored" families of Lanesborough, Massachusetts, and her photo clearly shows she is black with perhaps a hint of Native American features.[69]

During Askin's time with the Eagles, there was no obvious reason for Askin to pass for white. Florence, as every account suggests, was "noted for its good feeling towards the colored people."[70] Yet over the decades a gradual "whitening" of the Askin family took place. In the first census in which the family appears, in 1850, they are listed as "Haskins," and designated "B" for black. By the 1860 census, they are designated "M" for Mulatto; so they remained until the 1900 census, in which they were, temporarily, "black" again. In the 1920 census a more radical change occurs: Luther, his wife, Alice, and daughter, Sadie, are listed as "W" for white!

Was this "whitening" incidental, a matter of silence

and forgetting? Florence and the city it belongs to, Northampton, were not exempt from the forces shaping American racism.[71] In 1913, Northampton's entry in the Twin State League, the Meadowlarks, boycotted a game in Bellows Falls, Vermont, because the Vermonters had brought in one of the great black pitchers of the era, Frank Wickware of the Mohawk Giants.[72] For weeks after, the *Gazette*, a reasonably temperate publication, defended the Northampton club and permitted the use of slurs in its pages.[73] Given that Luther B. Askin regarded himself as a student of baseball and followed the local teams, he had to be aware of this incident and all that it implied.

By the 1920s, when Jim Ryan and Luther Askin were friends, western Massachusetts had its own shadowy chapter of the Ku Klux Klan.[74] On October 18, 1925, 300 Klansmen, some in regalia, "paid a visit" to the Florence Methodist Episcopal Church, an incident that left "Florence All Agog."[75] This event took place across the street from where Luther's mother was buried, three blocks away from the Askin household. Much of the tolerance and acceptance Luther B. Askin had known in Florence had been rolled back by racism and nativism. Having evaded racial labels when he was an Eagle, Askin may have found it easier to take advantage of the privilege and the protection afforded him by his new designation as an honorary, perhaps accidental, "white."[76]

That Askin was proud of his seasons as an Eagle was evident, for his obituary lists his baseball career before his other accomplishments.[77] The obituary makes the point that Askin was the last surviving Eagle. As the search goes forward for more instances of integration in baseball, the case of Luther B. Askin stands as an example of what an integrated team might look like and where earlier instances might be found.

ACKNOWLEDGMENTS

Thanks to John S. Bowman, a fellow SABR member, for his sympathetic yet keen-eyed reading of early drafts. Thanks also to Paul Gaffney, both as a reader and as a teacher of a valuable lesson in how to use municipal and county records for research.

SOURCES

Bowman, John S., "The Mighty Eagles & Hampshire County's Niche in Baseball's History." *Hampshire Life*, Northampton, MA, July 5, 1991., p. 9-26.

—"The Florence Eagles." http://historic-northampton.org/Historic_Highlights/968859402.html.; September 13, 2000.

Cooke, Rollin H. Index of vital statistics of Berkshire County. Pittsfield (MA) Atheneum.

Daily Hampshire Gazette, Northampton, MA.

Daily Herald, Northampton, MA.

The Free Press, Northampton, MA.

Friedrick, Anna Pauline, *Recollections of Some People Who Attended Cosmian Hall*, Florence Association, Florence, MA.

Gaffney, Paul, personal interview, Florence, MA, June, 2000.

Gazette & Courier, Northampton, MA.

Hampshire County Journal, Northampton, MA.

Hill, Arthur G., from *Papers of A. G. Hill*, Florence Association, Florence, MA.

Journal and Republican, Lowville, NY.

"One of the Players," Reminiscence of the Florence Eagles, Florence Association, Florence, MA.

Peterson, Robert, *Only the Ball Was White*. Oxford University Press, New York. 1970.

Ryan, James E., personal interviews, Florence, MA, 1998-2000.

Ryczek, William, *When Johnny Came Sliding Home: The Post-Civil War Baseball Boom, 1865-1870*. McFarland & Company, Jefferson, North Carolina. 1998.

Seymour, Harold, *Baseball: The Early Years*. Oxford University Press, New York. 1960.

—*Baseball: The People's Game*. Oxford University Press, New York. 1990.

Sheffeld, Charles A., *History of Florence Massachusetts*. Self-published, Florence, MA, 1895.

Springfield Republican, Springfield, MA.

Turner, Brian, "97 Years of Togetherness." *Hampshire Life*, Northampton, MA, December 31, 1999.

—"Valley of the Klan," *VMAG*, Northampton, MA, March, 2000.

—"The Years Northampton Won the Pennant—and Drew the Color Line," *VMAG*, Northampton, MA, August, 1999.

NOTES

1. "[T]he base ball fever, originating in Florence, has spread like an epidemic over all the towns in the region" (*Free Press*, November 13, 1866).
2. Florence is "beautifully situated three miles west of Northampton, being a manufacturing village within that town" (*Gazette*, April 2, 1867).
3. Bowman, "Florence Eagles," A match against the Unions in August 1867 was the only Eagles game to which admission was charged, with "over $300 taken" (*Gazette*, August 20, 1867).
4. Among them, the Hampdens of Chicopee (champions of Western Massachusetts), the Federals of Shelburne Falls (champions of Franklin County), the Rollstones of Fitchburg (champions of Worcester County), the Fraternity Club of South Boston (champions of Suffolk County), and the Pequots of New Haven (champions of Connecticut) (*Gazette*, August 23, 1916).
5. Most contemporary references to Luther B. Askin use "Askins." Yet in his obituary and that of his wife, and on their gravestone in Florence's Spring Grove Cemetery, the name is spelled without the second "s." On many of the legal papers signed by Askin himself, he leaves off the second "s." That is the spelling he wished to use, so I use it as well.
6. Turner, "97 Years," December 31, 1999.
7. Ryan, Personal Interviews, 1998-2000.
8. African Americans had been playing baseball "as early as whites and organized the games along roughly parallel lines" (Seymour, *People's*, 532). Most researchers admit that little "is known about the earliest Negro clubs" before the war, but "by 1867 teams were sufficiently well-organized, at least in the North, to have challenge matches for supremacy" (Peterson, p. 17).
9. The "early Florence associations" played "round ball" (Sheffeld, p. 179), not necessarily a reference to rounders, according to SABR's David Block, but one of the variants used to describe "town ball." Block holds that the use of the term "rounders" is a late edition to the baseball lexicon and therefore inaccurate. If so, then Askin misuses the term, recalling that "the first baseball game [was] played in Florence in 1860 which followed the game of rounders" (*Herald*, September 1, 1915).
10. *Free Press*, August 14, 1860.
11. *Gazette*, April 8, 1929.
12. The Eagles staged more matches per season than the clubs that preceded them. The 1858 "Nonotucks," a club whose players came from "the prominent families of the city" (*Herald*, June 11, 1909), staged two or three matches a season. Like the Nonotucks, the Eagles observed the costly social ritual of the post-game feast. After the Eagles' debut in 1865, the Northampton *Free Press* reported, "In the evening, the two clubs . . . partook of a supper at the Warner House, got up in the most approved style ... if the piles of choice edibles under which the tables groaned could be taken as an indication" (August 4, 1865). Before long the Eagles stopped staging feasts after every match, a ritual already fading away in areas where purely recreational baseball had evolved into a more competitive activity.
13. Whites and blacks had little social contact; therefore, the exclusion of players on the basis of race may have been moot.
14. *Gazette*, April 2, 1867. A population surge followed the war; by 1867 Florence had grown to 2,000 residents, most of them attracted by the thriving silk mills and factories.
15. *Gazette*, April 2, 1867.
16. Sheffeld, p. 187.
17. Arthur G. Hill's father was S. L. Hill, a confirmed abolitionist who helped organize the Northampton Association of Education and Industry, a utopian community; Hill and his teammate, E. S. Bottum, were children of the association, a place where Frederick Douglass and William Lloyd Garrison visited, where the "African Sybil," Sojourner Truth, lived (Hill, p. 3); after the association failed, the Free Congregational Church was formed, with Hill, Bottum, and Eagle pitching star, H. H. Bond as members. Luther Askin's mother and sisters also belonged, but Luther himself did not.
18. Friedrick, pp. 19-20.
19. Hill, p. 2.
20. Oberlin was where Fleetwood and Welday Walker, the first black major leaguers, went to college and played ball.
21. Peterson, p. 21.
22. In the 1850s, free blacks and ex-slaves, many of whom settled in Florence, constituted a greater percentage of Northampton's population (3%) than its larger neighbor, Springfield (Paul Gaffney).
23. Ryczek, p. 102.
24. If researchers can identify communities with integrated social organizations, such as the ones that existed in Oberlin and Florence, then these are the places where other integrated ball clubs may be found.
25. Hill, p. 3.
26. Bowman, "Florence Eagles."
27. Askin was a foreman with the Nonotuck volunteer firemen; one of his superiors was an Eagle teammate, E .S. Bottum, the company's engineer (Hampshire County *Journal*, May 17, 1879).
28. In 1894, when the anonymous Eagle recalls Askin, he uses language that raises as many questions as it answers. See Note 60.
29. Sheffeld, p. 182.
30. Sheffeld, p. 31.
31. Springfield (MA) *Republican*, September 3, 1866.
32. September 4, 1866.
33. Sheffeld, p. 185.
34. Bowman, "Mighty Eagles," p. 9. The "lightness" of the ball was a cause of controversy when the Hampdens won back the championship in October, 1866. The Eagles insisted that, as a matter of principle, they would never again compete for the championship. See Note 53.
35. Bowman, "Mighty Eagles," p. 26.
36. *Gazette*, August 23, 1916.

37. *Gazette*, August 23, 1916.
38. Hampshire County *Journal*, August 7, 1886. The representation of the Eagles as "paddies" seems to have crept into recollections about the team years later. In fact, even without Askin, the Eagles were a fairly heterogeneous group, with members of French Huguenot (Polmatier) and Anglo-Saxon (Hill, Hammond, Bond) descent, in addition to the "paddies" (O'Donnell, Whalen, Connell, Dunn). And yet, at one reunion, the Eagles and their guests, including Askin, were treated to "the famous Eagles song," entitled, "The Taking of the Ball," sung to the tune of "The Wearing of the Green" (*Herald*, August 23, 1916).
39. *Free Press*, September 4, 1866.
40. Letter to the *Free Press*, July 10, 1866.
41. *Free Press*, September 4, 1866.
42. Springfield (MA) *Republican*, September 3, 1866.
43. *Gazette*, September 11, 1866.
44. *Free Press*, September 4, 1866. Hampden fans insisted that their boys could win the silver ball whenever they chose. This notion was dispelled when the two teams met in September, 1866, and the Eagles won for the second time.
45. *Free Press*, August 21, 1866.
46. *Free Press*, August 21, 1866.
47. Hampshire County *Journal*, August 7, 1886.
48. In an act of hubris, the Florence Eagles challenged the Excelsiors and the Atlantics of Brooklyn. The games took place at the Capitoline Grounds, the Eagles losing to the Excelsiors, 32-21, on a Friday in early November, and to the Atlantics the next day. No final score for the second game was given, except to say that it "resulted in a triumph of the Atlantics by five runs" (*Free Press*, November 11, 1866).
49. Hampshire County *Journal*, August 7, 1886.
50. *Free Press*, September 26, 1865.
51. *Free Press*, June 12, 1866. In fairness to Askin, none of the Eagles scored more than two runs that day.
52. *Free Press*, June 12, 1866.
53. Apparently, the Eagles' vow never again to play for the championship did not take immediate effect. "The Eagle club have challenged the Hampden... to another contest" (Springfield *Republican*, October 8, 1866). No such game was played, though the clubs met in "friendly" matches.
54. Sheffeld, p. 185.
55. *Free Press*, August 9, 1865.
56. Brian McCullough, a descendant of A. G. Hill, discovered the manuscript among Hill's papers. McCullough concludes, based on the handwriting, that Hill did not write the manuscript. In 1916 Hill was entrusted with the club records, which would explain how the manuscript came into his possession.
57. Long after the Eagles disbanded, Bottum was celebrated for his power hitting. In 1879, a "few of the old Eagles played in the Fireman's nine[.] E. S. Bottum ... broke five ball clubs during the contest with his heavy batting" (Hampshire County *Journal*, June 24, 1879). Askin and Hill were also Florence firemen, but no box score exists to prove that they were among the "old Eagles" to take the field that day.
58. Hampshire County *Journal*, August 7, 1886.
59. Sheffeld, p. 186.
60. In the 1870s Askin was a musician with the Orcutt Orchestra, 1872; the Union Orchestra, 1874; the Addis Orchestra, 1876 (*Gazette*, April 8, 1929), probably playing the cornet, the instrument he gave his 14-year-old son, Luther, a renowned bandleader (Lowville *Journal and Republican*, February 10, 1966). It doesn't seem likely that Askin would lose the fine motor skills necessary to catch and hit a baseball, then regain them almost overnight, exhibiting them thereafter as a musician. Was "sickness" a euphemism for a nervous condition, one that caused Askin to "choke" or "freeze" in the big game? Perhaps so, but Askin's ability to make decisions and act under pressure was never questioned when he served as a fireman for 20 years; then again, 5,000 people weren't in attendance at the fires, nor did a community's self-image depend on every move he made. If "sickness" is a euphemism, it could also refer to drunkenness, something a committed temperance man like A. G. Hill would not have taken lightly. Askin's father, Nelson, having failed in the livery business, abandoned the family in 1850, but whether drunkenness had anything to do with it, it's difficult to say. Unless more evidence emerges to support drunken behavior, we have to assume that the "sickness" refers to something else—though what that might be we may never know.
61. *Free Press*, August 21, 1866.
62. Springfield (MA) *Republican*, October 8, 1866.
63. In September, 1866 the Eagles joined the New England Association of Base Ball Clubs (Bowman, "Mighty Eagles," p. 9). Along with the formalized rules provided by such associations, there also developed a form of institutional racism. In the winter of 1867 the National Association of Amateur Base Ball Players put in place "a written ban against [blacks]. The faded official records... prove that Negro players and clubs were barred from membership" (Seymour, *Early Years*, p. 42). The ban was in response to an application by an all-black team to join the association, not an attempt to integrate white teams.
64. In addition to the electoral successes of Judge O'Donnell (in spite of being a Democrat in a Republican city) and A. G. Hill, another of the Eagles appeared destined for a life of distinction. Before his death from tuberculosis at the age of 35, H. H. Bond was an attorney; and in that capacity managed the Homestead Fund, a trust set up by S. L. Hill to enable mill workers, including the Askins, to own homes. The Homestead Fund evolved into the Florence Savings Bank, directed by Bond's wife, Elizabeth Powell Bond, the first woman treasurer of a bank in America.
65. Sheffeld, p. 185.
66. Askin may have been so deferential as to be nearly invisible. Deference was a behavior African Americans learned to deploy in their interactions with whites.
67. Sheffeld, p. 176.
68. Sheffeld, p. 177.
69. Cooke, Rollin H. (1843-1904). A compilation of vital records of the Berkshires.
70. Hill, p. 3.

71. Askin had to be aware of the racism that manifested itself more openly over time. With the migration of freed slaves north, Jim Crow came into its own. "It is well-known historical paradox that as the Civil War receded... Southern caste attitudes spread increasingly in the North and West.... This blight included professional baseball in its contagious advance" (Seymour, *Early Years*, pp. 334-335). In such a charged racial atmosphere it was rare for blacks to play on the same team as whites, even informally, and by the 1890s segregation was the rule at almost every level of baseball except the collegiate and high school.
72. Turner, "Years Northampton Won," August 1999.
73. The *Gazette*'s rival, the *Herald*, took an opposite view, criticizing the team's action, yet the *Herald* also permitted the use of slurs in its pages and cannot be held up as exemplary in its representation of race.
74. During the 1920s, in the Northeast at least, the Klan was more openly anti-Catholic and anti-immigrant than racist; even so, Askin could take little comfort in the Klan's scapegoats of choice, especially since the Klan elsewhere was as racist as ever.
75. *Gazette*, October 19, 1925.
76. Light-skinned as he was, Askin may have been motivated to keep out of the newspapers for the sake of his son, Luther Benjamin Askin of Lowville, NY, who had been passing for white for years.
77. Over the course of his life Askin worked as a stonecutter, a carpenter, and a machinist, rising to the position of foreman with a toothbrush manufacturer, the Pro-Phy-Lac-Tic Brush Co. Paul Gaffney, a professor of history at Landmark College, says that it was highly unusual for an African American to enjoy even this rather modest success, more evidence, perhaps, of Askin's ability to mix in white society.

THERE IS AN OLD SALOON QUESTION *that goes 'what Hall of Famers hit homers on their first major league at bat?' Despite the power outage of recent years, the answer remains the same. Three.*

The first Cooperstown-bound player to accomplish the mark was Earl Averill, who started with the Indians on April 16, 1929. Also noteworthy that day was that both the Yankees and Indians planned to have numbers on the backs of their players' uniforms, but rain canceled the New York opener. The honor went to the Indians, who wore numbers only at home. Averill, wearing number 5 (his number 3 was later retired), cracked an 0-2 pitch for a homer, off Earl Whitehill. The numberless Charlie Gehringer matched the rookie in the third inning, hitting his off Joe Shaute. Cleveland handed new Tigers manager Bucky Harris his first loss, 5-4, in 10 innings. Averill would eventually hit 238 homers and be elected to the Hall of Fame in 1975. He was just the second player to connect in his first at-bat: Luke Stuart was the first, in 1921.

The second Hall of Famer to hit a homer in his initial plate appearance was Duke All-American football star Ace Parker, who debuted on April 30, 1937. Ace pinch-hit in his first major league at bat for the Athletics, connecting off the redoubtable Wes Ferrell in a 15-5 loss to Boston. This was the first time an AL player pinch homered in his debut at bat. Parker had just one more home run on his way to a .117 average in his one year. But Ace did better on the gridiron, scoring a pair of touchdowns for the Brooklyn Dodgers at Pittsburgh on November 21. Parker was eventually elected to the Hall of Fame—for football.

The third Hall of Famer to homer in his initial at bat was Hoyt Wilhelm of the New York Giants on April 23, 1952. The 29-year-old knuckleballer won his first game pitching 5+ innings in relief in a 9-5 win. In his first at bat he cleaned a pitch for a four-bagger off the Braves' Dick Hoover, in relief of loser Gene Conley. Though Wilhelm appeared in 1,070 games, this was his only homer. —JIM CHARLTON

Eddie Freed Made His Mark in Phillies History

by David Weeks

Here's a trivia question for you: who holds the Phillies record for most hits in their first major league game? Richie Ashburn? Sorry, "Whitey" went 1 for 5 in his first game on April 20, 1948. Denny Doyle? Close—Doyle gave a memorable performance in his debut on April 7, 1970, going 3 for 4 against the Cubs. Incidentally, in that game Phillies pitcher Chris Short threw a five-hit shutout in his first start since missing the 1969 season because of back surgery. But back to the question. How about Mike Schmidt? Nope, Schmidt went 1 for 3 in his first game on September 12, 1972. To find the answer, you have to go back almost 30 years to the day of Schmidt's debut. On September 11, 1942, a rookie outfielder named Eddie Freed made his major league debut with the Phillies. Now, unless you were a diehard Phillies fan during that dismal 1942 season, you probably don't remember Eddie Freed. But after a September call-up from Trenton, Freed's hitting provided one of the few highlights for the Phillies that year. His 4 for 5 performance in his first game in a Phillies uniform is still a team record and ties him with the likes of Casey Stengel and Willie McCovey for the major league record. Making that feat all the more remarkable was that the victim of Freed's bat that day was the Cincinnati Reds Johnny "Double No-Hit" Vander Meer. In 1938, Vander Meer had become the only pitcher to throw consecutive no-hitters. The 1942 season found him among the league leaders in most pitching categories, including leading the league in strikeouts. So where did Eddie Freed come from and why haven't you heard of him?

David Weeks is an assistant professor and reference librarian at Dacus Library, Winthrop University, in Rock Hill, South Carolina.

Edwin Charles Freed was born August 22, 1919, in Centre Valley , PA—a small community about 12 miles outside of Allentown. Like many country boys of those days his life revolved around school, work, and baseball—though not necessarily in that order. Freed remembers the first games he played in were matches between boys from Centre Valley and "city boys" (as he calls them) from Allentown. Since he was still too young for Legion ball, he became the batboy on a local semi-pro team. Part of his job soon became warming up the pitchers and catching batting practice. He quickly learned the skills of catching, and that became his position during those early years. As soon as he was old enough for Legion ball, Freed began playing with the Smith & Peifly Juniors, who would go on to become Lehigh County's Junior Legion champions. Freed's brother was a pitcher for Allentown High, and the coach quickly noticed Eddie's catching abilities. While still in junior high, he became the first-string catcher for the Allentown High School team.

After high school, Freed began playing semi-pro ball for a team in Allentown. (Well, that isn't quite true—he actually started playing semi-pro ball during his last year of high school under the name "Al Reach." On paydays he would "earn" his money by sweeping the dugout.) The player/manager of the semi-pro team was a catcher, so Freed started playing left field—except on days that the team's knuckleballer pitched. On these days he would replace his manager behind the plate. His big break came in 1940, when he attended a tryout camp for the Trenton Senators. At that time Trenton, a member of the Class B Interstate League, had a working agreement with the Phillies. Freed was impressive enough in the tryout to be signed by the Senators as a catcher. Soon after he reported, however, manager Goose Goslin began playing him in the outfield. In his rookie year, the right-handed hitter batted a respectable .280 and was voted most popular Trenton player by the fans. His best year at Trenton was 1941, when he finished the season with a .286 average, 71 RBI, and was named to the All-Star team. He also helped lead Trenton to the league championship that year, where they were defeated by Harrisburg, 4 games to 3. In 1942, Freed was having a subpar year offensively, hitting only .248, when the Phillies bought his contract in September. The callup seemed to be just what he needed.

(left to right) Eddie Freed, Chino Bernal, and Ralph Rowe patrolled the outfield for the 1947 Rock Hill Chiefs.

September 11, 1942, found the Phillies 53½ games behind the league-leading Brooklyn Dodgers. Freed's chance came that day when manager Hans Lobert scheduled him to start in center field and hit out of the number two hole. When told that Vander Meer would be pitching for the Reds, Freed admits he got a little nervous. The only advice Lobert gave him was to "swing at anything." Lloyd "Little Poison" Waner, who had been helping Freed learn the hitters and pitchers, told him to watch out for Vander Meer's curve. Freed admits he was literally shaking as he carried his 35-ounce bat up to the plate and dug in for that first at-bat. Vander Meer delivered a fastball and Freed fouled it off. As Freed puts it: "I thought to myself, 'Well, that wasn't so fast.'" At that point he says he stopped shaking and everything was okay. Actually, it was more than okay. After working the count full, Freed stroked an inside fastball into left field for a double. Freed's 5' 6", 165-pound frame led one reporter of the day to describe him as a "pint-sized pack of dynamite." The 393 fans in attendance that afternoon at Shibe Park quickly found out why. In his next at-bat, Freed sliced another fastball from Vander Meer into the outfield for his second double. Before the day was done he added a triple, a single, scored two runs, and was intentionally walked once. The only thing that spoiled a perfect day for Freed was a shoestring catch by the Reds Eric Tipton on a ball that looked like it would drop in for a hit. Despite Freed's hitting, the Phillies ended up losing 8-5 in the 11th when Reds catcher Ray Lamanno put a 3-1 pitch from Rube Melton into the left-field stands. For the rest of the 1942 season, Freed proved that his first game performance wasn't a fluke. The next day he went 2 for 5 off the Reds' Elmer Riddle as he pounded out a single, a double, and scored the Phillies' only run. Freed ended up the 1942 season with a .303 batting average and was slated to be the Phillies starting center fielder in 1943. But Uncle Sam had other ideas. Little did Freed know that he had just completed his major league career.

In January of 1943, Freed was drafted into the Army. From then until his discharge in January of 1946, he spent time in North Carolina, Texas,

California, and the Philippines in positions ranging from M.P. to medical technician to mail clerk. He did manage to keep his baseball skills sharp by becoming player/manager of the Camp Stoneman baseball team in California. After his discharge, Freed spent the 1946 season playing for Eddie Sawyer on the Phillies Eastern League Class A farm team in Utica, where he finished the season with a .277 batting average. By this time, however, the Phillies had a new crop of young prospects, some of who would win fame as the "Whiz Kids" of 1950. In fact, the future Hall of Fame center fielder Ashburn had started his professional career at Utica in 1945 before spending most of 1946 in the Army. Seeing that he wasn't in the Phillies' plans for the future, Freed decided to retire from baseball. His retirement, however, was to be short-lived.

While in the Army stationed in Charlotte, NC, Freed had met and later married a girl from nearby Shelby. After his retirement, they decided to move back to the Charlotte area, where Freed was to work for the Lance Company and play on their semi-pro team. Soon after returning to Charlotte, however, Freed got a call from an old friend named Danny Carnevale. Carnevale had just been named manager of the nearby Rock Hill (SC) Chiefs—members of the Class B Tri-State League. After a little persuasion, he agreed to play for Carnevale and the Chiefs. Freed regained his old form in Rock Hill with a spectacular 1947 season. He led the league in fielding with a .992 percentage, led the Chiefs in hitting with a .324 average, batted in 97 runs, and was named to the Tri-State League All-Star team. His hitting led one opposing pitcher to complain, "I've thrown about everything to Freed and he's hit it all, high inside, low inside, high outside, low outside, down the middle." As if his hitting wasn't enough, Freed also did damage with his speed. In the 11th inning of a 4-4 game he stole home to give the Chiefs the win. When asked if the steal was his idea, Freed gave a sly smile and responded, "I'd been around a little longer than most of those fellows." Making his numbers even more impressive was the fact that he served part of the season as player/manager after Carnevale's resignation in July.

Freed followed with a .303 BA and 101 RBI performance in 1948, again while serving as player/manager during part of the season. Rock Hill made it to the league championship that year, only to be defeated by the Fayetteville Cubs 4 games to 1. After "slumping" to .292 with 85 RBIs in 1949, his contract was sold to nearby league rival Charlotte Hornets. Freed spent one year with Charlotte, hitting .280, before his contract was sold to the Reidsville Luckies of the Class B Carolina League. Freed decided that it was time to retire from baseball—this time for good.

Today, Freed spends more time on the golf course than the baseball diamond. Even though his major league career was shorter than he would have liked, he says he doesn't feel cheated. "I feel like I was one of the fortunate ones who made it to the big leagues," says Freed. And for a short time in 1942, the Phillies were glad he did.

IN OCTOBER 1911 *W. Hanna described Honus Wagner's batting form in the New York* Sun*:*

"Wagner's form varies according to his mood. Usually the great Dutchman stands with his feet well apart, but he can hit from any position and sometimes changes. His body is in his swing and his arms more so. Sometimes he swings so hard he all but falls down if he doesn't land, and sometimes he takes a slow swing.

"He is a batting genius who can afford to disregard canons about the ball coming over the plate and occasionally offers at balls over his head or across the plate from him. On a hit-and-run play he and Chase have been known to lunge across the plate and clout a near wild pitch safely past the infield." —NORMAN MACHT

Remembering the Chicago Black Sox

by Robert Jernigan

CHICAGO WHITE'S JOE FOOLISHLY GAMBLED WITH MOBSTER ROTHSTEIN. Yes, that first sentence reads like a poor headline, but it does describe the events surrounding the 1919 World Series in which the Chicago White Sox dumped the series to the Cincinnati Reds. Only eight descriptive words, but it also serves as a mnemonic for the players involved. Joe, of course, was "Shoeless" Joe Jackson, Chicago's heavy-hitting left fielder who received $5,000 for his involvement in the scheme to throw the series. Arnold Rothstein was the notorious New York gambler who financed and possibly orchestrated the fixing of the series by payoffs to Jackson and seven other Chicago players.

Most fans remember the names of Jackson and Rothstein, but who else was involved? Readers of Eliot Asinof's book *Eight Men Out* may well know some of the other players. But for others, here is where that awkward first sentence can help us remember not only who was involved but also something about their career statistics. The first letters of each of those eight words corresponds to the first letters of the last names of the eight players involved.

CHICAGO
"C" for pitcher Eddie Cicotte (career ERA 2.38)
WHITE'S
"W" for pitcher Lefty Williams (career ERA 3.13)
JOE
"J" for left fielder Joe Jackson (career BA .356)
FOOLISHLY
"F" for center fielder Oscar Felsch (career BA .293)
GAMBLED
"G" for first baseman Chick Gandil (career BA .277)
WITH
"W" for third baseman Buck Weaver (career BA .272)
MOBSTER
"M" for utility infielder Fred McMullin (career BA .256)
ROTHSTEIN
"R" for shortstop Swede Risberg (career BA .243)

The first two words correspond to pitchers Cicotte and Williams, listed by their career ERAs. The other six words indicate the players involved in the scandal listed by their career batting averages.

One sentence of eight words that describes the scandal serves as a mnemonic for the players involved, and ranks those players by their career statistics. This sentence is almost the Swiss Army mnemonic for remembering this ultimate baseball scandal.

Robert W. Jernigan is Professor of Statistics at American University in Washington, D.C.

The Surgeon General of Baseball

by William B. Mead

It was July 24, 1934. The doormat St. Louis Browns were hosting the proud New York Yankees at Sportsman's Park. Earle Combs, veteran Yankee center fielder, was playing left field in place of aging Babe Ruth, who had the day off. Sitting in the Knothole Gang in far left field was a disappointed youngster, Bob Broeg, who had hoped to see Ruth in what would be his final season in the American League. Sitting behind home plate in Box 50 was its usual occupant, Dr. Robert F. Hyland.

Harlond Clift of the Browns hit a drive to deep left center, and Combs sped after it. "He turned just in time to hit his head on that concrete wall," recalled Broeg, who grew up to become sports editor of the St. Louis *Post-Dispatch*. Combs fell unconscious. Bleeding from his nose, mouth, and a forehead wound, he was carried from the field on a stretcher.

Hyland went quickly to the Yankee clubhouse. "Maybe it was the budding sportswriter in me," said Broeg. "I raced under the stands and got there just as Dr. Hyland got into the ambulance with him." Combs' hair was prematurely gray. His face was white.

His skull was fractured. Hyland operated and stayed with Combs all that night and the next day, until the Yankee star was out of danger. Combs played no more that season, but returned to the Yankee outfield in 1935 before retiring, at age 36. He was elected to the Hall of Fame in 1970, lived until 1976, and credited Hyland with saving his life.

So did Hal Schumacher. "Prince Hal," a star pitcher for the New York Giants of the 1930s, collapsed on the mound on a brutally hot St. Louis afternoon. Again an unconscious player was carried to the clubhouse, and again Hyland was there to treat him.

Today's leading practitioners of sports medicine, such as Dr. Frank Jobe and Dr. James Andrews, are specialists who have devised innovative surgical techniques. Hyland was a surgeon, but like most physicians of his day he treated maladies of all kinds. He earned his living as physician for the St. Louis Public Service Company, which ran the city's bus and streetcar lines.

"He had a corner office on the second floor of the streetcar barn, off Grand Avenue," recalled Marty Marion, the legendary Cardinal shortstop of the 1940s. Marion had a bad back—"a horrible back," he called it—as a result of a childhood injury. When the Cardinals were at home, Marion would often climb the stairs to Hyland's office for diathermy treatments.

Ty Cobb climbed those stairs. So did Babe Ruth, Lou Gehrig, Dizzy Dean, Pepper Martin, Stan Musial, and hundreds of other players. As a baseball physician, Hyland's career spanned 36 years, from 1914 until his death in 1950 at age 64.

Hyland was certainly history's most prominent and beloved baseball physician, so it is no surprise that he was discovered by Branch Rickey, manager of the

William B. Mead is an award-winning journalist and the author of Only the Browns. *He was growing up in St. Louis when the Browns played the Cardinals in the 1944 World Series.*

Browns in 1914 and 1915 before moving to the Cardinals. Hyland, once a minor league first baseman, was an avid fan of the Browns and Cardinals. Rickey asked him if he would moonlight as team doctor for the Browns. Certainly, Hyland replied. But I will take no money for my services to ballplayers.

He never did, even after adding the Cardinals to his roster of patients and, before long, becoming the doctor that every ailing ballplayer came to see. "He was the number one physician for athletes in this country," said Bob Bauman, whose career as trainer for the Browns and then the Cardinals spanned 53 years. "I worked with him. He was tops. All the players from other clubs, whenever they got into St. Louis, they'd go see Dr. Hyland."

Hyland's skills went beyond his clinical expertise. "He was a great worker on the mind," said Robert L. Burnes, retired sports editor of the St. Louis *Globe-Democrat*. "He'd talk to the guys and convince them they could do great things."

Marion agreed. "He was kind of the father of goodwill and health to the whole Cardinal team. You'd go in to see Dr. Hyland and he'd talk about your marriage, your life. He was a goodwill ambassador, a counselor."

Late in his career, Hyland addressed the American College of Surgeons, telling his colleagues about his work. "Ballplayers as a class are quite amenable to suggestions as to injuries," he said. "They can be talked into hurts, and they can also be talked out of them. There was one great player who didn't need any imagination to give him cuts and bruises aplenty. Ty Cobb. I treated Cobb at the height of his career. He would come to me with his body fairly covered with bruises and abrasions, from his skull down to his toes."

Hyland saved the careers of many players, and gave a career to at least one future Hall of Famer. In the mid-1930s, Johnny Mize was a promising slugger with Rochester, New York, a top Cardinal farm team. But Mize couldn't stoop; his pelvis was damaged from years of riding mules and horses bareback in his Georgia boyhood. The Cards sold him to Cincinnati, giving the Reds the option of returning him. The Reds quickly gave up on Mize, and the Cardinals sent their damaged young first baseman to Hyland.

"It was my most difficult operation," Hyland said. "Mize was returned because he had growths in both crotches. These were shaped like icicles and extended into the musculature of both thighs. Cavalrymen are subjected to this trouble. It was a tough job to remove these growths from such a difficult spot."

Restored to health, Mize took over first base for the Cards in 1936 and quickly became one of baseball's top sluggers, leading the National League in home runs and batting in 1939, and in homers and RBI in 1940. Rickey, following his usual practice, sold Mize to the New York Giants in 1942, netting $50,000 and two players for a first baseman whom Hyland had fixed free of charge. Mize went on to win two home run championships for the Giants, and to stay with the Yankees as a first baseman and pinch-hitter.

When Dizzy Dean hurt his arm in 1937, it was Hyland who diagnosed the ailment, and predicted that Dean's pitching days were numbered. The Chicago Cubs were told of Hyland's findings, but nevertheless gave the Cardinals three players and $185,000 for the colorful pitcher. The Cubs should have heeded Hyland; Ol' Diz was washed up.

In 1941, the Cardinals feared that arm trouble might ruin the career of another young pitching star when Mort Cooper came down with an ailing elbow. Rest didn't cure it. Hyland operated, and Cooper came back better than ever. In 1942 he won 22 games, pitched ten shutouts, and led the National League with an ERA of 1.78. Cooper was named the league's Most Valuable Player. Hyland was satisfied with a plaque from the 1941 Cardinals, a team that had been riddled with injuries. It read:

"To Robert F. Hyland. We dedicate this plaque as a token of our esteem. His athletic background, his years of experience in medicine and surgery, his deep understanding of baseball men and the game they play make him indispensable and very dear to all of us. To which we attach our signatures."

Commissioner Landis attached something more lasting to Hyland—an enduring nickname. The occasion was a happy one for St. Louis fans, because the Cardinals had just won the 1942 World Series, closing out the favored Yankees in New York.

"We were coming home from the 1942 World Series," recalled Burnes of the *Globe-Democrat*. "Hyland was on the Cardinal train, and Landis rode with us. The train stopped in Indianapolis, and I went for a walk on the platform with Hyland and Landis." The commissioner was praising the modest doctor's accomplishments, and turned to Burnes for emphasis. "He's the surgeon general of baseball!" Landis said. "I looked at him," Burnes recalled, "and he said, 'Well, he is, isn't he?'" Burnes related the incident in his column, and Hyland was forever after referred to as the Surgeon General of Baseball. Not even Dr. Jobe can claim such a sobriquet.

Hyland enjoyed a good time, too. He went to work early, and usually was able to get away in time for the afternoon game at Sportsman's Park. He was a diabolical practical jokester, often working in partnership with Clarence Lloyd, a Cardinal administrator with great skill in mimicking, or creating, accents and dialects.

One day a lion escaped from the St. Louis Zoo, swam the Mississippi River, and took refuge on a wooded, uninhabited island. Hyland persuaded two friends, both prosperous businessmen, to join him in hiring a noted European zoologist who would capture the lion and return it to the zoo—for a profitable fee.

Lloyd played the zoologist, using a phony accent as he educated Hyland's unsuspecting friends on the habits, diet, dangers, and diseases of the lion, all made up. One lesson followed another, day after day, the unwary investors hoping the zoologist would finally shut up and close in for the capture. In fact, not even real experts could trap the poor lion; it eventually was shot.

Hyland enjoyed a drink, too, as did Frankie Frisch, the star second baseman of three Cardinal championship teams in the 1930s. "He and Frank Frisch were great drinking buddies," recalled Bob Broeg. "They'd close the Coal Hole bar at the old Coronado Hotel many a night. Frisch was a great longhair music buff. He'd get Max Steindel, a cellist for the St. Louis Symphony, to play for him and Hyland in the bar."

In an early version of today's fantasy camps, Hyland also took occasional infield practice with three friends while the Cardinal players were off the field. His colleagues were Sam Breadon, owner of the Cardinals; George Vierheller, a noted curator of the St. Louis Zoo; and Sam Muchnik, a sportswriter turned wrestling promoter.

In Hyland's time, the established medical practice called for long periods of hospital recuperation after surgery. Hyland didn't believe in it. He was way ahead of his time in urging patients to get out of bed and get moving. "He took my appendix out," said Marty Marion. "I think it was 1941. I got a stomach ache one night and I called him up and he said, 'Come on over.' He took it out and I was back playing in four or five days."

The prognosis was more severe for Musial in 1947. The Cardinal great was off to a slow start, hitting under .200, when appendicitis felled him in New York. Stan the Man wanted to go home to Dr. Hyland, and Del Wilber, a reserve catcher, accompanied Musial on a special flight to St. Louis. Hyland met the plane with an ambulance, accompanied Musial to the hospital, and examined him. Bob Broeg picks up the story. "He said to Stan, 'If I operate you'll be out a couple of weeks. But I believe I can freeze it, and take it out after the season.'"

Musial missed two days, and then his batting average began to climb. After the off-season surgery, he felt unusually strong in 1948 and had his best season, leading the league in batting, runs, hits, doubles, triples, total bases, RBI, and falling one short of the league lead in homers.

Perhaps Hyland's most famous piece of medical advice was ignored by the patient. In the fifth game of the 1946 World Series, a fastball from Joe Dobson of the Red Sox hit the Cards' Enos Slaughter on the right elbow. The arm swelled badly, and the pain kept Slaughter awake on the overnight sleeper to St. Louis.

Slaughter went to St. John's Hospital, where Hyland examined his elbow and had it X-rayed. In his autobiography, Slaughter related his conversation.

Hyland: "I sure hate to tell you this, but you just can't play in the Series any more."

GENE KARST, a SABR senior statesman at 96, served as the Cardinals' publicity director in 1931-1932 and knew Hyland. He relates this story, told to him by Clarence Lloyd, the team's traveling secretary going back to Branch Rickey's years as Cardinal field manager from 1919 until 1925.

Rickey, the indefatigable moralist, liked to lecture young players on the value of abstinence and other virtues. He was delivering this lecture to Cliff Heathcote, playing his first full season in the majors in 1919, when Heathcote broke in, saying: "But, Mr. Rickey, I have to tell you my immediate problem. I have the clap!"

Rickey, the story goes, exploded in anger and called Hyland. "Bob, I'm sending you a young ballplayer named Heathcote," he said. "He doesn't know how to take care of his pecker. And when he gets to your office I want you to cut it off! Cut it off!"

Heathcote turned white, Lloyd remembered. Hyland's medical ethics no doubt overcame Rickey's order.

Slaughter: "I'm playing."

Hyland: "The hemorrhaging around your elbow is really bad. If it were to be hit against the ground, with another ball or against the fence, you'd be through as a player. I mean it. In fact, I'd have to amputate your arm."

Slaughter: "I'm just going to have to take that chance. If I can swing a bat, I'll be out there."

Slaughter singled home a run in the sixth game as the Cards tied the Series. In the seventh game, with the score even, Slaughter led off the home eighth with a single. After two outs, Harry Walker doubled, and Slaughter scored the decisive run on his "mad dash home," one of the most dramatic and famous plays in Series history. Sliding home, Slaughter was careful not to bump his bad elbow.

The last ballplayer treated by Hyland was pitcher Virgil (Fire) Trucks of the Detroit Tigers, whose arm went dead after pitching a 13-inning shutout early in the 1950 season. After a series in St. Louis that August, the Tigers left Trucks and another sore-armed pitcher, Ted Gray, behind for treatment by Hyland.

Hyland died of liver disease and uremia on December 14, 1950. Trucks was back to full strength by mid-1951. He quickly became the ace of the staff. In 1952 he pitched two no-hitters, the second one on August 25 against the Yankees. He called that game a memorial "to the greatest friend any ballplayer ever had."

"It has been almost as if a little of Dr. Hyland was living in me," Trucks continued. "He did so much for so many of us."

But not for himself. The Internal Revenue Service sued Hyland's small estate for allegedly unpaid taxes. Why, an interviewer asked him five years before his death, did he devote so much time and skill to ballplayers, without pay?

"I like to," he replied. "It's my hobby. My love for baseball is old and deep and sincere. . . . Wealth never fascinated me. Medical problems always have. But I've found it impossible to put a price on something that brings me happiness and sometimes helps avert tragedy."

Anyway, he got that wonderful nickname from Landis. And he always was welcome in Box 50 at Sportsman's Park—and anywhere else that ballplayers gathered.

DOC HYLAND'S EIGHT COMMANDMENTS

Dr. Robert Hyland was an early exponent of preventative medicine, and wrote out a sheet of "eight commandments" for young ballplayers. Copies were prominently posted in clubhouses throughout the major leagues. The text:

It is necessary for a player to be mentally and physically alert. Therefore, these rules are important. The player should keep himself fit in the off-season and follow the rules which were formulated in the playing season. He should learn to take care of his eyes at all times. They are very important in his profession, and yearly examination of the eyes is advisable.

1. **Pay strict attention to diet.** Do not eat too much. Do not mix foods that won't go together. You can get along without lobster, shrimp and other seafoods in places which have to bring them a long way. And eating eggs, too, can be overdone.
2. **Watch your elimination.** A clogged system means a clogged brain, and a clogged brain means a tough day.
3. **Sleep is important.** Eight, nine, ten hours of it. After a double-header, ten hours. The sleep that comes between midnight and 8 in the morning is the ballplayers' sleep.
4. **No ballplayer is any better than his legs.** Watch them. After a game, lie down and raise your legs on pillows for 30 minutes.
5. **Learn the proper way to run.** Most leg injuries and other hurts, too, are traced to the fact that the player did not know how to run correctly, or that he did not know how to slide or touch bases properly.
6. **Never hide an injury from your manager.** If hurt, see a surgeon at once. Have x-rays taken immediately.
7. **Don't be stupid about sex.** Physical troubles tracing to this factor are inexcusable and should be dealt with by managers quite harshly. Venereal diseases have ruined the careers of many potentially great athletes. Do not be a fool in this respect or your future may be ruined.
8. **Don't douse yourself with liniments, hot lotions.** Don't bind your ankles and knees. Don't neglect sprains, but binding them to stop circulation is not the treatment. Tie up with a reputable surgeon.

The Year Penn Hosted the Phillies

by David S. Rich

The freshmen in Penn's lower Quadrangle may not know it, but they reside on a significant site of major league baseball history.

In August 1894, a fire destroyed Huntington Street Grounds, the ballpark of the city's major league baseball team, the Philadelphia Phillies. While the ballpark was being rebuilt, the Phillies played their next six home games at the University of Pennsylvania's Varsity Grounds at 37th and Spruce Streets. These games were the first major league baseball games ever played on a university's field. The move to Penn was a natural one for the Phillies, because the coach of Penn's varsity baseball team was also the Phillies' manager, and because Penn's team frequently played exhibition games against the Phillies.

Varsity Grounds was such a hitters' ballfield that, in their one-week sojourn at Penn, the Phillies set two single-game offensive records which still stand today. The 1894 Phillies tenure at Penn also helped the team and its individual players set numerous extant single-season offensive records, at least one of which will never be broken.

The Dead Ball—In 1894, home runs were a relative rarity in major league baseball. There was an average of about one home run every two games.

Despite the absence of the long ball, hitters unleashed the greatest offensive onslaught in major league history. The National League averaged .309, and each game averaged 15 runs and 22 hits. Prior to the 1893 season, the National League lengthened the pitcher's distance from the rear corner of home plate from an effective distance of about 55 feet to the pitcher's current distance of 60 feet and six inches. (Colleges, including Penn, quickly complied with the National League's new pitching distance.) Hurlers had yet to adjust to the longer distance, which tilted the offense-defense balance in favor of the batter.

The 1894 Phillies—1894 was the Phillies' 12th season in Philadelphia, and they had yet to win a pennant. The team played its home games at Huntington Street Grounds, also known as the Philadelphia Base Ball Park. Huntington Street Grounds was located on an odd-shaped lot bounded by Broad Street, Lehigh Avenue, 15th Street, and Huntington Avenue in North Philadelphia. Originally built at a cost of $101,000, the park when it opened in 1887 was regarded as the premier stadium in the country, a stupendous showplace that was the pride of Philadelphia.

The Phillies home games started at either 3:00 or 3:15 p.m. Pennsylvania's blue laws prohibited games on Sundays, so the team often staged doubleheaders drawing packed houses on Saturdays. The Phillies were baseball's most popular team, leading the National League in attendance in 1890, 1891 and 1893. In 1894, the Philadelphia franchise would

David S. Rich is an associate of the law firm of Hellring Lindeman Goldstein & Siegal LLP in Newark, New Jersey. He and his wife, Galit Rich, nee *Chinitz, live in Manhattan.*

attract 352,773 spectators, or 5,469 fans per game.

The heart of the 1894 Phillies was their hard-hitting outfield, which was and remains one of the greatest of all time. The Phillies' left fielder was 26-year-old Edward James ("Big Ed") Delahanty. Delahanty, who stood 6'1" and weighed 170 pounds, was a natural right-handed hitter who had power to all fields. He was a dangerous bad ball hitter, waving a long heavy bat that would reach any pitch thrown anywhere. In 1893, Delahanty had led the league in home runs (19), runs batted in (146), and slugging percentage (.583).

Off the field Delahanty was a strutter, gathering a cluster of admirers as he passed from one saloon to another. He knew where the best corned beef and cabbage could be found in every city. A free spender, he was perpetually broke.

William Robert ("Sliding Billy") Hamilton, age 28, patrolled center field. Hamilton stood 5'6" and weighed 165 pounds. Despite his stocky build, he was the most daring, crowd-pleasing base runner of the 19th century. By 1894 Hamilton had swiped 100 or more bases in each of three different seasons. He was fearless on the basepaths, sliding head-first into bases during a period when that tactic was likely to draw a knee in the neck and a tag between the eyes. At the bat, Hamilton was a masterful poke hitter.

Samuel Luther ("Big Sam") Thompson, age 34, manned right field. Thompson, a Goliath in his time, stood 6'2" and weighed 207 pounds. Before he was a professional ballplayer, Thompson was a carpenter and roofer in Danville, Indiana. Thompson was a prolific run producer who at the time held the single-season RBI record, having driven in 166 runs for the pennant-winning Detroit Wolverines in 1887. He possessed an unusual left-handed batting stance. He began in an extreme crouch and, then, as the ball neared the plate, he uncoiled and leaped at the pitch, swinging from his heels.

Thompson was a quiet, sober man who never argued with the umpires or got in any brawls. But he gradually became the Phillies' team leader and spokesman. In 1894 he openly criticized the Phillies' owners for providing the players second-rate railroad and hotel accommodations, and pledged to quit the team unless things improved. They did. Thompson was also a favorite of the fans.

The weakness of the 1894 Phillies was their pitching staff, which was among the league's worst. Their only above-average pitcher was 21-year-old John Budd ("Brewery Jack") Taylor, whose nickname derived from his heavy drinking habit.

The 1894 Phillies manager was the always nattily dressed Arthur Albert Irwin, age 36. Irwin, a Toronto native, had as a youngster moved with his family to South Boston, where he began playing with strong amateur teams. From 1880 to 1891 Irwin played shortstop for five major league clubs, including three pennant winners. In his playing days he was a steady though unspectacular hitter, a reliable fielder, and a good baserunner. He is generally credited with inventing, in 1885, the modern (padded) fielder's glove.

Outside the ballpark, Irwin led a double life. Irwin had a legal wife, Lizzie Irwin, in Boston. Irwin and his legal wife had a son, Arthur Herbert Irwin, who was 10 years old in 1894. Beginning around 1891, Irwin also maintained a common-law "wife" in Manhattan. In 1893 or 1894, Irwin had a son, F. Harold Irwin, with the New York Mrs. Irwin. Irwin also eventually had two daughters by the New York woman. His two families did not learn of one another's existence until the 1920s.

Penn's 1894 Varsity Baseball Team—Arthur Irwin was also the coach of Penn's 1894 varsity baseball team, a post he had held since 1892. Irwin is credited with first making the Red and Blue an important team on the intercollegiate circuit in the early 1890s. Irwin's duties consisted of drilling and supervising the varsity squad in preseason practices held during February and March. (College baseball teams did not have full-time field coaches until about 1910.)

Penn's varsity baseball team played its home games at Varsity Grounds, also known as University Grounds. Varsity Grounds was a field bounded by 37th Street, Spruce Street, 36th Street, and Pine Street. The grounds were prepared at a cost of $15,000. Since 1885 all of Penn's baseball games, football matches, and athletic sports had been held at this site. The grandstands stretched in an L on the west and north sides of a first-class oval cinder track which enclosed a football field with a good baseball diamond at the west end. By 1894 the grandstands were covered.

The baseball field at Varsity Grounds was oriented such that the batter faced east or southeast. According to the Washington *Post*, "the man who could put a ball over . . . [Varsity Grounds'] center field fence on the fly would be a second Samson." By contrast, Varsity Grounds' left-field and right-field fences were each but a short distance from home plate. There was an embankment in left field, and one in right field as well.

The baseball field at Varsity Grounds heavily favored hitters. In the Penn baseball team's games there from 1885 to 1894 (Varsity Grounds' ten full seasons as Penn's home ballfield), Penn and its opponents together averaged 19.52 runs per game. By contrast, during the same 10-year period, in the Penn varsity squad's games at its opponents' home fields or at neutral sites, Penn and its adversaries together tallied only 13.96 runs per game.

Penn's 1894 varsity baseball team was the university's greatest ever up to that time. The team, which was distinguished by its terrific batting, included four future major league ballplayers. The team's brightest star was its center fielder, Roy Allen Thomas, who turned 20 years old during the season. In games that year against other college teams, Thomas, who stood 5'11" and weighed 150 pounds, stole 19 bases and compiled a staggering .585 batting average. Four years later, *Sporting Life* called Thomas "the greatest amateur player of this generation." Thomas went on to become a stellar outfielder and leadoff hitter for the Phillies in a 13-year major league career. Other standouts, each of whom would reach the big leagues for a single year, were Penn's first baseman, William John ("Billy") Goeckel; one of the 1894 varsity squad's pitchers, righthander Andrew Cotwell ("Andy") Boswell; and catcher Daniel George ("Dan") Coogan.

Penn's 1894 team also featured a 22-year-old substitute outfielder, Pearl Zane Gray. Two decades hence, Gray's fame would dwarf that of his major league-bound brethren, but not because of Gray's prowess on the diamond. Gray, a native Ohioan, played in only two games for Penn in 1894, but would be a starting outfielder for the university in 1895 and 1896. Gray would also play for the Findlay (Ohio) Sluggers of the Interstate League, a minor league, during the summer of 1895. Beginning in 1902, under the name Zane Grey, he would write a total of 89 books, 56 of which were Western novels, plus four collections of novelettes and short stories. Grey's wildly popular books have sold more than 130 million copies and have been the basis for over 100 movies.

Since 1886 Penn's varsity squad had periodically played, and invariably lost, exhibition games against the Phillies on each team's home fields. In 1894, from March 26 to April 7, the Red and the Blue and the Phillies scrimmaged six times. The most memorable of that year's exhibition games from Penn's perspective took place on Thursday, April 5, before 1,000 people at Varsity Grounds. In the first inning, Penn scored two runs off rookie Phillies pitcher Nixey Callahan on a walk and a wild throw. The collegians maintained a lead throughout the game. Thomas led the university's offense, slugging a triple and a long double. In the third inning, Coogan smacked a three-run home-run drive over Delahanty's head and to the left-field fence. Penn's starting pitcher, A. King Dickson, frustrated the professionals with his slow high and inside pitching, allowing only one run and no hits in a five-inning appearance. Penn won the game, 12 to 8, infusing the university's students with glee. The April 5 game was the first and only victory by Penn over the Phillies.

The Phillies convincingly defeated Penn in the team's other five matchups that year by scores of 13-9, 14-7, 16-9, 10-3, and 9-2.

The Ballpark a Heap of Ashes—By Monday, August 6, 1894, the Phillies had compiled a 43-38 record. They were in sixth place in the National League, 10 games behind the first-place, defending pennant winners, the Boston Beaneaters. That morning, the Phillies were at Huntington Street Grounds preparing for a home afternoon doubleheader with the second-place Baltimore Orioles. At 10:30, Phillies pitcher Taylor and another person noticed a fire in the grandstand. Taylor and fellow Phillies pitcher John Fanning raced to the fire and tried unsuccessfully to extinguish it.

The fire rapidly spread to other parts of the mostly wooden ballpark. "Run for your clothes," someone yelled. The players ran to the clubhouse while much of the rest of the stadium burst into flames. The players stumbled to the street through smoke and flames. Eventually all of the team members reached safety.

Fire companies responded rapidly. Soon every available department in the city had hurried firefighters and equipment to the scene as the conflagration raged out of control. The blaze took several hours to put out. By then not only Huntington Street Grounds but a nearby company with stables for 340 or 350 horses, several stores, and three or four houses had been destroyed. The approximate damage was $250,000.

The cause of the fire was never discovered. The most probable explanation, which eventually gained general acceptance, was that it was caused by a torch that a plumber was using to make repairs.

Workers toiled day and night to rebuild the park. Meanwhile, on Tuesday, August 7, the Phillies signed an agreement with the Bank Clerks' Athletic Association, which had a lease on Penn's Varsity

Grounds. Under the agreement, the Phillies were to play a doubleheader with the Washington Senators on Saturday, August 11. Ultimately, the Phillies would play six consecutive home games at Varsity Grounds.

Penn Hosts the Phillies—Before coming to Varsity Grounds, the Phillies embarked on a brief road trip. On the night of August 6, the Phillies left Philadelphia for Boston. From Tuesday, August 7, through Thursday, August 9, at Boston's South End Grounds III, the scorched Philadelphians dropped two out of three slugfests to the champion Beaneaters. The Phillies then headed for Washington, where, on August 10, they were upset in a 4-1 pitchers battle by the twelfth- and last-place Senators.

On the afternoon of Saturday, August 11, the Phillies and the Senators changed venues, facing off in the arranged-for doubleheader at Varsity Grounds. The double bill constituted the first major league baseball games ever played on a college's field.

Given that Penn's football season was to begin soon, the university's authorities were concerned that the Phillies' spectators would damage Varsity Grounds' turf. To prevent the crowds from encroaching on the field and tearing up the sod, ropes were extended all around the oval cinder track from both ends of the grandstand. An ample number of police officers were charged with keeping fans outside the roped-off space.

Hometown fans numbering 4,848, a large crowd for the era, turned out to see Saturday's unprecedented event. Varsity Grounds' modest seating accommodations were extended to their limit, and the overflow lined up around the cinder track. The teams established ground rules on balls hit into the crowd encircling the field. Because Varsity Grounds' right-field fence was so close to home plate, the teams agreed that a hit clearing that fence to the right of a certain point in right field fair territory would be a double rather than a home run.

In the opener, young Phillies ace Brewery Jack Taylor outpitched Senators hurler Mike Sullivan, 10 to 7. The Phillies pounded Sullivan, hitting safely 15 times. Thompson was the game's hero, rapping five straight hits, including a double and a triple. Taylor held the Senators to ten hits, of which left fielder Kip Selbach contributed three, a double and two triples. Senators third baseman Bill Joyce whacked a two-run homer over the right-field fence and to the roof of the veterinary department on Pine Street.

The Phillies also won Saturday's second game, sending the fans home in a state of jubilation. Gus Weyhing pitched a fine game for the Phillies, limiting the visitors to four scattered hits. The Phillies solved Al Maul's curveball, whacking 22 hits. Delahanty belted two singles, a line drive over the right-field fence counting for a double, and a two-run ground-rule triple into the crowd in back of left field. Hamilton smacked three singles and a three bagger. Thompson swatted two singles and a bases-loaded triple, and he, Hamilton, and Senators left fielder Selbach made brilliant catches. At 6:15 p.m., after Washington batted in the top of the seventh inning, the umpire, Bob Emslie, called the game on account of darkness.

According to the Washington *Post*, many of the grounders that were credited as hits that Saturday afternoon would have ordinarily been easy outs, because the grounds were hard and "the balls sailed over the infielders' heads like a hard rubber ball being bounced on a piece of marble."

The Phillies were scheduled to play another doubleheader with Washington at Varsity Grounds on August 13, but the twin bill was postponed on account of rain.

On Tuesday, August 14, before a crowd of 2,200, the Phillies opened a four-game series at Varsity Grounds against the eleventh-place Louisville Colonels.

In Tuesday's game, the Colonels bashed six home runs off Phillies twirler Kid Carsey on the way to an improbable 13-7 triumph over the Philadelphians. In their victory, the Colonels took full advantage of Varsity Grounds' short right-field fence. The visitors got five hits over it, four of which—including two by Colonels center fielder Tom Brown—counted for home runs. About three of Louisville's round-trippers would have been outs on a larger field. Colonels southpaw pitcher Phil Knell led his team at the plate, knocking a home run into the left-field grandstand, a triple and a single. The Colonels scored four runs in the top of the first, and held the lead throughout the game.

Delahanty hit the ball hard all day, smacking two triples and a double. Phillies shortstop Joe Sullivan's one-handed catch of Louisville first baseman Luke Lutenberg's liner in the ninth was the fielding feature of the game.

On Wednesday, August 15, the Phillies easily defeated the Colonels, 14 to 4. The Phillies' victory placed them in a dead heat with the Pittsburgh Pirates for fifth place in the league. Only 1,500 fans turned out for the game, but the assemblage was a great deal more boisterous than it was large. The game was close for five innings, but after that the Phillies connected on Colonels hurler George Hemming's curves, and batted home many earned runs. The Colonels touched Phillies ace Jack Taylor for three runs early, but as the game wore on Taylor grew more effective, and in the last four innings he held Louisville hitless.

The Phillies knocked 17 hits, with Joe Sullivan leading with a double and two singles. Thompson socked two triples, Cross belted a home run and two singles, Hamilton rapped a home run and a single, and Taylor and Phillies first baseman Jack Boyle hit a triple and a single apiece. The Phillies also played excellently in the field. They chose to go to bat first, an order they maintained during their remaining two games at Varsity Grounds.

The next day, Thursday, August 16, in perfect game weather and in view of 1,400 fans, the Phillies mauled Louisville, 17 to 3. (The lackluster turnout prompted the Phillies to redouble their efforts to rebuild Huntington Street Grounds, where the team's rooters would turn out in greater numbers.) The one-sided beating earned Arthur Irwin's men sole possession of fifth place. Philadelphia pounded Colonels southpaw hurler George Nicol for 19 hits. Sullivan headed the home team's assault with a triple, two singles, and a home run, and he was closely followed by Cross with three singles and a home run. Despite the Phillies' imposing run total, the game's fielding was sharp, with Philadelphia turning four double plays and Louisville turning two. Delahanty made a superb running catch and fired to second to trap a runner off base. Weyhing pitched another good game, holding the Senators to nine scattered hits.

On Friday, August 17, in their final game at Varsity Grounds, the Phillies put on a display of batting feats not bested before or since. Before a crowd of 1,200, the Phillies crushed the Colonels by a score of 29 to 4, sending at least one runner home in every inning save one. Reported the Philadelphia *Inquirer*, "At the end of the game [Colonels] Pitcher [Bill] Wadsworth's arm hung limp and the Louisville fielders' tongues were hanging out, the result of their running after long hits."

The Phillies smacked 36 hits, setting a major league record for hits by a team in one game. In the 108 years since, no team has ever matched this mark.

The Phillies connected for 28 singles, establishing a major league record for singles by a team in one game. The Boston Beaneaters would tie this record in an 1896 game against the Baltimore Orioles, but no team has ever bested it.

Sam Thompson led the Phillies' onslaught. He went 6 for 7 and hit for the cycle, belting three singles, a double, a triple, and a home run to right-center field. Sullivan rapped four singles and a two-bagger, and Phils catcher Mike Grady made the same record. Hamilton hit five singles, Phillies pitcher Carsey knocked three singles and a double, and Delahanty made four singles. Boyle whacked a double and two singles, and also stole three bases.

Carsey pitched an excellent game and held the Colonels to eight hits. Louisville made two runs in the fourth inning on a walk and Grim's home run over the left-field grandstand, and two in the sixth on a two-bagger by Brown, a single by Clarke, and an errant throw by Sullivan. Colonels third baseman Pat Flaherty's fielding and his one-handed grab of a line drive from Cross's bat were the defensive highlights of the game.

In their torrid six-game stretch at Varsity Grounds, the Phillies won five games, outscored their adversaries 93 runs to 35, belted 119 hits (including 84 singles), and batted .458. Hamilton scored 13 runs. Thompson drove in at least 12 runs, and probably several more.

A Season Without Parallel—The Phillies returned to Huntington Street Grounds on August 18 with a victory over the fourth-place Cleveland Spiders. Spectators sat in temporary bleachers that seated 9,000. The park employed the temporary bleachers for the remainder of the season.

The Phillies played well for the balance of the season, ending the year in fourth place with a 71-57 record. The Baltimore Orioles won the pennant by three games over the New York Giants, who overtook fading Boston. The second-place Giants then swept the favored Orioles, four games to none, in the first Temple Cup series.

With a boost from the six-game offensive barrage at Varsity Grounds, the Phillies team, and Phillies Billy Hamilton and Sam Thompson individually, set single-season offensive major league records during the 1894 season which survive today. Aided by their .458 clip at Varsity Grounds, the Phillies as a team batted an all-time best .349. No team has ever, or will ever, best Philadelphia's mark; not since the 1950 Boston Red Sox hit .302 has a big league team even batted .300. Thompson, who batted .407, Delahanty (.407), and Hamilton (.404), made up the only .400-hitting outfield in major league history. Phillies 21-year-old utility outfielder George A. ("Tuck") Turner bested all three of them, compiling a .416 average.

Including the 84 singles the 1894 Phillies rapped at Varsity Grounds, the team hit a record 1,309 singles that year. This mark survives today, even though the major leagues lengthened the season from 132 games to 154 by the dawn of the 20th century and from 154 games to 162 in 1961.

Abetted by the 13 runs he scored in six games at Penn, Billy Hamilton scored a record 192 runs during the 1894 season. Notwithstanding today's longer seasons, no player has ever seriously challenged "Sliding Billy"'s all-time high.

Boosted by the 12 or more runs he batted home at Varsity Grounds, Sam Thompson, in the 99 games he played, batted in an astonishing 141 runs. "Big Sam" thus drove in 1.42 runs per game he played in 1894, a single-season record which still stands.

Afterword—In 1893, the university's trustees, desiring the Varsity Grounds field for new dormitories, had set aside land at 33rd and Spruce Streets upon which the Athletic Association of the university was authorized to lay out new athletic grounds to be called Franklin Field. At first the only structures erected were a cinder track and a level field for baseball and football, with a wooden grandstand on the south side. These facilities were formally opened on April 20, 1895, with the first running of the Intercollegiate and Interscholastic Relay Races, the inaugural "Penn Relays."

Penn's 1895 varsity baseball team played its first three home games at Varsity Grounds. The Penn squad then relocated for good to Franklin Field.

In the mid-1890s, Varsity Grounds was used for the first of the Dormitory Quadrangles which today constitute "The Quad."

Pledging that there would be no more fires at the Phillies' home park, Phillies president and principal owner Al Reach erected a new ballpark, using mostly steel and brick, on the site of its destroyed predecessor. The park, which opened on May 2, 1895, was again called Huntington Street Grounds, or the Philadelphia Base Ball Park. As it was the first time, the ballpark was hailed as the most modern in baseball and a showplace that was both the pride of the city and an attraction which tourists made special journeys up Broad Street to view.

Arthur Irwin managed the Phillies to a third-place finish in the 1895 season, upon which the team fired him for failing to bring home a pennant. Unfazed by his sacking, Irwin went on to pilot the New York Giants and the Washington Senators. Irwin coached Penn's varsity baseball team through the 1902 season. He then relinquished control to his former star player Roy Thomas (then playing for the Phillies) and N.P. Stauffer. Thomas and Stauffer coached the 1903 Penn squad, and then handed over Penn's reins to Thomas's former college teammate Dan Coogan.

Irwin remained active in baseball throughout the first two decades of the twentieth century. He owned, operated, and managed a string of minor league teams, including clubs at Toronto, Rochester, Kansas City, Altoona, Lewiston, and Hartford, Connecticut. He also served as the head scout of the American League's New York Highlanders from 1908 to 1912.

By 1921, Irwin, then 63 years of age, was a wealthy man. On June 21, Irwin, suffering from abdominal trouble and severe nervous attacks, was admitted for several weeks to a Hartford hospital. The illness forced him to quit his post as the Hartford club's manager. According to Irwin's statement to J.H. Clarkin, owner of the Hartford team, the hospital's doctors diagnosed him with terminal cancer. At the hospital, Irwin was told that only a serious operation would prolong his life beyond two months. On or about Thursday, July 14, 1921, in New York, Irwin boarded the Metropolitan Line steamship *Calvin Austin*, bound for his Boston home. He reportedly stated to a fellow passenger that he was "going home to die." Irwin was aboard the steamer with a party of friends; the friends later stated that, before midnight, when Irwin left them, he was depressed. When the steamer docked in Boston on the morning of Saturday, July 16, 1921, Irwin was no longer aboard. His baggage and some of the clothing he had worn were found in his stateroom. Apparently, Irwin committed suicide by jumping into the Atlantic. His body was never found. Upon Irwin's presumptive death, his double life was exposed, with his Boston and New York families, to their amazement and dismay, discovering one another's existence.

Irwin was elected to the Canadian Baseball Hall of Fame in 1989. Ed Delahanty, Billy Hamilton, and Sam Thompson were posthumously inducted into the National Baseball Hall of Fame in Cooperstown, New York in 1945, 1961, and 1974, respectively.

Baseball 1897—A Second Opinion

Contributed by A. Thomas Wallace

Charlotte Hall, St. Mary's Co.
June 28th, 1897

My dear Miss Reba,

It seems that every project in which I am at all interested comes to an untimely end. The lawn fete to which I was looking forward with so much pleasure at the time of my last writing to you has been declared "off." One of the sisters went to New York quite unexpectedly, and the other did not care to undertake the responsibility alone. I was somewhat reconciled to this disappointment however by receiving an invitation to a fete at Hampton Manor. This estate is one of the largest and most historic in the state, and although but twelve or fifteen miles from Baltimore I had never before seen the Mansion, which will, I think, favorably compare with any of the colonial mansions in this or any other state. In describing such places I become so eloquent and my epistles so prolific that I will desist against my inclination from going into details. If you ever decide to visit Baltimore again, however, you must not fail to see it. Just as we were ready to leave from home a heavy rain came up. We drove to Towson in a closed carriage and so far suffered no inconvenience from the elements, but for the remainder of the journey we experienced to their fullest extent the inconveniences and annoyances of the Balto. transfer system.

This letter was found among a collection of over 1,000 letters exchanged between Armstrong Thomas of Baltimore and Rebecca Ellerson of Virginia during the period 1896–1902. Contributed by their grandson.

If you have incurred to so great a degree the heat of Uncle Sol's displeasure, it is you that should have our sympathy, which we freely extend to you. The ocean breezes that are caught as in a funnel in the valley of the Chesapeake and thence through the valley of Patapsco conducted to the city of Baltimore pour themselves with such vigor into the south window of 807 Fidelity Bldg. as to overturn the ink bottles and blow away the paper weights. In fact, a mortal suffering from the heat of the sun has but to throw open one of the 9th story windows on the bay side of one of our up to date (and up to sky) office buildings to enjoy all the pleasures of a trip "down the Bay."

But do not talk to me of baseball—It makes me warm—I attended my first and last professional game some time ago. It was an extremely warm day, I will remember and I suffered the torments of the lower regions. The planks (a foots length on one of which cost me 25 cents and which was called a seat) were too hot to sit upon, and the rays of the sun pound right through the crown of my hat. I was determined to see our game of baseball. I sat down and waited. My own situation was well nigh intolerable, and when I saw the poor creatures rolling and tumbling around in the sand I was worked up to a state of nervous excitement indescribable. I tried to get water, but none was to be had. Waiters were indeed hurrying hither and thither with glasses of foaming beer, and not hesitate either to step right over any one so unfortunate as to intervene between themselves and a probable customers, but they looked as if they had been boiling—I tried several times to get out, but was reduced to a state of submission by cries of "sit down, sit down." I got out when the game was over, glad at least the Baltimore had lost and the rooters had hollored themselves hoarse for nothing. Well I suppose it is an honor to be a favorite rooter in such a city as this. W.S. Bryan, for instance, the former solicitor for Balto City, until he became Council for the big Nine was scarcely heard of beyond the walls of his native city. When his name appeared in the daily papers it was with the simple title of *Hon.* preferred. Now on occasions of great municipal demonstrations [welcomes to pennant winners] he rides in a four horse coach with the world reknown Captain of the Baltimore Base Ball Nine. The picture of *Rooter* Bryan (such is now his proud title) appears in all the daily papers. His great oration to the Champions is heralded throughout the world. And who in this great land of—baseball—has not heard of rooter Bryan—Counsel for three times Champion baseball team of the world-orator on the occasion of the grand celebration in honor of their return to the city they have by their prowess made known and respected throughout the world.

I am truly sorry that your father and sisters have been so unwell but I have no doubt that their sickness gave you some much needed employment.

You will see by the above address that I am now at Charlotte Hall, but do not address me here as I will be in Baltimore long before you think of answering.

Most sincerely,
Armstrong Thomas

GREG MADDUX'S FIFTEENTH WIN *of the 2002 season allowed him to join Cy Young as the only pitcher to reach that total for fifteen consecutive years. Just about a century separates these two great hurlers, as Young did it between 1891 and 1905, while pitching for Cleveland and St. Louis of the National League and Boston of the American League. Maddux's streak, which began in 1988 with the Cubs, includes five 15+ win seasons with Chicago and the last ten with Atlanta. Given the changes that have occurred over the past century, you'd be hard-pressed to say whether Young's 414-228 won-lost record during his run was more or less impressive than Maddux's 265-134 mark during his.*

Young's streak ended when he won only thirteen games for Boston in 1906 (13-21), before winning 21, 21 and 19 the next three seasons. So what happened in 1906? Simply that the 1906 Red Sox were a terrible club, winning only 49 games. By comparison, Maddux won 16 games in the strike-shortened 1994 season, yet it's doubtful he would have done so had he still been with the Cubs in '94, a team that also won only 49 games.

Young was Boston's opening day pitcher in '06, losing 2-1 in 12 innings to New York's Jack Chesbro. Five days later he beat the Yanks, but then dropped his next seven decisions, matching the longest losing streak of his career. The first two, on April 25 and 27, were to the defending AL champion Philadelphia A's, as Rube Waddell and Eddie Plank tossed shutouts at the Sox.

Actually, Boston was a respectable 6-7 on the morning of May 1, before setting an American League record by losing their next 20 games. Young was saddled with five losses during that streak, leaving him with an atypically dreadful record of 1-8 on May 19. He won 12 and lost 13 the rest of the way, with win number 13 coming on September 21. After losing on the 26th, Young failed to appear in any of the season's seven remaining games.

Will Maddux break Young's record in 2003? Hard to say, but you can be sure that if he has 13 wins with seven games left to play, he'd start at least two of them. —LYLE SPATZ

Henry Aaron and the '52 Bears

by Jason Christopherson

Manager Bill Adair had to be feeling a little confident as the 1952 Northern League season approached.

After all, his Eau Claire Bears were the defending champions of the loop. Actually, were it not for a near-miss in 1950, his Class C Boston Braves affiliate would be seeking their fourth straight crown. Don Jordan, staff ace in 1951 with a 16-6 record, would be back in the fold. Right fielder Earl Bass, a member of the 1949 championship club, was also wearing the Eau Claire uniform again.

And yet Adair had again been given a young, largely unproven talent base to work from. Bass was the only player other than himself (Adair still played when needed) to have more than three years of playing experience. Though this was fairly typical for the low minors, it was clear why Adair wasn't offering any predictions for 1952 as the season began on May 4th against the Superior Blues.

The Bears stumbled out of the blocks, despite the solid play of John (later known as Wes) Covington in left. A month and a half into the season, Eau Claire was still under .500, lurking in 4th place. On June 11th, the Eau Claire *Leader* reported attendance was severely lacking, threatening, "Unless there is a big climb in attendance... there may be no Eau Claire Bears in 1953." Attendance was averaging a mere 647 fans per game, off by more than 300 fans per game from 1951. Potential reasons were many: a sub-.500 club, poor weather, an increased number of radio broadcasts, and the rise of television, which was competing for the entertainment dollars of the nation. The *Leader* even mentioned, "There have also been grumblings about the number of Negro players." (In all fairness, the paper did downplay this as a reason.) Little did anyone know that the arrival of another "Negro" in the next few days would likely save professional baseball in Eau Claire for another decade, not to mention previewing one of the most feared home run hitters in the history of the game.

> The Bears may put a new shortstop into action Friday, a Negro named Aaron, who was signed by the Boston Braves while hitting at a sensational clip for the Indianapolis Clowns. He comes on option from Evansville's Three-I club.
>
> —Eau Claire *Leader*, June 11, 1952

Henry Aaron was actually placed on the active roster on Saturday, June 14, replacing the aforementioned Earl Bass, who was hitting only .220. Aaron made his professional debut on that day, starting at shortstop and hitting seventh in the lineup against the Rox of St. Cloud (MN). Heading into the game at Eau Claire's Carson Park, the Bears had a record of 17-19, 12 games behind the upstart Blues and 3½ games back of the Rox. After spotting St. Cloud two runs in the second

Jason Christopherson was born, raised, and still lives in Eau Claire with his wife, Shelley, and two children. He is gathering interviews for a history of professional baseball in Eau Claire.

inning, the Bears got one back in their half of the frame. Bear center fielder Collins Morgan ripped a double to right-center off Rox starter Art Rosser, and Aaron followed by slamming a pitch to left for a hit, scoring Morgan. Perhaps a little overanxious, Henry was thrown out trying to stretch the hit into a double. In the fifth, déjà vu as Morgan doubled and Aaron singled him home to tie the score at 2. Not a bad way to start a career! If only it were that easy. With one out and a runner at first in the top of the sixth, Henry bobbled what would have been an inning-ending double play. Two Rox players ended up crossing the plate later on in the inning to make the score 4-2. The Bears had their chances in the final three innings, but John Covington struck out with the bases loaded in the seventh. A Lantz Blaney solo homer in the eighth closed the gap to 4-3, but Covington looked at the game's final pitch for strike three with the tying run at second. Aaron ended up 2-for-4 with two RBI and handled seven chances without officially being charged with an error, though his bobble was certainly costly.

Aaron's first few weeks were eventful, to say the least. Given the chance to bat in the second slot of the order (ahead of "Flash" Covington), Henry responded nicely. In a three-game set against a Superior Blues team that had lost only seven of its first 40 games, Aaron was only 3-for-12 but had four RBI and had a big hand in the outcome, directly or not, in two games of the surprising sweep by the Bears. In game one, Henry came up with the bases loaded in the sixth and promptly unloaded them with a triple to right-center, providing the margin of victory in an 8-5 win. Aaron was virtually nonexistent in game two of the series—even dropping back to sixth in the order. He went 0-for-4, but the Bears slipped past the Blues 4-3 on a manufactured run in the eighth. The final game of the series saw Aaron drive Blaney in with the Bears' second run of the game in the bottom of the fourth, but that had a minor impact compared to what happened in the Superior half of the eighth. Superior's Gideon Applegate led off the inning by being hit by Eau Claire starter Gordie Roach and immediately stole second. Blues catcher Chuck Wiles then walked but was then forced at second on a grounder to Bob MacConnell. MacConnell flipped to Aaron, but Henry's attempt for a double play hit Wiles squarely in the head. Applegate scored the tying run as Wiles lay unconscious. He was taken to Luther Hospital in Eau Claire, where three days later the *Leader* could only report his condition as "improved" from critical. He would need several days in the hospital to recover from his concussion. Back to the game: the Blues were forced to replace Wiles with Alfredo Ibanez, a pitcher. It cost them dearly as Roach, who led off the ninth with a single and was advanced to second on a sacrifice, went to third and finally home with the winning run ... on two passed balls!

The winning ways continued against 1the underachieving Fargo-Moorhead squad. The Twins were only 13-33 before being swept at home in a four-game set against the surging Bears. Aaron hit his first professional home run on June 22, a 10th inning shot off the Twins' Reuben Stohs. The following day, Aaron hit his second, an inside-the-park clout to center field. The win that day gave the team a streak of nine wins and moved the Bears into third place, 10 games behind front runner Superior. After only 13 games, Aaron was hitting a robust .345 (19-55) with three doubles, a triple, two home runs, and 14 RBI. Covington was the power source for the Bears with nine homers and 42 RBI, while catcher Julie Bowers was at .347/5/29 in his 150 at-bats. Aaron, Covington, and Bowers were the only black players on the team, and the trio was ripping league pitching apart. However, when the Boston Braves' respected former manager and now roving scout Billy Southworth stopped by Eau Claire to have a look at the team, the only player about whom he commented to the *Leader* was Dick Engquist. Engquist was steady with the glove at first base, but his season numbers (.256/0/26) didn't seem to warrant special attention. Accoring to an article in the *Leader*, Southworth did mention that several players "have showed well," so it should be safe to assume that Aaron, Covington, and Bowers were among those players.

At that time the Northern League was considering a proposal by Fargo-Moorhead to split the season in order to help attendance for teams that started poorly out of the gate (such as the Twins). However, the attendance of the Bears, another team off to a slow start, was beginning to soar. In a six-game homestand ending July 1, the average crowd was 1,304 with a peak of 2,050 fans for a tilt with Grand Forks on June 30. In that game the Bears rallied for six runs in the bottom of the eighth to win, 11-6. Aaron had three hits, including a homer, 3 RBI, and a stolen base. Of course, a Little League game was also played at Carson Park that night and a "double header" billing was advertised. The *Leader* mentioned the combination with the Little League worked so well "that it may be used for future home stays." It was used at least two more times early in July. Fargo-Moorhead's proposal was voted down.

Taking three games out of four against St. Cloud, Eau Claire secured third place in the Northern League, four full games ahead of the Rox. The Bears still trailed Superior by 6½ games and second-place Sioux Falls by 6. Aaron provided the Independence Day fireworks, going six-for-ten with three doubles, a grand slam, and five RBI in a doubleheader sweep of the Rox. The homer came in the eighth inning with the Bears trailing, 7-6. Henry had a chance to be a hero the next night as well, coming up with the bases loaded and trailing 3-1 in the bottom of the eighth against a scrappy Duluth team. But the Dukes Vern Belt, throwing a masterful game, coaxed Aaron to hit a sharp liner right at third baseman Dick Getter. The Dukes swept the two-game home-and-home series the following night, and the Bears headed into a key three-game set at Superior trailing the Blues by 8½ games. The lack of momentum didn't seem to faze Eau Claire as the Bears walked out of Superior with a sweep. Reliever Bobby Brown worked nine innings in the series, gave up only one earned run, and was credited with a save in the opener and the victory in the finale. Brown had given up an unearned run in game one on Aaron's second error of the night, but it wasn't enough to spoil the win. The Bears came home with a 40-28 mark, only 5½ games behind the Blues and 3½ behind Sioux Falls, the first opponent for Eau Claire on the homestand.

Henry opened the scoring against the Canaries with his fifth home run of the season, a towering shot to right in front of 1,640 of the hometown faithful. Sioux Falls rallied for two runs in the second inning, but future major league player and manager John Goryl quelled the rally with a sparkling double play. In the sixth, Covington doubled in Aaron and Collins Morgan to put the Bears in the lead 4-2. Gordie Roach bailed out tiring starter Ken Reitmeier in the seventh and went on to close the door in a 5-3 victory. Future major leaguer Don Elston dominated the Bears in game two of the series, giving up only three runs (one earned) and eight hits in a complete-game 4-3 win in front of 2,386 fans. He got stronger as the game progressed, allowing only three base runners in the final five innings. Aaron made up for a quiet night by homering in the series finale, a 7-4 Bears win.

Meanwhile, the votes from league baseball writers and managers were tabulated, and the All-Star team was announced. In the Northern League at that time, the club in first place at midnight on July 4th earned the right to host and play against the All-Stars from the other teams. Superior, of course, won the right to host the game held on July 16. Aaron, hitting .367 and now with enough at-bats to qualify for the batting title, clearly had made an impression all around the league in his 30+ games, as he was named to the team. Other Bears joining Henry were Covington, Brown, Bowers, and pitcher Don Jordan, along with manager Bill Adair. The Canaries placed six on the squad, including Elston. Duluth's Joe Caffie was the only other major leaguer-to-be representing the All-Stars.

However, there was still a little baseball to be played before the All-Star break. Aaron hit another opposite-field home run in the series-opening win against fourth-place Aberdeen. Collins Morgan's grand slam in the bottom of the seventh provided the margin of victory in a 7-3 win over the Pheasants. But in what very well may have been the turning point in the season, the Bears bobbled and fumbled away both ends of a doubleheader the following day. The Pheasants scored 14 runs in the twin bill, 11 of them unearned as a result of six Eau Claire errors. Though solid defensively, Aaron could only manage a single in seven at-bats on the day. To compound the agony, Superior swept Grand Forks and Sioux Falls split a twin bill with St. Cloud. This left the Bears 3½ games out of second place and 7½ out of the Northern League lead heading into the All-Star game.

For Eau Claire players and fans, the All-Star game couldn't have gone much worse. Seven All-Star errors added up to an 8-6 victory for the Blues, but that wasn't half the story. Bear players managed four hits in ten at-bats, but neither scored nor drove in any runs. Brown, Covington, and Bowers each had an error that led to runs for the Blues. Brown was tagged with the loss. And Aaron? After lacing a single up the middle in the top of the first, he sprained his ankle sliding into former Bear Jack Pelosi at second base while trying to break up a double-play grounder off the bat of Fargo-Moorhead's Frank Gravino. The Superior fans, recalling that Henry's throw a month earlier had likely ended the season of their catcher, Chuck Wiles, had little sympathy as Aaron hobbled off the field. (Incidentally, Wiles was announced prior to the game and got "the biggest hand from the crowd," {*Leader*, 7/18/52} A collection was taken up for Wiles and brought $723.) Clell Buzzell, sports editor for the *Leader*, reported:

> Eau Claire fans at the game got a sickening feeling as they watched the 18-year-old star hobble to the dugout. They were jolted again when the public address system called for a doctor and once more when he was sped by ambulance to the hospital. Not until they received word that the injury was nothing more than an ordinary sprain did Eau Claire officials relax.
>
> —*Leader*, 7/15/52

John Goryl filled in admirably for Aaron in the first game Henry missed due to the injury. Goryl doubled in four trips to the plate and scored the eventual winning run in a 2-1 win over Sioux Falls. The Bears pulled within 1½ games of the Canaries with Aaron back in the lineup the following night but slipped back a game in the series finale, a three-hit, ten-strikeout performance by Don Elston. Aaron had to sit out again, and the Bear offense had no answer for Elston. Eau Claire bounced back, taking two of three at Aberdeen before coming home and taking three of five from St. Cloud behind some masterful pitching performances. Bobby Brown fired a four-hitter in the first game of a doubleheader, winning 6-2. Brown was then given the ball to pitch game two and promptly shut out the Rox on three hits! Don Jordan followed up that performance by throwing 7⅔ innings of no-hit ball but lost, 3-1. Bill Conroy breezed through St. Cloud's hitters the following night, winning 6-1 on a five-hit gem. Aaron was fairly quiet in the eight games after he came back permanently and, aside from a homer in a 26-3 drubbing of Grand Forks, remained in a mini-slump for the majority of the week.

By August 2, the Northern League had become a three-team race. The Bears remained in third place, nine games behind Superior and one game back of Sioux Falls. Aberdeen was a distant fourth, 18 games out of the lead. Though Aaron had been slumping, he still led the league with a .344 average and had contributed eight home runs and 44 RBI. On Aaron's tail was Covington at .341/17/80. A three-game sweep of Fargo-Moorhead, combined with a Superior sweep of Sioux Falls, propelled the Bears into second place by two games over the Canaries. The third win, however, came at a huge price. Leading off the eighth inning, Covington was hit in the head by Twins pitcher Howard Simmons. He lay on the field motionless, only regaining consciousness in the ambulance en route to Luther Hospital. He would not return for more than two weeks. A dejected Eau Claire team lost an exhibition game to the House of David club the following night, 5-2. Aaron, nursing a sore hand, had a pinch single and stole a base in the ninth. The Bears were perhaps looking ahead to a three-game set with Sioux Falls, hoping to put some distance between them and the Canaries.

It didn't happen. Aaron doubled in a run and scored two in an opening 10-5 victory, but he could manage only a single the rest of the series while committing an error in each game (running his error streak to five games). The Bears dropped the final two games, falling into a virtual tie with Sioux Falls. The finale had the Canaries winning on a bases-loaded walk in the ninth by ace hurler Gordon Roach. A frustrated Roach threw his glove, striking umpire Pete Jaworsky and drawing a suspension from the league in the process. At a time in the season when Eau Claire really needed to come together, it was clear the Bears were falling apart.

The loss of Covington hurt the team greatly. The team struggled to a 5-10 record in his absence. Aaron performed like the champion he was, hitting .359 and stealing six bases in attempts to spark the team. After surging Aberdeen swept past the Bears in a three-game set, Eau Claire split a short two-game home stand with Duluth. Aaron went 5-8 with some key hits to keep rallies going. Meanwhile, Sioux Falls swept a doubleheader from Grand Forks, the nightcap giving the Canaries a 1½ game lead over Eau Claire. In that game Don Elston struck out 16 and came within a walk of a perfect game in the best pitching performance in the Northern League that season.

A key three-game series at Superior gave the Bears an opportunity to draw closer to the leaders. However, Eau Claire could only get one victory, a 3-0 win for Roach with Aaron pacing the way with three hits. A four-game split in Duluth left the Bears two games behind Sioux Falls and still ten games behind Superior as the Blues came to town for three games. Aaron went 2-4 with an RBI and a stolen base in the opening 4-0 victory. Covington returned after fifteen games but was 0-3. He shook the rust off the following night, getting three hits and stealing a base in another Bear shutout, 4-0. An 11-9 loss in game three dropped Eau Claire back to nine games out of first with only eleven to play. Clearly, it was time to focus on taking second place. The Bears swept three games at St. Cloud and returned home to close the season out with three

TRANSCENDENTAL GRAPHICS

The 1952 Eau Claire Bears. Aaron is on the far left in the middle row. Pendleton is third from the right in the back row, with Goryl second from the left.

games against Aberdeen, three against Sioux Falls, and two more against St. Cloud.

Covington and Adair homered, and Elmer Toth scattered nine hits in a 5-1 win over Aberdeen. Since Sioux Falls was rained out, this win moved Eau Claire into a virtual tie for second place. Aberdeen evened the series with a 5-2 win in the first game of a doubleheader, but Gordon Roach fired a no-hitter for the win in the nightcap. The Canaries also split a doubleheader to keep pace with the Bears as they geared up for the second-place showdown. The drama ended early for Eau Claire. Don Elston opened with a five-hitter and the Canaries beat the Bears 6-2. Aaron was 0-for-3 with a stolen base. In game two, John Mudd shut down the Bear offense once again. Covington homered in the bottom of the eighth to bring the Bears to within one at 3-2, but they could draw no closer. Mudd finished with a two-hitter. Again, Aaron was 0-3 and had to leave the game early with a bruised thumb. The Bears fell in the series finale as well, assuring a third-place finish, the team's lowest finish since 1948. Eau Claire ended strong against St. Cloud, winning both ends of the doubleheader by scores of 4-3 and 10-9. Aaron showed no ill effects of his injury, going 5-for-9 with five runs and three RBI in the twin bill.

The wins gave Eau Claire a final regular-season record of 72-53, much improved over the 17-19 start they had endured before Aaron arrived. Henry finished the year with a .336 average, six points behind hitting champion Joe Caffie of Duluth. Aaron had 19 doubles, four triples, nine home runs, and 61 RBI to go along with the healthy average. For his efforts, Aaron was overwhelmingly voted the league's Rookie of the Year for 1952. He grabbed 13 first-place votes, three second-place, and one third-place vote of the 21 writers, managers, and umpires who voted. Aaron became the third successive Bear to win the award. Bill Bruton and Horace Garner led the poll in 1950 and 1951, respectively. Covington finished fifth in voting and Goryl tied for sixth.

The third-place finish meant the Bears would have to face Superior in the first round of the playoffs, while fourth-place Duluth would tackle Sioux Falls. The opening round was a best of three series. The first game found Eau Claire quickly down 4-1 due in part to a costly error by Aaron which led to three runs in the fifth inning. Aaron's clutch two-run home run in the sixth pulled the Bears to within one run, and Lantz

Blaney's single tied the game one inning later. Superior's Alfredo Ibanez and Eau Claire's Bobby Brown both pitched into the 12th inning, but Don Phalen of the Blues came through with a clutch single in the twelfth to drive home the winning run and give Superior a 1-0 lead in the series.

Gordon Roach was roughed up early in game two, and when the Bears came to bat in the bottom of the seventh they were trailing, 7-0. Three consecutive walks followed a single by Bill Conroy. Covington then drove in two more with a single of his own to make the score 7-3. In the eighth, Bob MacConnell singled and Conroy and Manager Adair walked to load the bases. Dick Engquist hit into a fielder's choice as MacConnell scored and Conroy went to third. Conroy scored Eau Claire's fifth run of the game on a wild pitch that also sent Engquist to second. Blaney then hit a grounder as Engquist broke for third. The throw to third was not in time, and the Bears had runners on the corners for Julie Bowers. In what must have been the highlight of the season for him, Bowers launched a ball deep into the Eau Claire night to complete an improbable comeback. Don Jordan pitched the ninth and preserved the 8-7 victory. Though not having a direct impact on the scoring, Aaron had a good night, going 2-for-4 with a double and a stolen base.

Normally a right fielder, Gene Collins was tabbed as the Blues' pitcher in the rubber match, facing the Bears' Bill Conroy. Once again the Blues jumped ahead early, scoring two runs before Eau Claire came to bat. The Bears, though, answered with two runs of their own in the bottom of the first. The pitchers then took control of the game. Collins struck out 12 in seven innings and only gave up four hits while Conroy scattered eight hits in 7⅔ innings. Conroy ran into trouble in the eighth, and Superior's Jose Bustamentes narrowly beat a throw to the plate to break a 3-3 tie. Jordan came on and struck out all four batters he faced, but the Blues' Alfredo Ibanez, the league's winningest pitcher, slammed the door on the Bears' season. Superior would go on to sweep Sioux Falls in three games to capture the Northern League crown for 1952.

The 1952 Eau Claire Bears were an enigma. They combined a powerful offense with a solid pitching staff and a better than average defense (second in the league in fielding as a team), but they were only able to manage a third-place finish and an early exit from the playoffs. Maybe this team would have dominated any other Northern League season, but 1952 was clearly the year of the Blues. What this team did achieve, though, was to save baseball in Eau Claire, if only in the short term. The tear the Bears went on after Henry Aaron arrived boosted attendance dramatically and allowed the franchise to stay operational.

Though professional baseball left Eau Claire in the early 1960s, Carson Park still stands as a monument to the history of baseball in the city and as a source of civic pride. A restoration project a few years ago injected life into the stadium, and the amateur Cavaliers draw thousands of fans every summer for some quality baseball in a beautiful facility. And as the fans arrive, they are greeted by a statue of the 18-year-old Eau Claire Bear, Henry Aaron.

REGULAR SEASON STATISTICS

BATTING (MINIMUM OF 100 ABs)

NAME	AB	H	2B	3B	HR	RBI	PCT
Aaron	345	116	19	4	9	61	.336
Covington	400	132	18	9	24	99	.330
Bowers	327	102	19	1	11	68	.312
Morgan	243	73	15	3	14	63	.300
Goryl	218	64	6	3	8	25	.294
Adair	139	38	8	0	6	24	.273
Blaney	379	103	18	3	3	54	.272
Engquist	482	119	15	1	1	51	.247
Auten	208	47	9	1	3	29	.226
MacConnell	292	64	7	6	4	31	.219

PITCHING (MINIMUM OF 5 DECISIONS)

NAME	W	L	PCT	IP	H	BB	SO
Roach	14	4	.778	169	145	109	105
Jordan	10	5	.667	122	106	83	102
Conroy	16	9	.640	205	182	97	131
Brown	14	10	.583	167	133	87	158
Reitmeier	8	7	.533	135	125	72	92
Kornach	2	2	.500	90	102	53	34
Toth	3	5	.375	50	53	33	40

SOURCES

Eau Claire *Leader*, September 7, 1952.

Thanks to Bob Buege for assistance in editing the article.

The Wartime Portland Beavers

From the Pits to the Pinnacle

by Donald Wells

The Pacific Coast League emerged from the Depression of the 1930s in rather good condition. Four new ballparks were constructed in the 1930s, and the fans' support was increasing in the last two pre-war years, 1940 and 1941. However, Portland became the doormat of the league, finishing last for four consecutive years, 1939–1942. Its ballpark, Vaughn Street Park, was the oldest in the league, dating to 1901, two years before the league's first season. The franchise had six different managers in the six seasons from 1939 through 1944.

After the U. S. entered World War II, baseball had to make adjustments. Many minor leagues shut down because they could not find enough players. President Roosevelt wanted the game to continue for public morale, but players were not given special treatment when it came to military service. At the end of the 1941 season, the PCL decided to expand the rosters to 25 players for the 1942 season, but this number was reduced to 20 because of the demands of the military. But no distinction was to be made between veteran players and rookies, as in previous years.

Travel was also a problem. Railroad fares were increased and no separate Pullman cars were to be set aside for the players. Each man would have to carry his bags and find a berth wherever he could. Travel delays on long road trips from Seattle and Portland to Southern California often caused Tuesday games to be postponed, necessitating doubleheaders at a time when pitching staffs were overworked because of smaller rosters.

In 1942 prices were rising but players were still allowed only $2 a day for meals on the road. This amount had been cut from $3 in the early 1930s and had yet to be restored. All citizens had to turn in their old toothpaste tube before they could buy a replacement, and everyone was encouraged to save waste fats to make munitions.

At various times in 1942 blackouts were declared up and down the West Coast, requiring that stadium lights to be extinguished immediately, causing players and fans to grope to the exits in the dark. Team announcers were sometimes taken off the air when radio stations had to broadcast alerts to the public. Announcers were also forbidden to mention anything about the weather, but it was obvious why games were stopped or called off by "unplayable conditions."

Night ball was allowed in 1942 up until August 20, and then all games had to be played in the daytime. This policy lasted until the beginning of the 1944 season. Teams experimented with many different starting times, from morning to 7 p.m. The latter time would only be possible in June or July and usually in Portland or Seattle.

One group of fans were not allowed to attend any games all during the war—Japanese Americans, some

Donald R. Wells grew up in Glendale, California rooting for the Los Angeles Angels of the PCL. In 1997 he retired after 30 years as an economics professor at the University of Memphis, and returned to his first love, baseball.

of who were avid followers of the game.

The 1942 Season—This was the fourth straight year that the Beavers were to finish last. Frank Brazill had the unenviable job of managing this poor club, being the fourth of six managers the team was to employ from 1939 to 1944. This plunge into the cellar coincided with Portland's northern rival, Seattle, winning three straight pennants from 1939 through 1941, which was salt in Beaver fans' wounds.

Portland had three reliable pitchers, Ad Liska, Syd Cohen, and Byron Speece, but they were overworked by being forced to relieve in between starts. Portland was especially weak at catching, with both receivers hitting near .200. Their top hitter, Ted Norbert, started off very slowly, getting only 8 hits in his first 57 at-bats. Adding to the Beavers' misery was the large amount of "unplayable conditions" (i.e., rain) that caused 10 postponed games during the first three months of the season, which necessitated many doubleheaders, putting more strain on the overworked pitching staff. In addition to these makeup games, Portland was forced to play several exhibition games with army or navy teams on Monday nights, normally an off day.

Two key players, third baseman Marvin Owen and first baseman Larry Barton, were injured, and Portland had only 18 players available in July. This coincided with a 10-game losing streak. Then in mid-August, things got worse when their double play combination, shortstop Lindsey Brown and second baseman Al Wright, joined the navy. With just 16 players on hand, Portland had to use outfielders in the infield and pitchers in the outfield.

When the decree forbidding night ball went into effect on August 20, attendance dropped all over the league, but in Portland they were not drawing many fans anyway. The Beavers tried a 1:30 p.m. start to attract shift workers that had to start work at 4:30, but this met with little success. However, on the last Sunday of the final home stand, 3,000 fans turned out for that doubleheader because there were rumors the league would not operate in 1943.

After his poor start, Ted Norbert got hot and ended up winning the batting title at .378, 31 points ahead of the second highest batter. He hit at a .410 pace after his dismal start. He was the first Portland hitter to win the title since Bill Bagwell in 1926. Norbert also won the home run title with 28. Four other Beavers hit over .300 this season: Marvin Owen, Larry Barton, Rupert Thompson, and Johnny Gill.

After the season, Willam Klepper, who formerly owned both the Portland and Seattle clubs, was named the general manager. Klepper promised to improve the team but said he could not guarantee a first-division club right away. But that is exactly what he delivered.

The 1943 Season—This was the only wartime season that all games had to be played in the daytime. Teams tried various starting times for weekday games, from late morning to early evening. Portland settled on 5:30 for the months of April, May, and September, but was able to start at 7 p.m. during the summer months. The schedule was reduced from 178 games to 155. The player limit was increased from 20 to 25, but five had to be rookies. The limit was increased because there were fewer lower leagues where players could be sent. It was also common for some players to keep war industry jobs and play for their club only when it was home, or in a nearby city.

Merv Shea was Portland's fifth manager in five seasons. He was faced with the loss of Ted Norbert, who was traded to Milwaukee for four players, only two of whom agreed to report to the Beavers. Even though the team was improved over 1942, attendance did not increase as much as hoped for because of the elimination of night ball and the fact that there was no pennant race in 1943, with the Angels running away from the pack. Los Angeles won 26 of their first 29 games, including 20 in a row, which caused some writers and some owners to call for a split season.

The new ownership, along with the Portland Boosters Club, arranged for a patriotic parade before their home opener. Fans were to avoid all gasoline vehicles, and use horse-drawn buck boards, bicycles or walk. Those on bikes were given free bleacher tickets, but the first home game had to be postponed for "unplayable conditions." It was a poor home stand because they were swept by the Angels, who were in the midst of their winning streak.

One of the highlights of the season occurred right after this dismal home stand, when they went to Los Angeles and won a series, 5 games to 4. It was only one of two series the Angels were to lose all season. Portland followed that with a winning trip to Oakland and a close series in Seattle, to return home in third place. They were eventually overtaken by Seattle for third, but were able to finish fourth and qualify for the playoffs for the first time since 1937.

They suffered the loss of pitcher Wayne Osborne to military service and of Syd Cohen for a month while he had to report to Dallas for his draft physical. Cohen was able to return after being rejected for duty, but pitcher Joe Orrell was sold to Detroit, so Portland went into the playoffs with a depleted pitching staff.

Portland won the first two games from San Francisco at home in the playoffs, but then they had to go to spacious Seals Stadium, where they lost four in a row, and were eliminated.

The 1944 Season—Because the war situation looked better, the league was able to return to night ball and the schedule was increased to 169 games. Even though Los Angeles won the pennant and San Francisco won the playoffs again, the 1944 season had an exciting pennant race until late July, when the Angels pulled ahead. But the race for the first division was not settled until the very last day. A new attendance record was set in 1944, the first of four straight seasons through 1947 when new records were set.

Portland's sixth manager in six years was Marvin Owen, who continued to play third base. His first problem was the hold-out of Ad Liska, who did not sign until the season was two weeks old. But Liska received a two-year contract, which was very unusual for a minor league team. Another pitcher, Don Pulford, did not sign until May 20, and he won only three games in 1944. But Portland got good years from pitchers Marino Pieretti and Roy Helser, who won 26 and 20 games respectively.

The 25-player limit was retained, but five had to be rookies. One versatile player, Charlie Petersen, was acquired from the Seals. Petersen could play infield, outfield, and even catch, but because of his war industry job in Portland, he could not travel with the team, except during his two-week vacation in June.

The 1944 season saw several teams dominate others. Portland had trouble with Los Angeles and Oakland, winning just 7 of 21 from the Angels and only 5 of 21 from the Oaks. But Portland pounded San Francisco and Sacramento, winning 16 of 24 from the Seals and 20 of 29 from the Solons. The most dramatic example was Hollywood taking 20 of 22 from Oakland.

At the end of the first week of July, only three games separated the first seven clubs. Last-place Sacramento was only five games out of first. During July five different clubs were in first place, but after July 23 Los Angeles took the lead for good, and won by 12 games over second-place Portland.

Portland purchased Frank Demaree from the Browns in late July. Demaree had won the triple crown when with the Angels in 1934, but he had only a mediocre year with the Beavers in 1944. Shortly thereafter, Portland went on a road trip to Los Angeles, where they won only one of seven games, but they went to San Francisco and swept all seven from the Seals. As Marvin Owen's sister, Vi Owen, stated in her book, *The Adventures of a Quiet Soul,* whenever the team won seven games in a row, all the players were invited to the manager's home for a steak dinner.

On their last home stand, Portland faced Seattle, Sacramento and San Diego and was enjoying a record of 12-7, but then lost the last four games to the Padres, to finish at 12-11. On their final road trip to Sacramento and Oakland, they won 9 and lost 8, but it was good enough to finish second, 12 games behind L.A., but one ahead of San Francisco and Oakland, who tied for third.

All playoff games had to be played in California because the railroad would not extend the priority it had given the teams during the regular season to the playoffs. Portland won the first two games from the Angels, but then lost four in a row, just as happened in 1943.

No Portland player hit .300 in 1944. There were rumors the ball was deadened. Catcher Eddie Adams hit .297 and Marvin Owen hit .290. Ted Gullic led the teams in homers with just 8. Portland doubled their 1943 attendance, drawing 272,776 fans.

The 1945 Pennant-Winning Season—The Portland Beavers made the jump from eighth place to fourth from 1942 to 1943, and a further jump from fourth place to second between 1943 and 1944. For the 1945 season they made the final leap to first place, winning their first pennant since 1936 and, to this date, their last. Because the war was winding down, the agency known as the War Manpower Commission declared that ballplayers could leave their war plant jobs and play ball full-time, but they would still be subject to the draft. This declaration helped four Portland players, Roy Helser, Charley Petersen, Charley English, and Larry Barton, who had been holding such jobs over the winter.

Portland acquired a few new players for this pennant-winning season, most of whom played important parts in the team's success. Second baseman Charley English, who also filled in at third, was acquired from Oakland for outfielder Norm De Weese. Pitcher Jack

Tising was purchased from Buffalo, and Jake Mooty, another right hander, was acquired from Detroit. Three rookies made the team: left-hand pitcher, Wandel Mossor, backup catcher Hank Souza, and middle infielder Frank Lucchesi, who was also used in center field. Another young infielder, Curt Schmidt, was traded to Sacramento in July for the versatile Roy Younker.

Housing was even more scarce than in previous years. When Ad Liska and his family arrived from their Eau Claire, Wisconsin, home, they were taken in by the groundskeeper at Vaughn Street Park, Rocky Benevento. Single players often had to rent rooms in private homes. Teams going to San Francisco from April through June had great difficulty finding hotel space because of the peace conference that set up the United Nations. While there was talk of putting teams up in the Seals Stadium clubhouse, most were able to find space in Oakland or some other East Bay area.

Just before the season started, Portland fans received the sad news that Henry Martinez, an infielder on their 1942 club, was killed in action in the battle of Leyte Gulf in the Philippines.

All minor leagues were faced with a shortage of bats for the 1945 season, which some service teams helped rectify. Earlier in the war, professional teams provided servicemen with baseball equipment, so now the military was returning the favor. Charley English got several bats from his navy friends, and Marvin Owen retrieved an old bat that had been given him in 1940. Originally Owen found the bat too heavy, but he bulked up to 187 pounds over the winter, making it just right for him.

Two Portland players had much better years in 1945 than in 1944 because of weight changes, one up and one down. Johnny O'Neal, who had hit .236, gained 12 pounds of pure muscle over the winter and raised his average to .315. Frank Demaree, following his nurse-wife's advice, lost 30 pounds and increased his bat speed and became a gazelle in the outfield. He improved from .276 to .304. Pitcher Don Pulford played winter ball in Los Angeles and improved his 3-10 record to 20-11.

Because of travel restrictions, the Beavers again trained in San Jose but encountered a great deal of rain, limiting the amount of exhibition games they could play. They had only a few games with some service teams, and were unable to schedule any PCL clubs.

Vaughn Street Park, home of the Portland Beavers, in a 1940s photograph. In its final season in 1955 the wooden park was the oldest active stadium in the PCL. It was torn down the following year.

On the bright side, players had their meal money on the road increased from $2 a day to $3, but some felt this was inadequate in the San Francisco area.

Portland opened their pennant-winning season in Oakland on March 31 with a five-game series. The Beavers won the opener with the following lineup:

Frank Shone	CF
Larry Barton	1B
Frank Demaree	LF
Charley English	2B
Ted Gullic	RF
Marvin Owen	3B
Johnny O'Neal	SS
Eddie Adams	C
Don Pulford	P

This lineup, with the exception of the pitcher, was the same one that started the post-season playoffs. However, throughout the season Portland suffered many injuries, so had to use many combinations to stay on top.

Starting the season so early meant that the players had to suffer some very cold and windy conditions. Ad Liska and Roy Helser had trouble in the cold, but Jack Tising, Jake Mooty, and Don Pulford pitched very well. Portland won four of five at Oakland and then won the first four in Sacramento before losing the Sunday doubleheader. The scheduled seven-game series in San Francisco was shortened to five because of the death of President Roosevelt. Portland won that series three games to two, to finish 11-5 on the trip. This put them one game behind Seattle for the league lead.

The home stand began on April 18 with Hollywood. It was delayed a day because the Stars had trouble getting there. It was a 4 p.m. start and Portland announced that the crowd of 12,651 beat Seattle's opening day crowd by 200 fans. The Stars beat Portland that day but could only win one more game that week, as the Beavers took the series, 5 games to 2. It was on Sunday, April 22, that Portland passed Seattle for first place, and never relinquished that spot all season. The Beavers were out of first place only a few days in April, and never by more than one game.

Oakland came to Portland next and split a six-game series, with one game rained out. The injury bug hit Portland hard that week. They had just sold outfielder John Gill to Seattle when Larry Barton pulled a ligament in his knee, causing Ted Gullic to play first and 44-year-old Spencer Harris to play outfield. Marvin Owen hurt his leg, causing Charley English to move to third, and Mel Nunes to play second. Then English got a charley horse, so Charley Petersen went to third. The Beavers ended their home stay with 8 wins and 5 losses.

Portland opened their next road trip in Hollywood and took 6 of 7 from the last place Stars. Young Hank Souza usually caught one game a week, giving Eddie Adams a rest. Charley Petersen was in right field with Owen and English back in the infield. Occasionally rookies Curtis Schmidt and Frank Lucchesi would fill in or pinch hit.

In San Diego the Beavers found hotel space so scarce that three players had to share a room. This proved harmful to pitcher Jack Tising, who got up at night, stubbed his toe, breaking the middle one on his left foot. This did not prevent him from winning Sunday and going the distance. After losing the first two games, the Beavers won the final five. Barton was able to return to first base in San Diego, giving the Beavers their starting infield, which was the league's best.

After an 11-3 road trip, the Beavers returned home to play the Angels on May 16. Both teams arrived on the same train, missing a connection in Martinez. But rain prevented the series from starting until Friday night with a doubleheader, which the Beavers won. The Angels won Saturday, a doubleheader Sunday, and a makeup game on Monday night, to take the series 4 games to 2. Portland blew an 8-1 lead Monday night, losing 9-8, and saw their league lead shrink to 4 games.

This poor home stand continued with the Seals coming to Vaughn Street Park. The Beavers broke a four-game losing streak by winning Tuesday, but catcher Eddie Adams broke a finger and was sidelined until early June. After a Wednesday rain out, the Seals copped a Thursday night doubleheader with Hank Souza turning in two bad games, with a couple of passed balls and allowing several stolen bases. Charley Petersen went behind the plate, but after this series he was sold to the Seals. O'Doul had been trying to reacquire Petersen all season, and while a valuable man, Petersen did not get along with manager Owen. The Seals won again on Friday night, the Beavers won Saturday, and the Seals took the rain-shortened game on Sunday, with the nightcap being rained out. Portland lost the series 4 games to 2, while their league lead was cut to just half a game.

So on May 29, Portland finished a 4-8 home stand during which their lead dropped from 6 games to just half a game. They were heading to Seattle to play their closest pursuer. Don Pulford won the opening game 4-3, pitching all 12 innings and going 5 for 6 at the plate. This game-and-a-half lead was maintained as the two clubs split the Memorial Day doubleheader. Souza was still catching all the games until Sunday, June 3, when Adams returned. But English was out with a bad back, so Nunes was at second. Syd Cohen and Roy Helser pitched shutouts on Thursday and Friday, but the Beavers lost Saturday and split the Sunday doubleheader to win the series, 5 games to 3, and leave Seattle with a 2-game lead.

Portland had won 27 and lost 11 on the road, and they went to Los Angeles and had a 3 games to 1 lead, only to lose the final 3 games of that series, suffering their first road series loss of the season. Charley English was not able to play against his former team. Frank Shone missed a few games with a pulled muscle, so Schmidt and Lucchesi moved to the outfield.

When Portland returned home to face second-place Seattle, they found more players hurt. Spencer Harris had a bad leg and Barton hurt his other leg, not the one that had been bothering him. Jake Mooty had a sore pitching shoulder. Seattle won the first game on Wednesday, June 13, to cut the Beaver lead to half a game. Frank Shone tried to play but had to come out, so pitcher Clarence Federmeyer went into the outfield. But the Beavers of 1945 were not to be overtaken. They won 5 of the remaining 6 games to send the Rainiers home trailing by 4 games. During this series Portland wore all white stockings with no stripe and all white caps, so the players decided to wear them for the rest of the season.

After this crucial series, Sacramento and San Diego came to Portland for a split week. The Sacs won 2 of 3 but Portland won 3 of 4 from the Padres to finish the home stand with 9 wins and 5 losses. Frank Lucchesi played center field all week, while English was limited mainly to pinch-hitting. After the midpoint of the season, on June 24, Portland had a 4-game lead on Seattle with a record of 52 and 32.

The Beavers left for a two-week road trip to Sacramento and Oakland. At Sacramento, Charley English began to give Marvin Owen a rest at third and Frank Demaree returned to the outfield. Portland managed to take 4 of the 7 games from the Solons to increase their lead to 5 games. The Beavers pulled a good trade with Sacramento at the end of the series by acquiring Roy Younker for the seldom-used Curtis Schmidt. The versatile Younker could play first, second, outfield, and catcher.

The series at Oaks Park was an 8-game set because of the July 4 doubleheader. Portland won the series 5 games to 3, but saw its lead shrink to 3 games. Roy Younker caught most of the games because Eddie Adams sprained his wrist. Frank Demaree came down with intestinal flu and was hospitalized in Oakland. Marvin Owen was feeling ill because of the 106 degree heat experienced in Sacramento.

When Portland returned home on July 10, catcher Hank Souza and utility infielder Mel Nunes took their draft physicals. Souza was rejected, but Nunes was accepted even though he had one leg shorter than the other. Nunes was not called until the second week of September.

The Seals were the opposition for 8 games, the extra game because of the postponement in April when Roosevelt died. Younker did most of the catching while ex-Beaver Charley Petersen played right field for the Seals. The lead got down to 2 games when the teams split a Thursday night doubleheader. But then Portland got hot and won the series 6 games to 2, to increase their lead to 3 games.

The Hollywood Stars next came to Portland, and the Beavers swept them all six games, with Saturday's game being rained out. This gave Portland an 11-game winning streak, and Marvin Owen again had the whole team over for steak dinners. They were now 7 games ahead of Seattle.

The Beavers had to go to Seattle and then to Hollywood before returning home to play Seattle again. In a very antagonistic series in Sick's Stadium, Seattle won the odd game to take the series, 4 games to 3, but the Beavers still led by 6 games. Marvin Owen said that this series against Bill Skiff's team was more hostile than the 1934 World Series between his Detroit team and Gas House Gang of St. Louis. During this series Frank Shone's hitting streak was stopped at 39 games, a team record.

Portland then went to Hollywood for an 8-game series, the extra game to make up for the rainout in Portland. The Beavers won 7 of 8, while Younker played outfield, with Adams back of the plate. Nunes was at second, English at third, and Owen at first because Larry Barton hurt his foot. Ted Gullic did not make the trip to Hollywood.

Portland had an 8-game lead over Seattle as the two top clubs met for the final time in the regular season at Portland. The Rainiers won this series 5 games to 2, cutting the lead to 5 games. This series drew 52,217 fans after the two had drawn 68,381 two weeks earlier in Seattle.

Oakland followed Seattle into Vaughn Street Park for an 8-game series, as the clubs were making up a rain out. Portland made some roster changes, releasing Spencer Harris and Clarence Federmeyer and acquiring two left-handed hitters and a pitcher. Outfielder Nick Rhabe was purchased from the Angels and infielder Glenn Crawford from the Phillies. The pitcher, Isadore Leon also came from the Phillies, but was returned to them after making only a couple of appearances. The Oaks and Beavers split the eight games, but Portland's lead was cut to four. No special holiday was declared by baseball when the war ended on August 14, though some fans were unruly.

The Angels followed Oakland into Portland for another 8-game series, caused by an earlier rain out. Portland took a 4 games to 1 lead in this series only to have the Angels win the final 3 games to tie the series, and cut the Beaver lead to 3 games.

Portland now embarked on their final road trip of the season, with 7 games in San Diego, 5 in L.A. and 6 in San Francisco. At this point Portland had won 9 of 11 in the road series, giving them a 49-26 road record. September started out well for the soon to be champion Beavers as they took 5 of 7 at San Diego to lead by 5 games.

Portland then headed to Wrigley Field and won a Labor Day doubleheader from the Angels. They won their 6th in a row on Tuesday night, but lost the opening game of the Wednesday doubleheader. They did win the nightcap, however, to take the series 4 games to 1. The Angels and Portland each won 13 games from each other in 1945, which was as close as any team came to winning a season series from the Beavers.

At Seals Stadium for 6 games in 3 days, the teams split the series. Portland returned home with a 6-game lead over Seattle and a magic number of 9.

The final two weeks of the season had the Beavers hosting San Diego and then Sacramento. Portland again won 5 of 7 from the Padres, clinching the pennant on Sunday, September 16. Three of the final week's games with Sacramento were rained out and not made up, as Portland won 3 of those 4 games.

Former Beaver outfielder Danny Escobar returned from military service and got into some games. Fans greeted his return warmly, and after his homer won the second game of the playoffs, they showered the field with silver coins, amounting to $81. Returning servicemen were allowed to play in post-season games.

Sportswriter L. H. Gregory, remembering that the 1936 champion Beavers had no memento from that season, encouraged fans to contribute to a fund to give players engraved watches. A special banquet was held at the Multnomah Hotel, and Governor Earl Snell was there to present the watches and a special gold and diamond ring that the club provided for each player. In addition, a special night was held at the ball park on September 19 to honor Marvin Owen for his leadership during the 1945 season.

To cut down on travel, Portland was ordered to meet Seattle in the opening round of the playoffs while Sacramento played San Francisco. Portland won the first 3 games played at home and then went up to Seattle and lost all 4 and were eliminated. The 1945 Beavers met the same fate at the hand of Seattle as the champion 1942 Sacramento and 1943 Los Angeles clubs. The Portland players said that losing those 4 games in Seattle made them feel like chumps instead of champs. It was especially annoying to lose to their hated northern rival.

IN EACH OF THE FIRST TWO YEARS OF THE 21ST CENTURY, *which by baseball's definition began in 2000, the American and National League batting champions had identical averages. In 2000, both Nomar Garciaparra of Boston and Todd Helton of Colorado batted .372, and in 2001, both Ichiro Suzuki of Seattle and Larry Walker of Colorado had .350 averages.*

Curiously, this had happened only twice in the 20th Century, and never after that century's first decade. Cleveland's Nap Lajoie and Pittsburgh's Honus Wagner had .355 marks in 1903, and Detroit's Ty Cobb and Wagner had .350 averages in 1907. —LYLE SPATZ

APPENDIX: PORTLAND BEAVERS TEAM STATISTICS, 1942-1945

1942 SEASON BATTING	HR	AVG
Ted Norbert	28	.378
Rupert Thompson	11	.308
Larry Barton	10	.305
John Gill	11	.303
Marvin Owen	3	.302
Lee Stine	2	.278
Bob Bergstrom	0	.238
John Leovich	1	.190
Ted Mayer	0	.213
Danny Amaral*	2	.308
Al Wright*	0	.228
Lindsey Brown	0	.220
Henry Martinez*	3	.243

PITCHING	W	L	ERA
Ad Liska	15	22	3.64
Joe Orrell	11	22	4.00
Syd Cohen	10	14	3.90
Byron Speece	9	6	3.92
Wayne Osborne	10	14	5.40
Bill Schubel	8	8	4.98
Bob Fitzke	1	3	N/A

1943 SEASON BATTING	HR	AVG
Marvin Owen	0	.308
Rupert Thompson	2	.287
Larry Barton	11	.283
Spencer Harris	6	.279
Ted Gullic	17	.270
Bubba Floyd	0	.263
Johnny O'Neal	0	.254
Packy Rogers	3	.244
Eddie Adams	3	.246
Merv Shea	0	.256
Bill Krueger	0	.232
Frank Shone	0	.190

PITCHING	W	L	ERA
Ad Liska	17	11	1.98
Jack Wilson	8	10	2.75
Syd Cohen	10	8	3.16
Earl Cook	5	12	3.83
Marino Pieretti	8	11	3.07
Wayne Osborne*	9	5	2.48
Joe Orrell*	8	11	2.33
Bill Herring*	8	5	2.90

* NOT WITH TEAM AT END OF SEASON

1944 SEASON BATTING	HR	AVG
Eddie Adams	0	.297
Marvin Owen	1	.292
John Gill	3	.287
Frank Shone	0	.275
Frank Demaree	0	.260
Spencer Harris	5	.273
Charley Petersen	0	.273
Larry Barton	4	.253
Ted Gullic	8	.260
Norm De Weese	2	.253
Johnny O'Neal	0	.236
Mel Nunes	1	.220
Earl Norager	0	.191
Gilly Campbell*	0	.226

PITCHING	W	L	ERA
Marino Pieretti	26	13	2.48
Roy Helser	20	16	2.41
Ad Liska	18	9	2.48
Syd Cohen	10	13	2.54
Clarence Federmeyer	6	6	4.19
Don Pulford	3	10	3.72

1945 SEASON BATTING	HR	AVG
Glenn Crawford	0	.348
Larry Barton	6	.320
Marvin Owen	1	.310
Johnny O'Neal	0	.309
Frank Demaree	2	.304
Frank Shone	6	.303
Nick Rhabe	0	.294
Charley English	4	.283
Mel Nunes	0	.273
Ted Gullic	9	.260
Roy Younker	5	.253
Danny Escobar	0	.250
Eddie Adams	2	.238
Frank Lucchesi	0	.233
Hank Souza	0	.209
Spencer Harris*	2	.246

PITCHING	W	L	ERA
Carl Gunnerson	2	0	N/A
Jake Mooty	11	5	3.12
Wandel Mossor	13	7	2.92
Don Pulford	20	11	2.37
Syd Cohen	14	8	3.26
Ad Liska	20	12	2.34
Roy Helser	20	14	3.37
Jack Tising	11	10	2.92
Clarence Federmeyer*	1	1	N/A

Sam "Toothpick" Jones

by John H. Schwarz

Ask most baseball fans which African American pitcher was the first to throw a major league no-hitter, and chances are good you will get the wrong answer. It wasn't Satchel Paige, or Don Newcombe, or Earl Wilson, or Juan Marichal, or Bob Gibson. It was Sam Jones—Sam "Toothpick" Jones or, to some, "Sad Sam" Jones. He was a strong-throwing right hander who was known both for his habit of chewing on a toothpick when he pitched and for his perpetually expressionless demeanor. Despite his personal idiosyncracies, he is probably better remembered by those who played major league baseball in the late '50s and early '60s as a pitcher possessing one of the toughest curveballs of his or any other era in baseball. The late Bill Rigney, who spent a lifetime in baseball and who managed Jones at San Francisco, ranked Jones' curveball along with Bert Blyleven's as the two best right-handed curveballs he ever saw. Arthur Daley, writing in the New York *Times*, compared it to Sal Maglie's curveball. Hobie Landrith, who often caught Jones throughout his career, was quoted as saying, "You've never seen a curveball until you've seen Sam Jones's curveball. If you were a right-handed hitter that ball was a good four feet behind you."

Not only was Jones the first African American major leaguer to pitch a no-hitter, he was also the first to lead the league in ERA, and he was the first pitcher, black or white, to pitch at Candlestick Park. Given his obvious skills and his historic no-hitter, why is Sam Jones such a forgotten man, often confused with Sam Pond Jones, the fine Yankee pitcher of the '20s who also bore the nickname of "Sad Sam"? Largely, it is his late ascension to the major leagues, having spent much of his formative years in the Negro Leagues, and his wildness, which plagued him in his early years in the majors. His failure to make a greater mark in the game may also have been the result of Sam's unselfishness, allowing managers to use him as the workhorse of the pitching staff and his own determination to do more than he was capable of, often pitching with insufficient rest, risking arm problems and a mediocre performance.

His precedent-setting no-hitter was pitched on May 12, 1955, in front of a sparse crowd of only 2,918 fans. He was pitching for the Chicago Cubs at the time. The opponent was the Pittsburgh Pirates, a team just starting to emerge from an era of consistent last-place finishes and about to become the talented group of young players that would lead Pittsburgh to a world championship in 1960. The final score of the game was 4-0. Jones faced only 31 batters. He walked seven, but double plays and a runner caught stealing helped minimize the number of batters faced. Through eight innings he had thrown only 107 pitches. The game's real excitement began in the ninth inning. Jones, who until that time, had walked only four batters, including one player, Dale Long, a dangerous left-handed

John H. Schwarz is a 64-year-old financial executive living in Wellesley, Massachusetts, whose remaining goal in life is to live long enough to see the Cubs or the Red Sox win a World Series.

hitter, three times. He opened the ninth by walking the first three batters, arguably three of the easiest outs on the team. Gene Freese, the eighth hitter in the lineup, a .250 hitter, who had popped up and flied to left in the two previous at-bats, was the first player walked. Then Preston Ward, a backup first baseman, a .212 hitter, pinch hitting for the pitcher, was walked. Finally, Tom Saffell, a .168 hitter in 1955, drew the third walk of the inning. No outs, ninth inning, the bases loaded, the tying run coming to the plate, the heart of the Pittsburgh lineup standing between Jones, his no-hitter, and possibly even a win. What do you do if you're Stan Hack, the Cub manager? The post-game newspapers quoted Hack as having said that he went to the mound and asked Jones the proverbial "how do you feel?. Jones, who was never known for loquaciousness, said, "fine." Hack then asked catcher Clyde McCullough, "How's his stuff?" McCullough, not anxious to be responsible for Jones losing his no-hitter bid and knowing Jones' proclivity for periodic wildness, said, "fine." Hack then made what proved to be the right decision. He said to Jones, who was about to face Dick Groat, Roberto Clemente, and Frank Thomas, "Just get the ball over the plate and let them hit it." As was mentioned after the game in the press, Jones responded to half his manager's instructions. He got the ball over the plate, but he didn't let them hit it. On 12 pitches he struck out Groat, Clemente, and Thomas to finish the game and preserve the shutout and the no-hitter. Groat, who struck out only 26 times that whole season, was fanned on three pitches.

In a *Sport Magazine* article several years after the no-hitter, Dick Schaap asked Jones if he remembered each pitch he threw in those three strikeouts. "Sure," Jones said. Dick Groat—"I threw him three fastballs." One out. Roberto Clemente—"I threw him two curves and a fastball—all strikes." Two out. Frank Thomas—"I threw him a curve. He swung and missed. I wasted a fastball. I then threw him another curve, high and outside. He swung and missed. Then another curve. He took it and it broke over the plate." Three out.

For the 1955 season Jones led the league in both strikeouts and walks, 198 and 185 respectively. He also led the league in losses with 20, but was the biggest winner on his sixth-place Cub team with 14. In addition to his no-hitter, he had a two-hitter, a three-hitter, a four-hitter, and three five-hitters that year. His no-hitter was the first at Wrigley Field in 38 years, and after the game, a local sportscaster, recognizing Jones' trademark toothpick, presented him with a gold toothpick.

Jones was born on December 14, 1925, in Stewardsville, Ohio. He grew up in an impoverished coal-mining region of West Virginia. He left school after the eleventh grade. In high school he did not play on the school baseball team. In fact, his first participation in organized baseball was in the army. At age 19, while serving in the military in Orlando, Florida, Jones joined an all-black company team. He was primarily a catcher and first baseman. Because he was big and could throw hard, he occasionally was asked to pitch. He had an erratic but powerful fastball, but no other pitches. In 1946, Jones joined a local Negro League team. Later that year he was spotted by Quincy Troupe and signed to play for the Cleveland Buckeyes. Based on Jones's size (6'4" and 200 lbs.) and inconsistency as a hitter, Troupe convinced him to concentrate on pitching. Initially, Jones succeeded with only his fastball, but after a game in which he opposed and outpitched Satchel Paige, Paige reportedly took him aside and introduced him to the merits of the curveball and how to throw it. Later, Mel Harder, the pitching coach with the Cleveland Indians, also helped Jones with his curveball. Jones proved to be a good student, and his curveball eventually became his "go-to" pitch and one he could throw both sidearm or overarm.

In late 1949, Hank Greenberg, then the general manager for the Cleveland Indians, signed Jones to a minor league contract. In 1951, Jones had a strong year in San Diego, winning 16 games, striking out 246 batters, and posting a 2.76 ERA. He led the league with 21 complete games. Jones's contract was then acquired by Cleveland. After showing real promise in a late-season stint in 1951 with the Indians, Jones developed bursitis in his pitching arm while playing winter baseball in Puerto Rico. Over the next two seasons he saw limited action, most of it in the minor leagues. As a result, he almost gave up baseball. However, in 1954, with his arm recovered, he went 15-8 at Indianapolis. With no room on the very strong pennant-winning Indians' pitching staff, Jones was traded to the Cubs along with Gale Wade and $60,000 for Ralph Kiner, who was then well into the twilight of his career, but a favorite of Indian GM Greenberg. In 1991, *USA Today* published an article on Cleveland players who, following the Indians pennant-winning season of 1954, were traded away and who went on to be stars elsewhere. Jones was designated as one of the three right-handed starters to make that list, along with Jim Perry and Luis Tiant.

Upon joining the Cubs, a solid second-division club in 1955, Jones quickly became the ace of the staff. He achieved this position despite continuing control problems. He also showed the capacity and strength to pitch a lot of innings and, with his proclivity for both walks and strikeouts, his innings were long ones with lots of pitches. Jones never tried to preserve his arm, nor were there a lot of coaches counting pitches in those days. Jones wanted the ball in his best years. He regularly worked over 200 innings per season and then went on to pitch winter ball. With the San Francisco Giants he was a key starter and also volunteered to relieve. He was a consummate team player.

Although a competent pitcher early in his career with both the Cubs and the Cardinals, his real success came as a member of the San Francisco Giants in 1959. For the Giants to obtain him, they had to give up Bill White. White later was to become an important member of a pennant-winning Cardinal team, but at the time of the trade was living in the shadow of Orlando Cepeda with the Giants.

In 1958 with the Cardinals, Jones had led the league in ERA, but had only 14 wins against 13 losses. He was well liked by Cardinal manager Fred Hutchinson, but the Cardinals at that time were a weak-hitting team and Frank Lane, the general manager, who never saw a player he didn't want to trade, sent Jones to San Francisco. Bill Rigney, the manager of the Giants, had always wanted to obtain Jones and took advantage of the situation. For Jones, it was an opportunity for the first time since his early Cleveland Indian days to play with a good team that provided run support.

With Rigney's encouragement and a strong team behind him, Jones had a monster season in 1959, in which he started 35 games and relieved in 15. He won 21 games that year and led the league in ERA and appearances while sharing the lead for the most wins and most shutouts. He carried the Giants pitching staff that year and almost helped carry the team to the pennant. He was voted by the fans as the team's most popular player. When the Giants moved from Seal's Stadium to the new Candlestick Park, Jones was named to be the starting pitcher for their first game in the new park. During his "career" 1959 season, Jones almost had a second no-hitter. Only an infield hit by Junior Gilliam in the eighth inning spoiled it. Most who saw it believe it was a shortstop error by the notoriously weak-fielding Andre Rogers that prevented Jones from a second no-hitter. Jones was not young when he reached San Francisco, and the cumulative innings he had pitched throughout his career probably made his arm even older than his years. He entered the majors at age 26, and by 1955, when he finally was given a chance to start regularly, he was 30 years old. During the period from 1955-1960, when Jones was between the ages of 30-35, he had good success. Over that six-year period, he averaged 228 innings pitched per season, had an ERA of 3.38, averaged 15 wins per year and 192 strikeouts. Had he begun his major league career at a younger age and/or found himself on a contending team earlier, his career statistics might have gained him more attention.

Following his successful 1959 season, he had one more good season for San Francisco, winning 18 games in 1960 with a 3.19 ERA and 190 strikeouts. At age 35, that was Jones's last strong season. He hung around the majors a few more years with little to show for it. His career lasted into the mid-'60s in the minor leagues and, although not the same pitcher, he did win both ends of a doubleheader at age 37 while relieving. He became so popular when pitching for the Columbus Jets in 1965 that the Central Ohio Home Plate Club sponsored a Sam Jones night in July to honor him.

In the early sixties while Jones was still in the majors, a minor malignancy was discovered in his neck. It was removed at the time, but the cancer returned later in his life. Jones died of cancer at age 46 in a hospital near his West Virginia home.

During his playing career, not only was Jones a popular player, but in his quiet way a role model for his time. While in San Francisco, Jones spent considerable time visiting children who were hospitalized with crippling diseases. Amongst those children was a young man named John Bushman, who suffered from the residual effects of polio. Jones befriended him and Bushman was at Jones's bedside when he died.

Sam Jones's no-hitter has been memorialized in a display at the Baseball Hall of Fame. It will be his only entry into that hallowed institution. However, if there were such a thing as baseball's all-time team of quality human beings and players who represented the values Americans look to from the games, Jones would be a hard guy to keep off that team.

Hank Greenberg & Bobo

by Mike Ross

It was 1982 when I phoned Greenberg at home and left a message that I was writing a piece on his sometime adversary and one-time teammate, Bobo Newsom. Could he phone to arrange an interview? Little did I know at the time that Greenberg did not give interviews. The next day the hotel clerk relayed the message that I was to meet Hank at the illustrious Beverly Hills Tennis Club at 1pm. I was right on time and full of anticipation when I was shown into the club's dining room.

There was the great slugger Hank Greenberg, sitting alone, spoon in hand, digging into a small dessert dish while watching a portable TV: the Cardinals were finishing off the Atlanta Braves in the 1982 National League Playoffs. He looked up wide-eyed, and after a few seconds he said, "I told you to call me here, not to come here!" Then at once he became cordial and, realizing it was lunchtime, gestured, "Well, now that you're here, you might as well sit down and order something."

After talking for a while, we retired to the palm-shaded terrace, out of view of the tennis courts. From that moment on he was accommodating, and he eagerly began to share his recollections. His equanimity and candor during our chat (forgiving, as it were, my tumbling onto his turf unexpectedly), along with his general attitude toward life and career and toward those he played ball with, proved that Hank Greenberg truly was a gentleman. I later learned that, except for his book with Ira Berkow, this was his first (and would be his last) interview since he left his advisory position with the Chicago White Sox two decades earlier.

While the questions were about Bobo Newsom and baseball, the subject was Hank. Newsom became the vehicle for Hank to state his views and recollections. Meanwhile he laughed, recalling the escapades of the lively Newsom, an adversary from 1934 until into the 1939 season and again after Greenberg's return from WWII. "I looked up his record when you called me," said Hank, "and I realized that I just played one full season with Newsom, in 1940." The pair were also teammates during the latter part of 1939, and in 1941, before Hank enlisted.

He graciously complimented Newsom's pitching ability and the importance of Bobo's participation in the Tigers' 1940 pennant and subsequent World Series. Hank recalled how the Tigers clinched the pennant. "Bobo won both ends of a doubleheader (one in relief), setting up a clinch situation for the final series of the season. We were two games up on Cleveland, and had to win one out of the three remaining games of the season. Bobo had won two games the day before. So we picked Floyd Giebell, an unknown, to go against Bob Feller. We figured Feller would be tough, and then we would save our best pitchers to go against

Mike Ross has been a baseball publisher, editor, columnist and TV baseball analyst in the United Kingdom since 1987. He lives in London where he is the chairman of SABR's Bobby Thomson chapter for the U.K. and Europe.

their lesser pitchers. Giebell beat Feller in that first game."

Regarding the 1940 World Series, I asked about the incident with Dick Bartell, It has been contended that Bartell held onto a relay throw too long, thus enabling the winning run to score in the seventh game [an incident preceding a similar happening with Johnny Pesky in 1946 Series]. "Oh, that wasn't Bartell's fault," said Hank. "It was a base-running error. How was Bartell supposed to know the base runner wouldn't hold up?."

Greenberg still takes much of the blame for the loss to the Reds. "Dammit. We knew everything that was coming up. Ernie Lombardi was hurt in September [Willard Hershberger had killed himself a few weeks earlier, so the Reds were down to their third-string catcher] and Jimmy Wilson took over. He wasn't able to bend down all the way, so his fingers were exposed, giving the signals away. The dugouts were so low at Crosley Field, you could sit on the lower step and it would be like our chins were even with the ground. Of course, taking the signals was one thing, hitting the ball was another. After all, it was marvelous to know what was coming. Some players, like Gehringer, wouldn't take the signals. Derringer was pitching and he threw me three perfect fastballs right up on the letters! I knew they were fastballs, I didn't have to look for anything else. I was swinging 3-0. I fouled off the first two and missed the third. I can see it now. I can just see myself hitting a home run, the score would have been 3-0, and Bobo would have won the final game." Greenberg slammed the table with the palm of his hand, seemingly still suffering remorse for a failure some 40 years earlier.

Greenberg received the 1940 league MVP, and missed a triple crown by .012 percentage points. Newsom was 21-5 and pitched three complete games in that World Series with a fabulous 1.38 ERA.. Their combined efforts created a mutual admiration society between them, and the pair were invited by Tiger owner Walter O. Briggs to name their salary for the 1941 season. Greenberg remained at the pinnacle of the wage scale while Bobo, according to Hank, took the opportunity to make himself the highest-paid pitcher in history.

Afterward, Hank joined the armed forces, put on an army uniform, and went to war. Newsom also changed uniforms, playing for seven different teams from 1941 through 1947, when Greenberg concluded his career.

"Buck (aka Bobo) pitched good against us. And then when he came to Detroit I had no trouble with him. Off the field we didn't exactly run together. He had his own [room]. I think Bobo liked to play around with the women and drinking. He was always chasing women. [Note: To be fair, he took his first wife, Lucille, on the road in the minor league days. Their breakup came while he was with Detroit. After his divorce in 1944, he immediately married Kay. Thanks to a "gift" from Connie Mack, she traveled with the team, and she did until Bobo finished playing for the Yankees, in 1947.] I didn't do any of that. I was too conscious of my career. I wasn't married, but like most ballplayers, I was wrapped up in my baseball career. Everyone knew who the players were looking for girls."

I asked Greenberg about an apocryphal tale told to me by former Tiger Hoot Evers. Evers spoke about a fracas between Newsom and Cleveland slugger Hal Trosky that Greenberg was alleged to have broken up. Newsom, in his well-known fashion, was teasing Trosky about the petition the team had signed to have the manager, Oscar Vitt, sacked.

"No, no, that wasn't it," Hank corrected. "The only story I know was something between Bobo and Slicker Coffman. We were staying in the Cleveland Hotel downtown, and we were having dinner in the hotel restaurant. Bobo was there. My roommate was a kid by the name of George "Slicker" Coffman, from Alabama. Well, Bobo was an overbearing kind of guy. I liked him a lot. I got along very well with him. But Bobo had been a bit obnoxious, and he and Slicker started going at it. We went into the bathroom, where they were going to settle it, and Slicker pulled a knife and said, 'I'm gonna get you, you so and so.' He wanted to challenge Bobo right then and there, and I stepped in and stopped it. I had to cool down Slicker. Because he was my roommate. I had a different kind of relationship with him—the old vet and the young rookie. I was a pretty big guy and I was an important member of the team, so I had a little voice in it. Bobo was a little concerned when Slicker challenged him; he kind of turned a little pale. Anyway, that is one of the silly things that happened. I don't know why Slicker got so upset. I wouldn't have reacted that way.

"See, Bobo was the star of every team he was with, a big man too, and they always wanted to put the big men down. They were always picking on me, making fun, but it didn't bother me. Also, Bobo was putting a pitcher down. Different if it was a hitter." The next time the two squared off, Coffman won the battle. Newsom faced Coffman in his first outing of 1940 and was beaten by Slicker, who had left the Tigers and was pitching for the lowly St. Louis Browns. After the loss, Bobo won 13 straight games.

"See, I had a good relationship with the young guys and always liked rookie players. Part of it stemmed from the fact that when I first came up—I had just come back up from the minors—I was given a locker next to Waite Hoyt. That was the last three weeks of the 1930 season, and, you know, he never said hello to me. I was just a raw rookie, 19 years of age, in my first year in the minor leagues. Naturally, walking into the clubhouse as a raw rookie with all those famous names and getting a locker there next to a veteran like Waite Hoyt. Well! He pitched for the Yankees when I was growing up in New York, and he was one of the idols. Then to have the guy not even look at me. That's not really a knock at Hoyt; that was the way they treated rookies in my time. I mean, they had contempt for them. I think the attitude was, 'Jesus, this guy may take my job!' Now a young kid comes in and right away they want to make him feel at home, and that was my attitude.

"I remember the very first time I came into a major league ballpark. I was playing semi-pro ball in Worcester, Mass. And the scout sent me to work out with the Washington baseball team, who were playing in Boston. Walter Johnson was the manager then. I was 19. It was before I signed a major league contract. I got dressed and went onto the field and sat on the bench. And I just sat there. I was a gangly tall teenage kid, and I felt awkward and self-conscious. No one talked to me until finally one guy came up to me and said. "Hey kid, you want to warm up?" I said, "Sure." We went and threw the ball back-and-forth. It turned out to be Fred Marberry, who was then one of the top pitchers in baseball. I never forgot that. What a feeling I had. I always tried to do for others what Marberry did for me.

"Bobo was good with the rookies. When he reached the Tigers, he was already a vet, a ten-year man. At that age they are usually ready to shoot them or send them to the stud farm. Bobo was making $15,000 a year, which was a lot of money then [1939]. Also, I was making big money. So we looked after the rookies. These kids would come up and they'd be making 600-700 dollars a month and I would be making $25,000 a season. When we would go to dinner, I would pick up their checks. I could afford it. It was easy for me, and I suppose it made me feel kinda important.

"Buck was an expansive man. One of his favorite expressions was: 'Gonna do it to you two times, Bobo.' Called everybody Bobo—that's how he got his nickname. Babe Ruth called everybody 'kid' because he couldn't remember names.

"What came to mind about Bobo when I heard you were researching him was the time he was pitching for the Athletics, it must have been 1945 and he was with the A's. They were in last place and we were a contending team. It was late August. He announced that he was going to pitch a doubleheader against us and he used the expression 'I'm gonna do it to you two times, Bobo!'

"So he goes out to pitch that day, and they get off to a good start and he's showboating all over the mound, having a good time. We are gradually picking up runs and picking up runs, and by the eighth inning we go ahead and beat him. Now, he has already made about 300 pitches, and we're giving him hell because he said he's gonna do it twice.

"He wasn't a rapid pitcher. He used to walk around the mound picking up bits of paper and stones, so that first game must have taken over three hours. He goes into the clubhouse and sure enough, he comes out to pitch that second game. That was really something! Connie Mack let him pitch the doubleheader. Well, again they get off to a big lead, five or six runs. Every pitch was by now a Herculean task. Do you know, we catch up again and beat him in a doubleheader? He must have thrown 400-500 pitches. I always used to tease him after that: 'Gonna do it two times, Bobo?' He had a cavalier attitude then because they were in last place, so he could fool around." Hank's memory was fairly accurate. Indeed, Bobo started the doubleheader on August 21, 1945. In game 1 he was taken out after six innings with a lead, allowing two earned runs; the A's blew the lead, but won 7-6. He lost game 2 after pitching eight innings, starting well, but allowing seven runs at the end. In the 14 innings Bobo allowed 23 hits, six walks, with only six strikeouts. The pitch count may have been high. A modest calculation, based on 52 outs, 23 hits, etc., and that Bobo, with his rubber arm, could pitch deep into the count, would make 300 pitches believable.

"He wasn't always fooling around. He loved to pitch. He pitched for the St. Louis Browns in 1938, when they had a terrible team. In those days they didn't tolerate his kind of behavior. You had to be a conformist. Guys with a bit of flare and a different temperament, they wanted to get rid of. He was good and should have stayed with all those teams he was with. I don't know what it was that made them get rid of him.

"Actually, I found him a good competitor. He was always friendly, never mean, he didn't want to knock you down. He wanted to show that his talent was good enough to offset your talent. As a competitor he was awful tough on me. I had a terrible time with him, and he liked to rub it in a little bit too. He'd let you know that you were facing the great Bobo.

"When I was going for the home run title in 1938 and he was with the Browns, I couldn't hit him. He keep pitching me outside, low and away, and it was hard for me to pull a ball and hit a home run off him. When I look back at it I maybe didn't hit one or two home runs off him in my whole career." Newsom started against Detroit six times, in 1938, going 4-2, with four complete games and a total of 50 innings pitched. According to reports, "[Newsom] gave Greenberg the horrors while he was trying to break Babe Ruth's home run record."

"If you're a home run hitter like me," Hank recalled, "you're not satisfied hitting the ball to the second-base side or up the middle, or the right-field line. It doesn't mean anything. I was always trying to pull for the seats. I wouldn't go the way Buck wanted me to go. That's why he was so effective against me; I wouldn't go the way he wanted me to hit. I was going against my own logic. He'd get me because I was trying to force him to throw inside to me. It was a mistake for me to keep trying to pull him. But a single never satisfied me. I wasn't going for singles or doubles; I wanted to hit the ball out of the park every time. Bobo had a good fastball, a good motion, and a rubber arm, but he never fast-balled me.

"He had a real strong arm, a real good pitcher. He had the stuff, the stamina, and the guts. Newsom was one of the first pitchers who consistently threw a moving ball, which they call a slider today. [Earlier that summer Ted Williams had described the pitch to me as "that little curveball of his."] Now everybody is throwing them. He was one of the first to throw them all the time. You see, the concept was if you threw a lot of curveballs and sliders you would hurt your arm and hurt your career. As a result, most of the pitchers in my time were fastball pitchers and resorted to the curve in certain situations. But he threw you that slider all the time, and very rarely threw you a fastball. For a right hander he always made it difficult.

"There were a couple of pitchers that used it. It was described as a 'nickel curve.' It was an almost derogatory term. So if a guy in the early days threw a slider they'd sneer at him because it was hard on the arm to throw a sharp curve all the time. A good curve was a sharp breaking pitch. When Buck first threw the slider, which he learned it from George Blaeholder of St. Louis [Newsom played with Blaeholder on the Browns in 1934], it was a fast breaking curve. It moves. It either goes down or sideways depending upon which way you throw it. Buck's ball would move just a little like that [he demonstrated the slider making a sideways shuffle movement]. Now everybody uses the slider.

Greenberg at the Beverly Hills Tennis Club in 1982.

"There are not as many great hitters as in my day. First of all, we played days and could see the ball better. And the starters stayed in longer, not as much relief work then. Now the manager can use his brilliant brain bringing this guy in and that guy in; he uses five pitchers in a game and the score ends up 3-2. Guys like Newsom would stay in no matter what the score was, because [on those bad teams] no matter who they brought in was not as good as he was. Buck was a fine pitcher and his record was nothing to what it should have been. He played with terrible teams. He didn't have the incentive you'd have pitching for a winning team, when every game could mean the difference between winning the pennant and losing it. When he came to our team, in 1939, it was the first time he was on a team that had pennant potential. With a 21-5 record, you know he wasn't clowning on the mound. I think his whole attitude of being partly a buffoon, instead of being all-business like they were then, hurt his reputation. Everybody took their baseball sooo -sooo seriously. It wasn't until Veeck came in and made a little show biz out of it. Before that when we went to the ballpark, it was like being in the operating room. Everybody had to be precise. Bobo brought some fun into it. So he gets beat, so what? Playing for a lousy club, what's the worst that could happen to him? He was good, though."

I mentioned the promises of a Hall of Fame induction at the testimonial for Newsom upon his retirement in 1953, and the subsequent campaign started in 1971 by the publisher of *The Sporting News* Taylor Spink. His efforts gained many new votes but then sputtered with Spink's untimely death shortly thereafter.

"Unfortunately," Hank explained, "when it comes to the Hall of Fame, it depends on the team you were playing for. For hitters you could be with a last-place team and still hit .300. Bobo had that [bad] reputation and when they are voting it works against you. And people didn't understand him. Now everyone gets in, there are lower standards."

He expressed a caustic and sardonic displeasure with the Hall of Fame's treatment of its members. "You know what they gave us when we were inducted? A photograph of our bust! Can you believe that? What are you gonna do with that? Then they came up with a tiny lapel pin. Now, who's going to wear that? When Cronin became president of the league I spoke to him about it and said we should get something for ourselves. So they made up these typical high school rings, no diamond or anything, just saying 'Hank Greenberg, Hall of Fame.' Who's going to wear a thing like that? I spoke to the head of the Hall of Fame, that we should have a replica of what they have on the wall. You know what he says? That they were afraid the guys would sell them and that they'd end up hanging in a barber shop somewhere!"

Greenberg was in extraordinarily good shape at 72, and so I was astonished and saddened to read, four years later, that Hank had died of cancer just after assisting Berkow with the completion of his own autobiography.

THE JULY 8, 1909 ISSUE *of the* Leslie's Illustrated Weekly *reported the following:*

"Charles S. Havenor, of the Milwaukee Baseball Club of the American Association, has bought for $175,000 the eight-acre tract in North Clark Street, Chicago. This property is considered the best vacant location in Chicago for a baseball park, and the purchase on its face appears to portend the entrance of an American Association club into that city, with a big baseball war as the result. It has been known that the American Association at various times in the last few years has cast covetous eyes on Chicago territory, and at one time last fall plans were all set for an invasion, but later abandoned. It looks as if the sport pages will be full of 'baseball war' talk again this winter as in the past. Let us hope so, for your baseball fan must have something to read during the icy months."

The land in question was the current site of Wrigley Field. Havenor paid $175,000 to the Lutheran Church for the land then occupied by the Theological Seminary of the Evangelical Lutheran Church. The Seminary had decided to leave the area as the once quiet neighborhood had started to expand. The noisy locale was no longer conducive for meditative study. — ED HARTIG
